THE FIRST PRINCIPLES OF

GOOD COOKERY

BY
THE RIGHT HON. LADY LLANOVER

WITH AN INTRODUCTION
BY
BOBBY FREEMAN

BREFI

Key words:
    Cookery
    Victoriana
    Wales

First published 1867
First published in this edition in Great Britain in 1991 by
    Brefi Press
    PO Box 103
    Tregaron
    Dyfed SY25 6BR

Brefi Press is an imprint of Coachex Ltd

5 4 3 2 1

Cover photograph: reproduced courtesy of the Warden
                     of Llandovery College

ISBN 0 948537 30 2 - Casebound
ISBN 0 948537 35 3 - Paperback

INTRODUCTION

TO THE 1991 EDITION

———

Though it was almost certainly the only Welsh cookery book written in the English language at the time, *Good Cookery* made little impression on the Victorian cookery scene when it was published in 1867. This is hardly surprising, if unfortunate - for the book has unusual merit - since it must have been something of an enigma even to the upper classes to whom it was directed.

Largely due to the rapid expansion of publishing, the 18th century had produced a plethora of titles, most of them concentrating on demystifying: Hannah Glasse stated this the most succinctly in her *The Art of Cookery Made plain and Easy* (1747). Elizabeth Raffald, on the other hand, had directed her *Experienced English Housekeeper* (1769) more towards acquiring competence - so skilfully that her book can be used with pleasure and success today.

The 19th century opened to a proliferation on a similar scale. Until Isabella Beeton's *Household Management* appeared in 1861, the most popular would then have been Maria Rundell's *New System of Domestic Cookery Formed Upon Principles of Economy and Adapted to Private Families* (1806) because it was the first household manual with any degree of completeness. The fat little book, costing 7/6d with its valuable hints and remedies prefacing a large collection of recipes was ideal for a young bride; it sold and sold. Though later books were to be aimed largely at the middle classes, Maria Rundell pre-empted Lady Llanover by directing her work to the upper classes, rightly judged incapable of understanding how to instruct their servants.

Lady Llanover dismisses all existing titles on the first page of *Good Cookery* by declaring that 'the multiplication of cookery books on the common plan had very little increased the amount of knowledge of the fundamental principles of the real art of Cookery and Domestic Economy', before modestly hazarding the likely success of her book in this aim. She addressed her book - it was far from being 'on the common plan' - in direct response to requests from her fellow-gentry, most of whom must have dined times without number at Llanover, no doubt curious to know how the food there always tasted so good while theirs didn't.

Given the Victorian fashion for extravagant entertaining it's easy to imagine the interest aroused by the 'simple dishes' offered at Llanover, that yet impressed. This must have been partly due to the fact that the Llanover cook and kitchen staff had been trained by Lady Llanover herself (who had, as we shall see later, practical experience of cookery) and had probably been employed there for years, knowing every nuance of her methods, time-consuming though they may have been to tired feet and aching legs. Despite the Llanovers' great wealth, thrift was sternly practised in the Llanover kitchens. As a constant reminder, appropriate to the times, the following inscription appeared above the doorway:

> '*Da i bawb cynhildeb yw*
> *A thad i gyfoeth ydyw*'

('Thrift is beneficial to all and is the father of wealth')

But who can make sense of the apparently tedious detail, made unnecessarily dense by being enmeshed in a contrived tale - of a young traveller weary of his inability to obtain a decent meal, fortuitously encountering a Hermit, well versed in culinary matters, sitting outside his cell and eager to educate the unfortunate (and receptive) young man.

Is this a device to carry her own culinary message, or is it remembrance of another's teachings, long ago? If so, whose is this voice from the past? The Hermit gives several clues: "I am at least 93 years old . . . I am from another century". Who was the Hermit? The voice from the past, or Lady Llanover herself? We shall see.

Upon close examination the culinary detail is in fact riveting, if needing some unravelling. For the real value of the book lies in its first part, expounded as 'The First Principles of Good Cookery': her obsession with flavour, her preoccupation with economy, the unorthodox as well as traditional use of old Welsh cooking utensils as with the *ffwrn fach* (small pot oven), and the quick-chill properties of the Well of Gover.

The most singular aspects of her style of cookery are her use of a 'double' - her term for a *bain marie* (a pan inside a bath of hot water to achieve gentle cooking) - and the digester, an early form of pressure cooker. This was essential for rendering down bones for jelly and stock. My personal comment on her recommendation of a 'double' for the salt duck (p408) is that there is no question about the superiority of the method over plain simmering in one pan. The flesh of the duck from the 'double' method has a smooth, silky quality, a delight to the tongue.

No other cookery book gives you the sense of the continuous kitchen process, the daily routine of soup and stock-making, the one operation leading into the next, the saving of fats of different kinds, and of various meat jellies. Unless you are in large-scale catering you can only experience it in a minor way, the above processes obviously being impractical in our smaller, contemporary kitchens. She reads, in fact, like a chef, for the methods and culinary lessons she details indicate a professionalism far beyond that of the average 'lady of the house' of her time. Nor can she be compared entirely to an experienced Victorian country house cook because of her intellectual concern for flavour, economy and nutrition.

For the first, see the chicken fricassée (p384) and the lobster sauce using the shell (p418) for the second, the comparison between a roasted English v Welsh leg of mutton (p467), the economy being in the sheep's nationality, the Welsh being less fatty; and for the third, see this and every recipe which calls for the removal of fat, the different results of the two methods of baking a fillet of veal (p401) and her views on wholemeal bread containing most of the bran - this one for flavour, too, for as she rightly says, the flavour is in the bran.

The Welsh pan or pot bread (p473) is a traditional bread made in the *ffwrn fach* standing on a tripod over hot coals, the lid heaped with hot coals. Such bread made with white flour was regarded as a special treat for ordinary folk.

The tins for 'rowley powley' puddings intrigue me (and her ingenious method of extracting a dozen at a time from the boiling water) (p458). Were they so difficult to obtain then that a local tinsmith had to make them for her?

There has been a recent fashion for pumpkin recipes. *Good Cookery* lists a few from Gower (p463), the area of Wales to which they were virtually exclusive - Lady Llanover claims this is the only area in Britain to grow them for their food value, unlike the Continent. She has a nice way with slices of pumpkin, boiled, sprinkled with salt and herbs egg-crumbed and fried 'like soles'. Or boiled in slices, eaten with brown gravy. She also credits them with the properties for which we know tofu and Quorn, of absorbing the flavour of anything cooked with them, and especially recommends them for ekeing out scarce fruit.

Then follows, typically, a lecture on the shortcomings of British horticulturists who have failed to learn from Germany how to grow hardier fruit varieties with more abundant yields.

The recipe for 'paste' for fruit tarts (p439) recalls the later medieval practice of icing tarts which persists to the present day whenever we sprinkle the top of a fruit tart with sugar. I like the reference to beating the egg white with a fork on a plate - until I read it I'd forgotten how my mother used to do it with a knife on the back of a plate.

The 'Welsh carrot plum pudding, Another' (p457) is extremely good. The recipe is old enough to be the one taken by the Welsh emigrants on the 'Mimosa' to South America and renamed 'Patagonia Pudding' in honour of the new country.

'Queen Charlotte's Orange Pudding' (p460) was a favourite of the Queen on the many occasions when she dined with Mrs Delany, Augusta's great, great aunt at Windsor. Though the recipe was given to the Queen, the royal kitchens were never able to make it as well, so the pudding would be cooked at Mrs Delany's house and sent over to the Queen's Lodge.

Before reaching the jumbled Appendix of recipes, 'The Traveller's Notebook' develops into a vehicle, Victorian style, for the author's discourses and strong, and sometimes valuable opinions on an ever-widening array of matters of contemporary concern, upon which she was invariably diametrically different from the currently-held view. Sometimes, indeed, she was far ahead of her time. The best example of this is her diatribe over the rearing of cattle and her invaluable account of Welsh cattle breeds (pp204 & 314-322) in which she denounced over-fattening of animals and methods of cruel confinement. Veal for the Llanover kitchens was obtained from Holland where calves were reared humanely. Interestingly, the situation is reversed today.

There is information on bee-keeping, drying herbs, roads, hedges and banks (with illustrations) and the frustrations of obtaining a good shirt-maker.

It's worth noting here that many of the recipes quoted in the Appendix are given very full treatment in the 'First Principles' section, rather than with the recipe itself - this does not of course make for easy use.

Lady Llanover may have obfuscated, but she did not copy, she did not plagiarise. We know that all the recipes in *Good Cookery* are Llanover favourites, tried and tested. In this and every aspect of the book she was a true original.

But the book does suffer from a certain eccentricity. One cannot deny that fairly ruthless editing and re-writing would have improved it. Of course it would then have lost its curious appeal.

But . . . it is maddeningly difficult to find one's way about in. There was no index. The list of contents, apart from those for the 'Traveller's Notebook', is hugely unhelpful, being simply listed by escalating page number. And those important 'First Principles' are left in a woolly lump, defying disentanglement.

I do not think she intended it to be so disorganised and incomplete.

In fact she makes apology for this at the end of the introduction, saying, in effect, that the reader can sort it all out for herself. Now, writers do not usually take this line. They would have to be pretty desperately distracted to do so - and I think Lady Llanover was. Cookery writing takes time, yet she worked on the manuscript for less than a year. By the November she had left Llanover for London, the copy already with the printers. From then on she was to be wholly taken up with nursing her beloved husband, Benjamin, in what was to prove a fatal illness. In the April of

1867 Benjamin died. A letter to a friend expressed her desolation: '*All is over. The light of my life is gone*'.

They had been married for 44 years and were as much in love then as on their wedding day. She was to live on, alone, for nearly 30 more years.

I have found nothing in the correspondence of the time to indicate that she derived the slightest satisfaction from the book's publication. We do not know how many copies were printed, or sold. It was on general sale, though I suspect that most of the copies went to those to whom it was directed - the South Wales' gentry. Maybe it didn't have much promotion from its ageing publisher, Richard Bentley, who died a few years later. Its price could also have been against any popular sale: 10/6d was quite high for a book of relatively few recipes (compare it with Mrs Beeton's over 2,000 plus legal, medical, etiquette and other non-cookery sections which sold for 7/6d). True, it was illustrated, but not copiously - sometimes, curiously, in the manner of a novel rather than a cookery book. Some of the illustrations were by Lady Llanover, some by her great friend Betha Johnes ('Robin Goch'), Dolaucothi, others by W J Allen and the anonymous artist - E J Fecit.

If the author herself had no interest in it, it is perhaps not surprising that with its difficult content the book passed into oblivion despite the interest it later aroused in such luminaries as André Simon, Ifan Kyrle Fletcher and Elizabeth David, who rightly saw the value of the recording of the traditional Welsh recipes, of South Wales, obtained from friends in the area.

André Simon, when president of the International Wine and Food Society, included one of them in his *Guide to Good Food and Wine* under the title 'The Welsh Hermit's Favourite Chicken and Leek Pie'. Another of his publications included Lady Llanover's instructions for crimping salmon, acknowledging their rarity.

Ifan Kyrle Fletcher wrote an article on 'Food and Drink in Wales' for the same society's *Wine and Food Quarterly,* spring number 1935. Like André Simon, he gave pride of place to the 'Chicken and Leek Pie' (which it deserves) with recipes for salmon, boiled shoulder of mutton, the 'Short Cakes of Gwent and Glamorgan' and 'Welsh Toasted Cheese'. He paid tribute to her work, in which the recipes had lain unnoticed ever since publication. 'Such a fate they did not deserve' he declared, 'as the collection contained at least five recipes which would bring honour to the name of Welsh cookery'.

Alas, he wrote in vain. Honour was most certainly not brought to Welsh cookery until comparitively recently, and then only with difficulty.

Elizabeth David, who is herself partly Welsh, with connections near to Llanover, singled out the recipe for 'Salt Duck' (p408) for publication in one of her cookery articles in the 1960's. When I was desperately searching for a genuine Welsh dish suitable for the dinner menu for my Fishguard restaurant a year or so later, she was kind enough to tell me about *Good Cookery.* Eventually I located a copy in Haverfordwest Reference Library to study, but of course I could never have it at home. In 1983 my younger daughter traced and gave me a copy.

Who was the author of this idiosyncratic book, and how did she fit into Wales and Welsh affairs?

Many people in Wales have probably heard of Lady Llanover, if only vaguely, and not always in flattering terms. Her enthusiasm for promoting the Welsh language, Welsh literature, costume and the *eisteddfod* are well enough known in Wales, if not elsewhere. Her aristocratic birth, brilliant social life at Llanover, London and Europe, her royal connections, her reputation (with her husband, Benjamin) for generous hospitality on a large scale which included tenants and servants, and their unflagging dedication to 'good works' inspired by the strictures of their respective upbringing, may now have been forgotten. What is remarkable about the hospitality at Llanover is that its success did not depend upon alcohol, for the couple were always uncompromisingly teetotal. Abstinence at the Court was one thing, but when Augusta, with the best of intentions - to combat the excessive drinking at that time - took it upon herself to close all the pubs in Llanover and to turn them into tea rooms, not surprisingly, she earned intense dislike (though I gather the villagers' wives were not averse to the move) and it is by this one infamous act that she is mostly remembered in Wales today.

However kind and good the Llanovers were to their tenants and servants, consideration has to be given to the innate Welsh dislike of gentry, and more so, the mine owners and ironmasters of that time. Benjamin's maternal grandfather being a Crawshay did not help, nor did the fact that his sister married a Guest. Yet Benjamin was a model employer, building sound housing, schools and even a church where his Welsh-speaking workers could worship in their own language, at his Abercarn coalfield.

As Augusta Waddington, Lady Llanover was born and grew up in the old house, '*Tŷ Uchaf*' (sometimes called the 'White House' though the Welsh means 'Upper House') in the great Park of Llanover near Abergavenny, in what was then Monmouthshire and is now Gwent.

Her father, Benjamin Waddington, a Nottinghamshire gentleman and businessman, his fortune made early in business in London and America, had bought Llanover ten years before, in

1792, to retire into the life of a country gentleman. He had found the Park in its sylvan setting on the banks of the beautiful river Usk, with its vista of hills and mountains, irresistible, though it was in poor repair.

Even today, the gentle, pastoral countryside unfolds as far as the eye can see, untouched by any industrial development, though the coal valleys lie so close to the west.

One of the delights of the Park was a brook which tumbled rapidly through the garden at the back of '*Tŷ Uchaf*', forming pools and cascades and little islets - a paradise for Augusta and her two older sisters to play in. The famous Well of Gover, fed by eight streams converging from different directions, was to play a conspicuous role in the cookery she was later to develop.

All her life, though she travelled extensively throughout Britain and Europe, Augusta was to love Llanover above anywhere else.

Fair-haired, blue-eyed, diminutive and pretty, she was a high-spirited child who yet took readily to training: when only three her manners were already considered exquisite and reliable enough for her to be taken to play with the royal princesses, daughters of George III, and to meet Queen Charlotte. She made especial friends with the young Princess of Wales.

Her aristocratic birth was due to her mother, the gentle, kindly and modest Georgina Waddington, whose ancestry went back to before the Norman Conquest, to the Plantagenate king, Edward I from whom she was directly descended through the illustrious Granvilles, of whom Sir Richard Granville of 'Revenge' fame is the most celebrated. It was from him that Augusta inherited her Celtic blood and strong feeling for Celtic culture.

But it was another Granville who had the most profound influence on Augusta's life and character, someone she never even met, yet to whom her upbringing owed everything, even though two generations removed.

Mary Granville, later Mrs Delany, had virtually adopted her great niece, Georgina, Augusta's mother, as a very young child and had brought her up with love and great affection in the style of the later Georgian period of the early 18th century. When she had daughters of her own, Mrs Waddington saw no reason not to bring them up in the same way. In a sense Augusta might well have been raised by Mrs Delany herself, so effectively was the mother's upbringing passed on to her daughters.

Thus, even when adult, Augusta is writing, in *Good Cookery* from the standpoint of a previous century - her education, her religion, her manners, her motivation and outlook had their roots in the early 18th century. Most importantly, as far as *Good Cookery* was concerned, her full and practical understanding of all matters on household management were rooted in this period, too. Many of the recipes in *Good Cookery* belong to the 18th rather than the 19th century. A few are even earlier: the 'Dish of Frogs', 'Eggs, Marrow and Curds' quoted in the 'Traveller's Notebook' (p307) from Robert May's *Accomplisht Cook* (1671), though, are included as a joke - rather as ignorant contemporary cooks until fairly recently made fun of Mrs Beeton's recipes.

William Rabisher, on the other hand, who published his *Cookery Dissected* only two years later found favour, perhaps because of his homily to aspiring cooks, which she opines 'ought to be the ambition of every good cook in the present century to deserve' (p311).

By teaching them herself on the same successful plan Mrs Delany had prescribed for her, Mrs Waddington gave her daughters a sounder and wider education than most girls of their age, who were simply taught what would be useful in acquiring and pleasing a husband. Now the educational ideas of the 18th century were to influence the great-great niece, though there were nearly 200 years between the birth of one and the death of the other. Together with her sisters Augusta studied Greek, Latin, Spanish and Italian, Euclid, economics, history, literature and geography, and the stars.

By the time she was 17, Augusta had a complete mastery of household management and a great interest in and practical knowledge of cookery, so that she was able to take over the running of the house while Mrs Waddington nursed the middle daughter, Emilia, through her last, fatal, illness.

Here in *Good Cookery* we can detect the authoritative voice from the past - from a previous century - reiterating the well-taught principles. Was the Hermit invented to do it? To represent great, great aunt Delany? Or is he Lady Llanover herself? The one living through the other, I would say. And the widows, Gwenllian, the improbable Cell of Gover . . . the thinly disguised Llanover kitchens and their staff, for sure.

The difference in household education marked Augusta out from her contemporaries and enabled her to write her book as she did. From Mrs Waddington her daughters learned how to draw from nature, to observe light and shade - and most exceptionally, to explain the reasons for every line they drew. The results in Augusta's case are apparent in her pencil sketches of the corn stooks.

They became adept at the popular art of cutting silhouettes from black paper. Reading aloud and recitation were encouraged. Later, a teacher came from Brecon to give them lessons in music and dancing.

Their mother also saw to their religious education, which again had its roots in the early 18th century, when manners were of immense importance, second to godliness. She imbued them with her own deeply-held Protestantism and belief in the goodness of God. These convictions were to endure all their lives, governing their actions in a quiet, unassuming way, setting example by precept. Above all, Mrs Waddington insisted upon complete truthfulness and of never breaking a promise.

Fresh air and exercise plus plenty of rest were the order of their day. There were no set hours for lessons, nor were they supervised, but trusted to undertake their studies as prescribed, from their sense of duty.

In between these activities there were indoor and outdoor games to play, exploration of the great Park and surrounding countryside and the regular interchange of visits from family and friends. Augusta loved to play with her little family of goats and to sketch them. She had successfully tamed the initially wicked billy to the point when he would docilely pull a little basket-work carriage and take her young friends for a ride.

Augusta was always to insist upon being part Welsh through her Granville ancestor, Richard de Granville who came over in the train of the Conqueror and was to found Neath Abbey in the county of Glamorgan. The name is enshrined in the 'Sauce for Fish' (p425). But her strongest claim to Welshness came through her maternal grandfather, John Port, who had (inexplicably) changed his name from Sparrow, a family long settled in Anglesey. But even in life, and more so in death, her detractors have insisted she was wholly English.

Almost all versions of Lady Llanover's life are incorrect in many instances. It is not true, for example, as is frequently claimed, that she learned Welsh in her early twenties as a result of a meeting with the Rev Thomas Price at the Brecon Eisteddfod of 1826, though it might well have increased her enthusiasm for the language. The truth is she began to speak Welsh in her childhood through visiting the cottages on the Llanover estate, and had early begun to study Welsh literature.

When they were both 21 (they were born in the same year) Augusta married Benjamin Hall of Abercarn, one of the Pembrokeshire Halls of Templeton. The wedding took place on December 4th 1823 almost immediately following Benjamin's 21st birthday celebrations. From then on, Christmas festivities at Llanover began on that date.

Head over heels in love with the tall, handsome Benjamin, Augusta looked radiantly lovely for her wedding, her high spirits unquenchable - not even by Benjamin's grandfather's attempt to spoil the arrangements bv bringing the ceremony forward by an hour, from 11 to 10 o'clock in the morning. Despite an understandable battery of argument, upbraiding and appealing to his better nature, he got his way, even though it meant Benjamin's mother could not be informed in time.

Fortunately most of the close relatives and friends were already staying at Llanover, but two of Augusta's three bridesmaids, the Misses Jones* were at Llanarth, the adjoining estate across the park. Cousin Frederick was despatched post-haste to fetch them. They arrived in the nick of time, for the vicar of Abergavenny was already there and Dr Hall was trying to take advantage of this and unite the pair 'without bridesmaids or men'. By great good fortune, Benjamin's mother arrived just as the last Llanover carriage swept out of the gates for the church, but the rest of the invited guests, who arrived at the proper time, missed the ceremony.

None of this dimmed Augusta's happiness, or her determina-

---

*The family name was later changed to Herbert.

tion that everyone - relations, friends, servants and tenants - should be joyous and gay for her wedding. Nor is there any record of Benjamin or herself being angered by Dr Hall's curmudgeonly behaviour. 'Augusta's blue eyes shone with happiness, her loveliness set off by a beautiful white silk hat and feathers framing her golden curls'. Her dress was a 'slender white silk palisse over a white satin petticoat 'all handsomely trimmed with lace'.

Benjamin, thankful the fashion for them still survived, was courtly in his favoured breeches, blue cut-away coat with gilt buttons, velvet waistcoat, frilled shirt, lace ruffles, and buckled shoes.

Superficially, the pair would seem to personify the attraction of opposites - Benjamin so tall (at least 6ft 4in), outwardly grave and reserved, Augusta so small and dainty, gay and vivacious. But Benjamin's gravity belied a genial kindliness, while Augusta's high spirits were partnered by a strong and resolute character. They shared a sense of humour and, more seriously, a deep awareness of the responsibilities their riches entailed (and they were fabulously wealthy) together with an unusual gratitude (for the times) for the smallest service rendered them.

The wedding was followed by celebrations for young and old at Llanover and afterwards at the Assembly Rooms in Abergavenny, the Llanover party not returning until after five in the morning. There was also late dancing at Llanover for the servants and tenants and, a few evenings later, a firework display and another servants' dance: it was Augusta's wish that everyone should enjoy themselves to the hilt on the occasion of her wedding.

We do not know where the honeymoon was spent after the couple's departure to Trecastle, but, wherever, it wasn't long, for the newlyweds were settled in their new home, Newport House, near Almley, Herefordshire by the 19th of December. (Surprising as it might seem now, Welsh was still spoken in Herefordshire at that time.)

Augusta and Benjamin had several homes before returning to Llanover Park to build their final home. Work was begun in 1828, but it was to be nearly ten years before the couple and their children could move in, and then in a frantic rush of last-minute painting and decorating, to be able to hold their housewarming at the time of the Brecon *Eisteddfod*. But Llanover Court was exactly what they had wanted. Benjamin, who had a flair for architecture and excellent taste, had commissioned Thomas Hopper to design the house, insisting on a simplicity of line in the Jacobean style which made the result attractive even by present-day standards. It was in no way the 'Gothic monstrosity' alleged in some malicious accounts - by people who had never actually seen it! Hopper had been responsible for the re-building of Penrhyn Castle in North Wales, and the reconstruction of Margam Abbey at Port Talbot.

Benjamin was also to build several bridges and churches in the locality: the structure he was most proud of was the bridge at Pontywain near Abercarn which carried Hall's tramway across the Ebbw valley. Originally horse-drawn, it was converted to a passenger-carrying railway, part of the GWR network. It reverted to goods traffic in 1939.

The couple intended their new home to become the recognised centre for Welsh culture and the hub of all their activities, particularly the promotion of the Welsh language and the mid 19th century Welsh literary revival. They were prominent in the founding of the Abergavenny Welsh Society, one of the Victorian Welsh societies which were to become the mainspring of the present-day Welsh language movement.

Her crusade for Welshness, especially the language, was often seen as ostentation by those careless of its preservation and of the increasing anglicisation of Wales, which many even felt to be an advantage. She was ridiculed, for example, when she addressed her letters to a niece in Lampeter, the market town in the Teifi valley, with its Welsh name *Llanbedr Pont Steffan*. The tide of Welsh placename anglicisation was not to be halted until the mid-1970's, when the turn-back began to be effective. Lady Llanover would be gratified today to see the bi-lingual signs throughout Wales; in the case of Lampeter, *Llanbedr Pont Steffan* appearing above the English name.

The couple attended, and in Augusta's case, took part in local *eisteddfodau*, donating prizes and originating competitions.

Llanover Court's chief feature was the enormous two-storey entrance hall with its coved, dark wooden ceiling and magnificent ornamental fireplace, specially designed to accommodate their musical and artistic entertainments, for which Augusta always wore Welsh costume and expected everyone to do the same. They soon had their first resident harpist to play the triple Welsh harp for every function. The happy, hospitable lifestyle which was to characterise the rest of their married life was quickly established. They had the *entré* to the highest society in England and Wales - many times the hospitality extended beyond the confines of the Court, when the surrounding lanes were decked with arches of evergreens and ribbons in honour of their most distinguished visitors - as when the young Prince of Orange came to stay in 1860.

Always a keen educationalist, Augusta was instrumental in founding Llandovery College in 1847, then one of only two public schools in Wales. She also ensured that St David's

College remained in Lampeter. Another of her activities was the creation of the Welsh Manuscript Society, which was to lead to her making, with Benjamin, what was to prove a rather risible purchase. Enthusiasts for Wales can find it all too easy to be economical with the truth. Such a one was the self-styled bard Iolo Morganwg, a Glamorgan stonemason with a penchant for ancient manuscripts who was a frequent visitor at Llanover Court. Amongst his collection of genuine manuscripts were some he had invented, the most notorious a bogus druidic ritual for the *eisteddfod*. Fearful for its safety after the deaths of Iolo and his son, Benjamin and Augusta bought the collection, which is now in the National Library of Wales, Aberystwyth. They were not the only ones to be deceived - even the British Museum were taken in. When the truth about the engaging (but obviously Victorian) *gorsedd* ritual was eventually discovered, it was too late to extract it.

It was at the 1834 Cardiff Eisteddfod that Augusta won a prize for an essay in English (the *eisteddfod* was not then, as it is today, an all-Welsh affair), and gained her bardic name '*Gwenynen Gwent*' (The Busy Bee of Gwent) on the advantages of the preservation of the Welsh language and Welsh 'national' costumes.

One of her competitions for the Abergavenny *Eisteddfod* of 1853 was the offer of £5 for the best collection of Welsh flannels in 'real national checks and stripes, with the Welsh names by which they are known, no specimens to be included which have not been well-known for at least 50 years.'

The object of the competition was 'to authenticate the real old checks and stripes of Wales and to preserve them'. Unfortunately, Augusta had let her zeal run away with her. There were no authentic national checks and stripes, there were no authentic national costumes. In what was a genuine effort to revive the flagging Welsh flannel industry, she illustrated her ideas of Welsh regional costume charmingly, attributing them to various counties, and even to parts of counties. They are almost wholly bogus though they have made attractive framed prints for the more recent tourist trade, as in their day they were used to assist the early Welsh tourist trade.

After her father's death in 1828 Augusta and Benjamin had taken over the running of the Llanover estate,and did so on strictly Welsh lines. All the servants had Welsh titles, Welsh was the language of the house and estate and, in the true tradition of Welsh squires, they were directly available to estate workers and tenants. Augusta's Welsh was fluent enough for the conduct of the day's business with staff and tenants. But as the years went on maintaining the Welshness of the estate became increasingly difficult as anglicisation of the county proceeded inexorably, until in the end the jobs had to be filled by imports from the still strongly Welsh-speaking Cardiganshire.

Augusta herself wore Welsh costume whenever possible, the servants at the Court wore it and the tenants were expected to when they visited the Court. Welsh costume was more or less obligatory for the Welsh musical and other entertainments. This policy was not wholly popular as the so-called 'costume' tended to be hot and heavy to wear.

In 1837 Benjamin went into politics, and was elected Liberal MP for Marylebone, which he represented for 22 years. These were the turbulent years of rebellion and reform, of the Chartist rising, the Corn Laws and the Poor Laws (and of the accession of Queen Victoria - Augusta, as the wife of a sitting MP, attended the coronation). Measures to improve the lot of the poor always had Benjamin's support. He fought to have the London parks opened on a Sunday, with bands playing; and in the Welsh cause, for the right of the Welsh to worship in their own language.

As Commissioner for Works he was chiefly able to organise London's water supply. But the post led to something else for which he achieved lasting fame: 'Big Ben' was affectionately named after the 'gentle giant' of a Welshman who had organised the casting and installation of the great bell in 1856.

But for political reasons, his reward in 1859 was not an expected and deeply desired new government post but to be raised to the House of Lords as Baron Llanover (he had been made a baronet in 1838) and in 1861 to be appointed Lord Lieutenant of Monmouthshire.

In 1849 Benjamin and Augusta's only surviving child, the flame-haired Augusta Charlotte, married John Arthur Jones (later Herbert), heir to the adjoining Llanarth estate and a life-long friend. It was a true love-match and her parents were delighted and not unappreciative of the advantage of joining two estates into one, particularly as their two sons had died young, leaving them no heir. But it did mean the trauma of their daughter adopting the Catholic faith.

Good Cookery was not Lady Llanover's only published literary work. By the early 1860's she had carried out a masterly editing of Mrs Delany's vast and valuable correspondence* which commanded much attention and critical acclaim. Some idea of the size of this work can be obtained by the initial reaction of the printers when they received the copy: they said they could not possibly set it, as required, in three volumes of 400-450pp

The Autobiography and Correspondence of Mary Granville, Mrs Delany, London, Richard Bentley. The printers were almost certainly Messrs Clowes, who printed *Good Cookery* for Bentley.

each! Presumably they did not have sufficient type available, because they eventually agreed to producing three volumes of 600 pages each as a first series in 1861, with a further three volumes of the same length a year later.

Copies are very hard to come by. Maxwell Fraser showed me hers, now lodged with National Library of Wales in Aberystwyth.

There was another, handwritten collection of recipes, typical of its kind and time though containing a few rather unusual recipes which could be 'originals'. Some may be of Dutch or German origin from friends and relatives in those countries. To my knowledge they do not appear in other collections of the period, or before or since. This collection, dated 1858, has entries up to 1883. There is absolutely no similarity of style or content with *Good Cookery*.

In conclusion, I have to declare my sense of kinship with Lady Llanover, which is more than the recognition of professionalism. Though 100 years separate us, I feel we are fellow-spirits, pioneers both, destined to annoy as well as please with our innovatory cookery notions.

Once, before I had my own copy, when they placed one of the library copies in my hands, it felt especially dear, for it was a signed one. I found I was turning the pages that time with a rising feeling of happiness . . . the fondness I then began to feel for this extraordinary author eventually reached the point when I bitterly resented the long death which separates us.

When I visit Llanover and climb up through the churchyard to that great railed family mausoleum under the ornamental crab-apple, I long to haul the Baroness out of it from beside her beloved Benjamin to set her on her dainty little feet to imperiously rule the Llanover kitchens once more. Then, if she looked as though she were open to such an advance, I'd proffer my hand to grasp hers in recognition. Because I only know her physical appearance from her portrait, hanging in '*Tŷ Uchaf*', in my vision of her resurrection she is garbed in the Welsh costume she patronised (not to say invented), her fine eyes gaze compellingly from beneath a tall 'Welsh' hat, and in her hand she is holding a nosegay of the culinary herbs she valued so highly - together with a sprig of mistletoe, an incomprehensible addition unless you know how much she esteemed its medicinal properties: its use in the treatment of St Vitus' Dance is the only medicinal recipe in '*Good Cookery*'.

I linger in the churchyard, hoping perhaps to catch the echo of the sound of hospitality which once rang in the Court across the Park.

ACKNOWLEDGEMENTS

My thanks are due to the late Maxwell Fraser for her earlier invaluable guidance, and more recently to her extensive work on the Llanover papers. Others who have played a part are Miss Nia Henson, Assistant Keeper, Department of Manuscripts and Records, National Library of Wales; Mrs Beryl Griffiths, NLW; Ben Owens; Bryn Jones, South Glamorgan County Library; Miss Rhian Evans, librarian, Fishguard Library; Ann Bagnall, Wyn Thomas. Thanks also to the Warden of Llandovery College for permission to reproduce the portrait of Lady Llanover.

Bobby Freeman
Newport, Pembrokshire

April, 1991

The Right Hon. Lady Llanover
1802-96

THE FIRST MEETING OF THE HERMIT AND THE TRAVELLER.

THE FIRST PRINCIPLES OF

GOOD COOKERY

ILLUSTRATED.

AND RECIPES COMMUNICATED BY THE WELSH HERMIT
OF THE CELL OF ST. GOVER,

*WITH VARIOUS REMARKS ON MANY THINGS
PAST AND PRESENT.*

BY

THE RIGHT HON. LADY LLANOVER.

LONDON:
RICHARD BENTLEY, NEW BURLINGTON STREET,
Publisher in Ordinary to Her Majesty.
1867.

" Tywyned graienyn, ei ran."

The grain of sand has its portion of the beach.

CONTENTS.

Contents.

LIST OF ILLUSTRATIONS.

INTRODUCTION.

GENTLE READER,

As the present work is intended for the especial benefit of those of *gentle* birth who may not have any very extensive knowledge of economy in domestic practice, and as the Hero of the accompanying annals belonged to the last century, the commencement of this Introductory Epistle is not misplaced; and the Author has adopted the present form, including dialogue remarks, annotations, and explanations, from experience of facts, which tend to prove that the multiplication of Cookery Books on the common plan has very little increased the amount of knowledge of the fundamental principles of the real art of Cookery and Domestic Economy. Whether the Master of the Cell of Gover will be more successful than his

predecessors in awakening the minds of the
present generation to the necessity of understanding themselves what ought to be done,
and what avoided, to ensure a well-cooked
dish, time alone will show!—but if *the Hermit*
only convinces a few persons, who desire to
benefit their fellow-creatures, that those who
want food might be benefited to an enormous
extent, were it not for the ignorance of the
majority of those who have enough, in matters
of practical utility, the knowledge of which
would prevent the destruction of millions of
tons of the best food, this little book will not
have been written in vain.

The Author has received, for the last few
years, numerous inquiries and applications, from
friends, for information about certain simple
dishes, which they had, in the course of their
travels, tasted at the board of her friend the
Hermit of Gover's Cell, and these applications
have now increased to such an extent, that, finding it impossible to reply to them satisfactorily,
a promise was given of "*a Book*," the appearance

of which has been hastened by recent urgent demands for a receipt, *How to make a Cook?*

The Author does not profess to write a Tale. The present little volume is for the avowed purpose of instruction in Cookery, Domestic Economy, and other matters involving home comfort, for which the narrative is merely a vehicle. Where quantities are mentioned, they have been generally extracted and translated from a day-book, kept in Welsh by the Hermit's first hand (Gwenllian, the senior widow), which day-book was made from original Welsh memo randa in white chalk, on the door of the Larder, made by Marged, the Hermit's second hand, as the materials were weighed, and their proceeds afterwards measured.

The Author feels that no apology is necessary for making public practical instructions which are the result of many years' individual ex-perience, in matters *universally admitted* to require an *entire reform*, which are very little understood by the poor, and *still less* compre-hended by the rich. It is, however, fair to the

Author, that the " *Gentle Readers* " should be informed (whether male or female), that, had time and circumstances permitted, this book would have been more complete, but, under the impression that *facts* will constitute its chief value, the Author decided on publishing one volume as quickly as possible, without waiting to rearrange the subjects or to improve the composition, being very certain that, *if* there is *any value* to be found in its pages, other persons will be awakened to their own practical responsibilities and to the knowledge of practical possibilities by what the Welsh Hermit has begun.

Aug^{A.} Llanover.

THE FIRST PRINCIPLES OF

GOOD COOKERY.

ONCE upon a time, not very long ago, there
was an aged Welshman who lived in a house
cut out of a rock adjoining the cell and opposite the Well of St. Gover.*   He was always
called the Hermit (Meudwy) by his Cambrian
countrymen, and had been remarkable in his
youth for acquiring a practical knowledge of
whatever art he deemed it useful to understand.
He was of ancient lineage, and had been born
where he resided.   He was one day sitting by
the side of the limpid spring which rose out of
the ground near the door of his rocky abode,

---

* Gover, Hênwg, and Gwarwg ; the three primitive saints of
Gwent.

when a traveller approached, and asked him if he would allow his horse to graze for a short time upon the tempting herbage which he saw around him, while he himself rested awhile by the well of sparkling water and quenched his thirst.

Elidr Gwyn, with the courtesy which distinguished his race, bade him welcome, and after the steed of the Traveller had been tethered at a little distance, entered into conversation with his new friend.

" You have ridden far, my son," said he, " and no doubt you can give me tidings of what has been passing in England and Wales as well as in the distant quarters of the globe for the last fifty years. I am myself ninety-three years old at least, but my own impression is that I am much older. I have no written record of my birth, and I sometimes think that I might rival in longevity the Salmon of Llyn Llyfon, the Ouzel of Cilgwri, the Toad of Mochnant bog, and the Owl of Cwm Cawlwyd, so celebrated in our ancient MSS."

" Who were those illustrious characters of

whom you speak?" said the Traveller: " I
have visited Scotland and Ireland; I have pene-
trated into the farthest parts of England; I have
crossed the seas, and visited the most celebrated
parts of the world; but I do not recollect ever
to have heard of the personages you have mentioned."

" Probably not, noble sir," said the Hermit,
with a humorous smile; " but may I ask whether
you have ever been in *Wales*, and have made
yourself acquainted with the literature of the
ancient Britons?"

" Never," replied his new friend; " but
being now upon Welsh ground, and, if I mistake not, having the pleasure of addressing a
native of the ancient race of the Cymry, I trust
you will excuse my freedom in again asking
who those remarkable champions were of
whom you spoke, for I suppose that they were
great warriors, who from some circumstances
connected with their history, or perhaps some
personal resemblance to a fish, a bird, or a reptile,
were designated in the manner you mention."

" Time," said the venerable Hermit, " is

too short,—for the sun is already on its down-
ward course,—to permit of my relating the remarkable history which has raised your curiosity.
I can only say that it is a Welsh MS. entitled
' The Ancients of the World,' by which it
appears that the Owl of Cwm Cawlwyd was
the oldest of all the birds and beasts at that
period, and it occurred to my mind, in allusion
to my own age, that I bid fair to rival that bird
of wisdom, as my health is perfect and my
faculties unimpaired."

" Good father," said the Traveller, " do
relate to me this history."

" My son," answered the Recluse, " one of
the proofs of my consistent nature is the
unabated vigour of my curiosity. It cannot
signify nearly so much to you to hear an old
Welsh tale, as it does to me to know (even at
this advanced age) what the world has been
about for the last sixty-four years, during which
time I have never gone beyond the neighbourhood of this secluded abode, where I have every
necessary of life, and a very large collection of
books of the last century. My recreations are

chiefly confined to the study of the properties
of wild plants, and the good people on the
mountains seek my advice. I have ample
means for myself, but in return for my medical
assistance they supply me with many additional
rural luxuries. Tell me then, I pray you,
something of the state of the world."

The Traveller complied with his request,
and some of his assertions were exceedingly
strange and apparently contradictory. He said,
the improvement was so great in the last sixty-
four years, that the Hermit would scarcely
believe it possible for human intellect to have
achieved the wonderful things that *he* himself
had seen and heard of. He then proceeded to
tell him of railroads—sixty miles traversed in
an hour; of iron ships; of marvellous guns;
of many queer things done with, or rather *in*,
balloons; but on the latter subject he was
rather confused, as although he had gone up
in one, it had come down on the top of a tree,
and he was taken out senseless.

After having recounted a succession of these
wonders to the attentive Hermit, he paused

to take breath, and his companion took advantage of the opportunity to venture upon a simple interrogatory :—

" All this surpasses my comprehension. Though I cannot doubt the word of so accomplished a gentleman, still you have hitherto confined yourself to the wonders of mechanical invention; but as the human intellect is by an all-wise Providence adapted for every exercise which is conducive to the welfare and benefit of mankind, I must ask you to gratify me by mentioning whether the great progress and improvement which you said was so universal, does not equal in other departments the mechanical ingenuity which has wrought such marvels, by which it appears that people travel so fast, they have not the slightest control over their own movements, or those of others who are killed wholesale without their surviving relations knowing the cause; and that they are also enabled to shoot so far, that they may destroy their friends almost as well as their enemies, as their patent guns carry to so great a distance they cannot see who they knock down. But tell me, my good sir, of the arts of life—those arts which mark the difference practically between a cultivated intellect and paralysed or petrified faculties—between the *useful* and the *useless*—between defined civilization and uncultured ignorance."

" The Traveller appeared not to understand the purport of this question, and was at a complete loss to answer it : " What do you mean," said he, " by the arts of life ? "

" My good friend," said the Hermit, " what do you mean by savage life ? what are its characteristics ? "

" I can answer that," said the Traveller, " without difficulty. Bodies without clothes, and meat and vegetables, either raw or so ill cooked that the preparation bestowed on them can scarcely be called cookery ; for truly cooked food fit to eat, and raiment shaped and fit to wear, are undeniable requirements in civilized life."

" It rejoices my heart," said the Hermit, " to find that we so perfectly agree ; and I am now longing to hear of the progress and improvements which have taken place in those most necessary arts of life. Doubtless the intellect of the last sixty-four years has caused such advances that there is not a matron or a damsel in any rank of life from the Land's End to John o' Groat's House, who cannot cut out and make to perfection what our Teutonic neighbours used sometimes to call a '*first-dress;*' or a master of a family, from the noble to the peasant, who has not his dinner, whether it be one dish or whether it be twenty, dressed in a manner which combines delicacy of flavour with the greatest economy and the utmost attention to health, with such a tempting appearance as does credit to the instructions or execution of the wife, the daughter or the sister presiding over his household."

At these words the Traveller turned pale, for he was a man of honour and veracity; he wished much to tell a *fib*—for the honour of England he wished to tell it—but his virtue forbade, and he could only sigh deeply.

The Hermit gently inquired the cause of his emotion, upon which, with some hesitation, the Traveller informed him that he had touched upon a point which made him low-spirited, as he had from childhood been always much annoyed when he could not verify his own assertions by facts, but that he had really been influenced chiefly by the opinions of the newspapers, of which there were now two or three in every village, and that he had used the words " *universal progress,*" and " *incredible improvement,*" in the general sense in which they appeared in print, and were consequently repeated by the reading millions ; but that the Hermit's last questions had struck home, and that he begged to be excused giving a more definite answer. This, however, was not permitted, and after some earnest but well-bred discussion, a compact was made that the Traveller should reply to the Hermit's inquiries without the slightest reserve, upon his own personal and individual knowledge, on condition that the Hermit in his turn should give him the benefit of his wisdom and experience, to suggest remedies for such existing evils as truth might oblige the Traveller to divulge.

The Hermit, perceiving that his companion was evidently acutely touched, with the delicacy which was one of his characteristics, said that he would *not* exact any expression of his sentiments or opinions—he would simply ask for facts.

"I will begin," said he, "with an inquiry easily answered. Everything in your apparel denotes civilized life. May I ask what dexterous fingers plied the needle which executed the numerous plaits in what used in the last century to be called a shirt, but in my youth there was far more needlework required than I perceive in the specimen before me?"

The Traveller again appeared embarrassed and perplexed. "I know not," said he, "whether it is made by man or woman, or by a machine! All I know is, that there is not a single family of my acquaintance, and my connexions are extensive, where there is a single female who can either cut out or make a shirt! I buy them out of shops in London, and every now and then there are subscriptions made for half-starved women, who are never

seen, but are said to be employed in the forma-
tion of shirts. But there is a general complaint
that ready-made shirts never fit, and that the
male part of the population of all ranks suffer
severely from the entire ignorance and utter
inability of their wives and daughters to undertake either the execution or the direction of
that portion of our dress."

"Marvellous change!" ejaculated the Hermit. " I could understand the possibility of a
new-fashioned shirt, or another form of garment, but I *never* shall be able to comprehend
the abandonment of that art denominated plain
needlework, the perfection of which is best demonstrated in all its branches in that one article
of apparel. Good heavens! Is it possible that
the heads of families (I mean, of course, the
lords of creation) should be so utterly neglected
by those who in *my* time considered it their
pride, as well as their duty, to be responsible
for every process necessary for the production
of a shirt ? "

The Traveller begged that this painful subject might not be continued, but promised to

place in the Hermit's hands a letter which had appeared some years ago in the papers of the day, and which he assured him was an exact statement of a general case as felt a few years since; but that it was now far worse, as now the very inquiry for a female who could make a shirt, would render the inquirer an object of ridicule, for supposing that the art was still known and practised.*

The Hermit, wishing to cheer his friend, changed the subject, and next asked for information with regard to the progress and improvement of *cookery*.

"I suppose," said he, "that since my time the advances in the culinary art have been commensurate with that of machinery, and that no man, in these days of progress and improvement, ever has a bad dinner, or tastes an ill-cooked dish; that the viands of the present century are prepared under the instructions of highly cultivated female intellects, in a manner far superior as to taste, salubrity, and appearance, to those

---

* For this letter, see "Traveller's Note Book."

that I remember in (what *you* probably would call) the ʻdark ages of ignorance.'"

Scarcely had these words been uttered, when the ashy paleness of the Traveller alarmed the inmate of the cell. "Good father," said he, "spare me! oh, spare me! The very recollection of what I have suffered from the universal, indeed cherished ignorance of the culinary art in the kingdom of Great Britain and Ireland, occasions a faintness which I cannot overcome."

"Possibly," said the Hermit, "it may be that you require sustenance at this very moment. You have ridden far, and no doubt fasted long ; allow me to offer you some refreshment, which, if not luxurious, will at all events be innoxious."

The Traveller looked in dismay at the rough exterior of the stony cell, and his silent reflections were as follows :—"I am sinking from inanition, but with my delicate digestion, what consequences may I not expect to result from partaking of such fare as will probably be offered me by this old man ? But I have no alternative, I must eat or starve. Too much fatigued to ride further without food, I must accept his offer, and bear as I can the disgust and subsequent suffering attendant on such a meal."

The reader need not be detained with a description of the various courtesies which passed between the aged host and his wandering guest, who was at length persuaded, with timid step, to follow him into the interior of his abode, where it is unnecessary to follow them at present.

At the expiration of two hours they reappeared; but what a change had taken place in the countenance of the stranger, who, it may be observed, was remarkably handsome, and, with the independence of a sensible man, was not disfigured by the terrier or monkey-like appendages, which have been the fashion since the hardships of the Crimean war necessarily obliged both officers and men to appear both unkempt and unshorn. His eyes were lighted with a vivacious intelligence; his clear complexion was suffused with a roseate tint; his light curly hair, as is always the case with renewed strength, had assumed a crisper curl, while a beaming yet reflective smile indicated the pleasing tenor of his thoughts.

The Hermit paused when they again reached the well, and said in a mild yet solemn tone— " Remember our agreement."

" I shall not forget it," said his new friend. " I should be the most ungrateful of mortals if I ever forgot the admirable repast for which I am indebted to you; and I consider that what you require of me is very inadequate to what I have received and am still to obtain from you. But lest there should be any misunderstanding between us, allow me to repeat what I believe are the terms of our convention, and correct me if I am in error."

The Hermit bowed with the air of a man who had never been in the habit of turning his back on leaving a room.

The Traveller resumed—" I have promised to travel for fourteen days; then to return here and to give you an exact report of my bad dinners, whether at inns or private houses, on condition that you will give me the same dinner each day, cooked in the same perfection of which I have

had a specimen already, and that you will allow
me to see each dish executed under your own
inspection, always being permitted to dine with
you afterwards; and that you will also inform
me of the causes which have produced the
faults of which I may have to complain, in my
descriptions of the dinners of which I may
have partaken, or of any other troubles or inconveniences I may have experienced."

The Hermit testified his approval, declared
the recapitulation to be perfectly correct, assisted the Traveller to regain his steed, and with
mutual compliments they parted in the hope of
another early meeting. At the end of fourteen
days the Hermit watched for the return of the
Traveller; but although he spent a longer time
than usual on his favourite seat by the well
surrounded by ferns and wild flowers, no Traveller returned, and he sighed when he retired
to rest, from the conviction that the compact
made with the Traveller would never be ful-
filled—that he had forgotten the conditions, and
cared no longer for the results.

Day after day, and week after week passed

away, until a month having elapsed the Hermit had ceased even to expect him; when one sultry afternoon he beheld a figure approaching on the horse which he recognised as that of his friend; but the rider was so unlike the Traveller of his former recollection, that he could scarcely persuade himself of his identity until he was close to him, when he dismounted with difficulty, and the Hermit was grieved to perceive that one of his formerly well-shaped legs had evidently been broken, and on his glove being withdrawn, that he had lost one finger and a part of his thumb. The bridge of his nose was much depressed, and a scar over the eyebrow proved that he had narrowly escaped loss of sight.

The Hermit, who was a man of most sensitive feeling, as well as of refined good breeding, was at a loss to know how he could testify his sympathy without demonstrating to the full extent the frightful change he perceived in his companion's outward appearance, when the latter, anticipating the difficulty, first broke silence.

C

"My venerable friend," said he, "you no doubt believed that I had broken faith, and was unworthy of the kind reception you had bestowed on me; but I think that the wreck of my former self which you now behold will be sufficient to convince you that I have narrowly escaped with my life, and that it is only wonderful that I have been able to pursue my journey hitherward."

The Hermit, with kind expressions of sympathy, begged that he would unfold to him the sad circumstances which had led to his injuries. "Have you," said he, "had an encounter with highwaymen or footpads in traversing some bleak moor, or have you been too adventurous in the hunting field, although it is not usual for accidents of this description to entail the loss of *fingers* and *thumbs* ?"

The Traveller assured him that to neither of those causes were his misfortunes to be attributed; but that he had been thus maimed from the railway train in which he was travelling having been run into by another train, which was going still faster.

"Why did they not pull up," said the Hermit, " when they saw your equipage before them ? "

" Because," replied the Traveller, " those wonderful engines which the progress of the human intellect has invented since your retirement from the world move with such velocity it is impossible to see anything in the way in time to pull up, and the whole dependence of the travellers for security from such accidents is on those persons who are placed on the road to make signals—which, *if rightly interpreted*, enable the driver to stop in time—intelligence being thus conveyed that another train is just before him ; but it frequently happens that the signal is not interpreted aright—or, rather that a wrong signal is made."

" How unjustifiable ! " exclaimed the Hermit. " How thoroughly inexcusable ! "

" My good friend," said the Traveller, " you are too severe. Dilapidated as I am, irreparable as the injuries are which I have received, I can not only forgive, but *pity* the unfortunate man who, by a wrong signal, has been the immediate cause of the death of six persons, and the mutilation of thirty more, many of whom are far worse off than myself. The wretched man of whom I speak was one of many officials who were obliged to work eighteen and twenty hours at a stretch, by which means his power of vision and his intellects became so completely confused that he could not distinguish right from wrong."

The Hermit appeared to be astounded, and desired to know " whether he had been in error in believing that Great Britain was governed by a virtuous and benevolent Sovereign, and a liberal and enlightened Government; and yet, if such was the case, how could such cruelties be perpetrated ? "

The Traveller had some difficulty in making his host understand that the Sovereign and the Government had no power to protect the lives of the subjects on these occasions—that the railroads were speculations unconnected with the Government, and that either no laws had yet been enacted with sufficient punishments and penalties to compel proper regulations, or else that the Houses of Parliament contained so many members who were themselves shareholders in railways, or who had constituents upon whose votes they depended for their return, who were also deeply involved in such speculations, that it was quite hopeless to endeavour to get a majority in the House of Commons to inflict punishments sufficient to ensure a reform for the preservation of life. " Indeed," added the Traveller, " I must confess that the hope of pecuniary gain induced *me* to take shares in the very railway on which I have now nearly ended my life ; and although I know that it *must* become bankrupt, yet I do not like to hasten the crisis by any public complaint, from the hope that if others don't know as much as I do, I may be enabled to sell my shares for as much as I gave for them."

The Hermit was unfeignedly shocked at this undisguised avowal of such selfish and mercenary motives; but he confined himself to the remark that railroad speculation appeared to him to be worse than the " *South Sea Bubble,*" the details of which he was better acquainted with, and that he could not perceive any indication of exalted or improved intellect, although there might be much increased ingenuity, in inventing machinery which outran all control, and that he considered the controlling power ought to be fully equal to the inventive before any great claim could be proved to the real progress of intellectual superiority.

He then hospitably inquired what the Traveller could eat, and was informed that his health had been so shaken by his late disaster, and subsequent diet in a large railway hotel kept by a company where no one was master, that he could swallow nothing but chicken, and even *that* he thought of with disgust, from the recollection of the greasy water which had been called chicken broth, and of the nauseous fluid which surrounded the fowl he had last eaten, and which was denominated "*parsley and butter.*"

The Hermit expressed his satisfaction in being provided with a pullet ready for boiling, and to the astonishment of the Traveller he introduced him to his kitchen, where there was

every convenience for cooking, with four
Welsh women of advanced age, the eldest
being past eighty, and the youngest past fifty,
but full of activity, and in costumes that would
have made the fortune of an artist. But he
informed his friend that as he had promised to
teach him to cook the dinner, and as he always
liked to superintend, the Traveller must be
present while that process was carried on,
unless he repented his compact, in which case
he (the Hermit) would remain, and the
Traveller bear himself company in another
apartment cut out of the rock during the period
of the performance.

The Traveller congratulated himself upon
the happy opportunity now offered for seeing
an exemplification of what the Hermit considered one of the most practical proofs of civilized life, and great was his astonishment when
he saw his host take a dainty chicken * ready
trussed, and *weigh it*—it was very fat, and the
weight was three pounds and a half; it was then

* See Receipt in Appendix No. I.

placed in a tin vessel, and one-fourth of a pint
of spring water to every pound, and a sprinkling of salt.   The vessel was then placed in an
iron vessel, an inch larger in circumference,*
which is well known in Wales, and called
Ffwrn fach, in which boiling water was
poured till it rose within an inch of the top.
The inner and outer vessels, having their lids
put on firmly, were placed over the slow heat
of the Hermit's stove, where they remained
undisturbed for nearly two hours ; which were
agreeably passed in visiting the Hermit's garden,
where herbs and vegetables abounded — his
goats, his cows, and even his pigs were not
forgotten.

In the course of these rambles, and others
which followed subsequently, many remarks
were made, and information given by the recluse of the cell, which the Traveller noted
down, and which will appear in a condensed
form from the " Traveller's note-book" in the
course of this volume ; but every hour tended

---

* See Plate No. I.

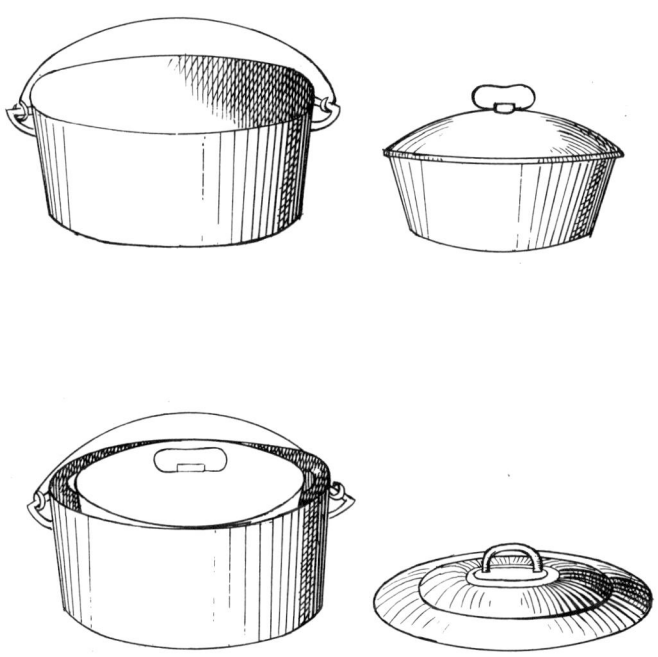

E J.Fecit

Ftwrn Fach

to strengthen the conviction of the wanderer, that he had at last found a man who practised what he understood, and who was not led away by any theory to give credence to that which was not demonstrated by the results. When they returned, the Hermit having ascertained by pricking his chicken with a fork that it was thoroughly done, proceeded to prepare melted butter—for according to his compact he was to give the Traveller a dinner of the same materials as those of which he had so much complained. The Hermit placed two ounces of fresh butter in a tin saucepan, which fitted into another holding boiling water; he added a teaspoonful of flour, which he mixed with the butter as it melted, adding also by degrees two tablespoonfuls of milk; when well incorporated, he added six tablespoonfuls of water, stirring it round the same way till it attained the thickness of *moderate*—not too thick—cream. He had previously requested his companion to assist the widows by washing some parsley, and pick it leaf from leaf; this he put into boiling water for a few minutes, then minced it fine and bruised it to a pulp in a small mortar; after which it was put into his wooden sauce-boat, the work of his own hands, which had been previously heated with hot water, and pouring the melted butter upon the parsley, stirred the whole together rapidly.

The frugal board was soon laid; but before they commenced their repast, the venerable host desired his friend to remember that the dinner he was about to eat was strictly in accordance with their compact—which was that the Hermit was to display *well dressed* that which the Traveller had particularly complained of as having had ill dressed; but he said that a boiled chicken, with parsley and butter, was the *very last* choice he himself would have made; as he thought the latter the very worst sauce that he knew; but he believed, as now prepared, it would be neither unpleasant in taste, or unwholesome. The result proved his supposition to be correct; the chicken was tender, juicy, and retained its full natural flavour; while the sauce was of its kind irre-proachable: but as the Hermit observed, with

such materials the most that could be done
was to make " an unobjectionable medium for
parsley." " You did not name any pudding,"
said he, " and therefore I have given you
none ; otherwise, my garden, and my kind
neighbours, would have enabled me to add
another dish." The Traveller, with many
apologies, begged to propose another clause in
their agreement, for his own advantage. It
was, that the Hermit should let them have the
remains of the fowl the next day, that he
might understand his method of making a repast the second time of cooking.

" With the greatest pleasure I comply
with your request," said the frugal Anchorite ;
" for I not only think it sinful to waste a
grain of good food, but I am certain that
I shall be able to give you a much more
relishing dish than any of those you have yet
named to me. There is, however, one slight
difficulty : we have both, it appears, good
appetites ; and, although it *was* a noble fowl,
there is not quite enough dinner for one person
left on its bones ! but, as my larder is not yet

exhausted, I will add another dish, on one condition, which is, that you tell me how you
would *fricasée* that chicken, if you were obliged
to cook it yourself, or to give directions for so
doing."

" I would," said the Traveller, " mix cream
and butter together over the fire, and then put
in the chicken."

" It would be *remarkably nasty*," said the
Hermit, " and, moreover, there would be no
thickening, and no flavour."

" Oh, I forgot the *flour*," said the Traveller,
" which I suppose is always stirred in to
thicken it."

" I think, my friend," said the Hermit,
" you have forgotten a good many other things,
or rather you are *totally ignorant* of cookery,
however many lectures on other sciences you
may have attended."

The Traveller appeared a little offended at
this remark, and said, he " never pretended to
be a cook ; " that he had simply stated what he
supposed must be done, without knowing anything about it.

The Hermit smiled at his choler—"You are," said he, "the best demonstration of the justice of my opinions—*extremes do indeed meet.* You would fain persuade me that the world is wonderfully more intelligent, and better informed, in everything denoting superior civilization, to the world I knew in the last century; but here you have been a sufferer for years from weakness of digestion, according to your own account, from the poisonous preparations of food that you have been doomed to swallow; yet it has never once occurred to you to make out what was the cause of cooked food being very bad or very good; and that *very* necessary knowledge, it appears, has not been imparted to you by any of the learned lecturers, who you say teach everybody everything without a book."

The reader need not be detained with the dialogue that followed. Suffice it to say, that the Traveller was slightly acrimonious, from finding himself totally unable to maintain his own original assertions against the cool practical logic of the Hermit; but a truce was at last concluded, and the Traveller wisely determined,

that if he couldn't teach he would at all events
learn ; and a plan was arranged for daily culinary instruction, as well as for walks in the
neighbouring valleys and mountains ; and as the
Traveller could not but admit to himself that
the Hermit knew a great many useful things of
which he was ignorant, he determined to note
down at night those facts which had never
before struck him, or of which he had not
previously heard, especially relating to objects
to which he had been accustomed from his
childhood ; and he was more particularly glad
that he had thus determined, when he found
that his host had not only a large garden, but a
small farm and a flock of sheep, besides bees,
goats, pigs, and two Welsh ponies.   With
pardonable self-conceit, he also determined that
everything which he observed in the Hermit's
management, or which was asserted by him to
be good or bad, he would try to *dis*prove, if it
was possible ; and he had at that time little
doubt of its being so in some instances, in
which case he intended to write down his own
counter-experiences on parallel columns, and he

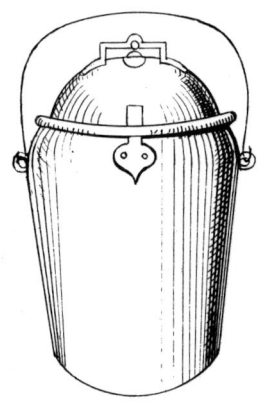

E.J. Fecit.

Digester.

thought, with no small delight, of the triumph
he would have on the conclusion of his visit,
when he should read his MSS. to the Recluse,
if he could produce some refutations of the
correctness of the Hermit's assertions from results obtained by the Traveller's own superior
knowledge, through his enlightened education
in this much more enlightened age.

As many remarks made during the rambles
of the two friends will appear in a concise
form (taken from the Traveller's note-book),
this narrative will pass on to the relation of the
Hermit's dinners—what they were, and how
they were cooked.

The afternoon of the chicken dinner, all the
remaining meat was carefully taken off the bones
of the Hermit's fowl; the bones were then
weighed, and the weight being one pound and
a half, they were afterwards broken small, with
an iron hammer, and one pint and a half of
spring water being added to it, the whole was
put into a digester on the Hermit's stove,* to
stew slowly for two hours. The liquor was

---

* For *Digester*, see Plate No. II.

then poured off, the bones taken out and *re-broken*, another pint and a quarter of spring water added to them, the vessel replaced on the stove for two hours more; the liquor again poured off into another basin, and the bones then given to the Hermit's dog.   By this time the Traveller had not the slightest doubt that his good host was mad, and he chuckled to himself at the idea of the instructions by which he was to benefit in the fricasee of the following day.

His amusement was, however, not unmixed with apprehension about the second dish, as he feared the Hermit had been so intent upon making broth out of bones which contained nothing, that he would forget there was not chicken enough left for two.

Preparations for the next day were as follows: the Hermit produced, first, a basin in which there was a pint of thin jelly, at the top of which was a quantity of clear oil, and underneath that a very thin layer of very delicate fat.   The Hermit first took off the oil and put it into a bottle—he said it was useful for many purposes where oil was required—he next took off the small quantity of more solid fat, which he laid upon a plate by his side; he then produced a second basin, in which was a pint of still firmer jelly, which he added to the contents of the first-mentioned basin; he then produced a large cup, in which was more than one-fourth of a pint of *as solid* but *more opaque* jelly, nearly white; this he also added to the other jellies, and then poured the whole into the inner part of a double saucepan, the outer vessel being nearly filled with boiling water.*

The Traveller could no longer contain his curiosity, and inquired whence all those jellies came, and what they were made of?

" The first," said the Hermit, " was the jelly produced by simply *boiling the chicken* in a double vessel, which in itself is the finest preparation of chicken broth for invalids. The

---

* The bones above mentioned then weighed one pound, and had they been again broken and subjected to the same process with one pint of water, instead of being given to the Hermit's dog, they would have produced a quarter of a pint more jelly; making in all, from the bones *alone*, more than one pint of jelly.

second was the jelly from the first stewing of the bones, which contain a large quantity of gelatine. The third was from the second boiling of those same bones. I have mixed all together, although the quantity will make more sauce than we shall require for our fricasee, because I shall require it to-morrow for another purpose." The Hermit added a little salt to the dissolved jelly, and desired his friend to taste it, who admitted that it was the perfection of chicken broth, but how it could ever become anything else he had no conception. The Hermit then chopped *very finely* celery, leek-roots, a small quantity of turnip, still less of carrot, and one small potato, all of which he put into a single saucepan with the surface chicken fat which he had taken from the chicken jellies. He stirred these over a slow heat for about ten minutes, so that the chopped vegetables absorbed the whole of the chicken fat without burning; he then gradually added as much flour as made the whole into a stiff paste, which he stirred about five minutes longer, till the fat, the vegetables, and the flour

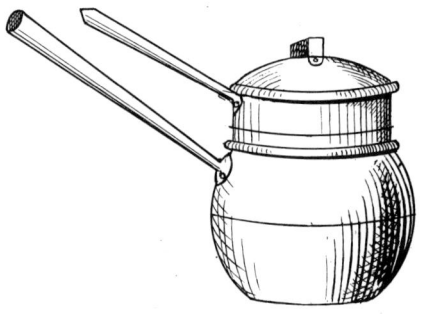

E.J.Fecit.

Double Saucepan.

were thoroughly incorporated; he then turned
the whole mass into the melted and hot
chicken stock, and, well stirring it, covered it
over, and left it to stew slowly in a double
saucepan,* (a vessel surrounded by boiling
water,) for three-quarters of an hour, at the
end of which time he requested his friend
to taste and pronounce his opinion.

The Traveller was so agreeably surprised by
the excellence of the taste, that he forgot for
the moment what it was intended for, and exclaimed, "What excellent chicken soup!"

" If that is your opinion," said his host, "the
first stage of my fricasee is well accomplished;
but from soup it must become sauce." Upon
which he poured the whole through a wire
sieve into a basin, by which process the thicker
portions of the vegetables were left behind.
He then emptied the contents of the basin back
into the saucepan, and added two spoonfuls of
cream; again it was stirred, and again it was
tasted, and the Traveller's opinion requested.

* See Plate III.

He was evidently a man of acute taste, and the Hermit (who was always aiming at perfection) took pleasure in his criticisms.

" This condiment," said the Traveller, " now disappoints me : the first taste was *so pure*, and yet so *relishing*, that I expected when further advanced nothing more could be desired ; but strange to say, *now* that it has assumed the usual hue of fricasee sauce, now that it has received the addition of what I should consider its best ingredient, cream, it has much *less* flavour than before, and, although extremely good, is by former comparison insipid."

" You enchant me, my friend, by your remarks," said the good man ; " you have the real organ of taste of palate. Your observations are as correct as they are acute. When you first tasted my sauce it was redolent of the aroma of the fresh vegetables, judiciously selected, and so finely chopped that their juices were thoroughly extracted. The cream has, as it were, diluted and diminished the flavour, though it has materially enriched the composition ; but such a diminution of the poignancy of the flavours you admired was necessary to our present purpose; in so delicate a meat as chicken, the flavour of roots and herbs must not preponderate."

The Hermit then took the meat of the cold chicken, which was cut or pulled lengthways, in pieces pointed at each end, and put into the sauce, with the addition of a little more salt. He then added boiling water to the outer vessel (which had by long boiling wasted considerably), and he allowed the whole to stew— frequently stirring, for half an hour. The Traveller was again called upon to taste. " It *is* perfection," said he; " never do I remember a fricasee which combined the whole flavour of the chicken with the most perfect consistency; and was thus rich without being nauseating, thus pure without being insipid, thus relishing yet thus delicate."

The Hermit bowed. " It is twelve o'clock, my friend, and as we rose at cock-crow, and breakfasted with the larks, we will, if you have no objection, dine at my usual hour; observe, the sun's rays have just struck the meridian line upon my window."

The Traveller expressed his concurrence and satisfaction, but, at the same time, he was too well bred to give utterance to the misgivings which he felt, lest his hospitable provider had forgotten that the only imperfection in his fricasee was, that it was not enough for the dinner of two hungry men! The simple board was soon spread by the Welsh widows, but before they sat down the Hermit gave an order in " *mountain Greek ;* "* when they disappeared, and going into a side chamber, also cut in the rock, brought from thence a small square of cold meat, delicately garnished with mountain thyme. The fricasee was soon finished, the good man observing that it had been no part of his compact to ornament the dish; that he dealt only with the palate, and with the digestion; that his cookery was as agreeable to the former as it was innoxious, indeed beneficial, to the latter; but, were it necessary, he was not incapable of adding such garnish as would be as pleasing to the eye as to the taste.

---

* Welsh—the ancient language of Biitain.

The Traveller declared he had no wish for any addition to such a dish; the only complaint he had to make was, that he wished to have eaten a great deal more.

" I anticipated as much," said the Hermit, " and though my practical art will not make the meat of half a chicken suffice for two persons, I think you will not find this cold meat unpalatable, and that you may possibly have tasted worse fare."

The Traveller cut off a slice of the meat alluded to, which he found was beef, which the knife passed through like cheese, and he was astonished at its tenderness and flavour. He asked the Hermit to explain how it had been prepared, but he excused himself, saying that he intended on another occasion to give him a similar piece of beef *hot*, which he should see prepared himself.

The next day was passed in similar rambles to its predecessor, and incidents occurred which served to illustrate the Hermit's opinions and the results of his practice, which will appear later in the notes of the Traveller.

The third day's dinner consisted of a leg of Welsh mutton, so small, that an English eye would have believed it to be the leg of a sucking lamb ; notwithstanding it was six years old, and consequently in the full perfection oʃ flavour to which that unrivalled animal attains.   Over the Hermit's fire-place was a simple crank with notches, from which he suspended a piece of woollen yarn, doubled several times and twisted.   To the end of this string he attached a hook, to which he suspended the leg of mutton, and in the dripping-pan he placed a cake of such ivory fat, that the Traveller could scarcely believe that the delicate-looking substance was really that usually nauseous material.

The Traveller remarked that the mutton was very far from the fire.

" Only *twenty-three inches*," said his friend. " One of the chief reasons of the rarity of good roasting is the senseless habit of scorching the meat on the outside before it is warmed within. I shall not put the mutton nearer to the fire until it is *well warmed;* and then I shall only put it *two inches nearer,* and leave it at *twenty-one inches* till it begins to smoke, and you will then witness the last process."

The Hermit then made the Travéller assist the widows in basting the mutton, before which there was a wooden screen lined with tin, with two shelves on the side next the fire. But, contrary to the usual practice, he showed the Traveller that every time he basted the meat he was to empty all the melted fat which poured down into the hollow of the dripping-pan, into an earthen pan, which stood at the bottom of the screen on a level with the dripping-pan, and from which he was instructed to replenish the ladle when there was no longer any supply in the well of the dripping-pan to baste the meat. The Traveller could not contain his surprise at the intervention of this pan, and desired to have an explanation, upon which the Hermit, who seemed very much to enjoy his astonishment, said that he would give him two guesses; and that if he failed to discover the reason, he would tell him, but that, at the same time, he must expect

that the Hermit would be justified, in such a
case, in having less respect than ever for the
effect of the scientific lectures upon chemistry
which his friend had so highly valued.

The Traveller's two guesses were unfortunate.
The first time he supposed that, the earthen
pan being rather further from the fire than
the dripping-pan, the Hermit made use of it
to avoid burning the eyes. His second idea
was, that, for some reason unknown to him,
the earthen pan imparted a flavour to the fat;
and he was much annoyed when the explanation was given, to find that he had exactly hit
upon the wrong end of the reason.

The Hermit, who really wished to instruct
him, very kindly determined to make him find
out the right reason by a series of questions.
" Did you ever," said he, " remark that gravy
had a very strong, unpleasant taste, which often
was found in a still greater degree in the *outer*
part of roast meat ? "

The Traveller declared his clear recollection
of those coincidences, but he did not see what
they had to do with the questions at issue.

"Did you ever," said the Hermit, "smell a very unpleasant odour pervading a house, which is often explained by the supposition that 'fat had fallen into the fire' in the kitchen? But," said he, "it is not so often that *fat has fallen into the fire*, as that *fire* has fallen *into the fat!* from a hot cinder dropping into the well of the dripping-pan, *or*, what is more frequent, and has exactly the same effect, the dripping-pan becoming almost red hot, from the long exposure too near the fire. A large portion of the fat is thus kept in a perpetual state of frying for the space of some hours; one portion of it becomes the consistency of treacle, and adheres to the dripping-pan, while the more liquid part imbibes the objectionable flavour which is created by this continual frizzling, and the gravy of the meat (the most delicate part of the dish) is a nauseous liquid, redolent with grease, which the action of the fire has rendered unwholesome and rancid, however pure it may have been when first put down to melt. But by emptying it into the earthen pan, this effect is prevented. It is sufficiently near the fire to retain its liquid state, without any bad effect to the taste; and the gravy which, as the joint proceeds in roasting, is likewise received into the dripping-pan with the fat, is also preserved from injury in the same manner."

The Traveller, who did not lack intelligence, although (like many theoretical wise men) he was little accustomed to plain practice, saw in a moment the sense and reason of the Hermit's system of roasting, but he did not like to say much about it, because he felt that he would not *rise* in the Hermit's estimation if he confessed how especially he had suffered, in more organs than one, from the very cause which the Hermit had now so clearly demonstrated, and which, by so simple a process, could be prevented, without *ever* attempting to understand the cause of his annoyance, or making use of his own intellect to provide a remedy. By this time the leg of mutton, which had been basted every ten minutes, began to smoke. The Hermit then put the yarn a few notches nearer the fire, and fetching a small watering-pot, put in about a pint and a half of boiling water, with a little salt, and dexterously sprinkled the whole joint, as it turned round and round, through the rose of the watering-pot.

"This little vessel," said the good man, "serves *two* purposes; it waters my flowers and helps to cook my mutton! which, with the hot saline bath I am now giving it, will rain down a double supply of most excellent gravy, which be it your care, my good friend, to take up as fast as it flows down, and to turn it over the meat three *or* four times. Then return the whole into the earthen pan, and it will be the business of one of my widows, when the joint has again browned, to apply the last finishings of fresh basting and frothing with flour, which I do not think you are as yet suffi-ciently accomplished to practise with dexterity, and which has very little to do with the essen-tial roasting of the joint, upon which its good cooking depends."

The Traveller smiled to himself, as he thought that, however well the leg of mutton might be roasted, of which indeed he had no doubt, yet that the gravy would be *extremely* greasy, and though not burnt or fried, that it would certainly not be pure or clear.

The mutton was taken down, and placed by the Welsh widow upon its hot dish, and presented a most tempting appearance; it was *well done,* but *not over done.* It was browned and frothed, but not burnt; it was juicy, yet cooked to the bone. The widow then removed the earthen pan, with the fat and gravy, from the fire. After pouring round the mutton some clear pure brown gravy, which, the Traveller had not before observed, had been warmed in a little double saucepan by the side of the Hermit's stove, and which he had seen put on about half an hour before, but had not inquired into the contents—

"That is not quite fair," said he, "I know not how that gravy was made."

"I assure you, my friend," said the Hermit, "I do not wish to conceal anything; but I cannot perform impossibilities. No one can have a gravy properly prepared from the same leg of mutton which is just roasted, because there is not time for the fat and gravy—which are necessarily mixed together—to cool, which process must take place before every particle of the fat can be removed from the gravy. The gravy I am now using for our dinner was the produce of my *last* leg of roast mutton, with the fat taken off, which, being clarified, was, with some addition, the delicate cake that you saw used for basting the present joint; and the next time we have a leg of mutton, you shall have the very gravy that you have assisted in preserving, and which I have now put away to cool."

The Traveller comprehended this sensible explanation, and participated in the best dressed dish of roast mutton he had ever tasted, to which the Hermit added an apple tart. He informed him his Welsh widows always made two tarts at a time, as waste was an abomination to him, and they could not divide the yolk and white of an egg with any advantage.

" Each tart," said he, " only requires half a yolk and half a white, consequently I have two tarts at a time, as the tarts will keep till I can eat them, but not the divided egg."

The Traveller really thought his venerable
host had lost his memory; but he had ocular
demonstration on another day, when he saw
the widows make tarts, that he had not exaggerated in the least degree, and that the excellent tarts he tasted were really composed of
nothing more than one ounce of fresh butter
rubbed in flour, one yolk of an egg, mixed in
skim milk, to wet the flour, the white of the
egg being used for glazing the top of the crust,
with a little white sugar; which ingredients
made paste enough for two tarts, each large
enough for five or six persons.

The Traveller did not forget to claim the
Hermit's promise of explaining to him the
reason that certain dishes, especially in England, were generally so extremely bad, and at
inns and schools almost uneatable; and that
he would begin with soups.

The Hermit desired he would catechise him
regularly, and that, if he failed to account in a
rational manner for any bad cookery from
which he had suffered, he would pay a forfeit
of an extra dinner for every such lapse;

although he had never had the advantage of attending scientific lectures, his knowledge was practical, and his experience gained at home.

The Traveller commenced his questions in the first place by desiring to know why soups and broths were so often *greasy?*

" The cause," said the Hermit, " is one, to my understanding, the most easily accounted for ; and yet, I suppose, from the general complaint of an evil so very easy to remedy, that it is not self-evident to everybody, or they would hardly voluntarily permit the continuance of an evil which I would undertake that any attentive and obedient Welsh child of thirteen years old would never incur after a week's instruction in my kitchen."

The Traveller eagerly requested that he would impart this *most valuable* secret, doubly valuable if so easy of execution.

The Hermit, who had a vein of old-fashioned pleasantry about him, gravely assured his friend, that to impress his lessons more completely on his memory, it was necessary,

E

that before he imparted the desired information the Traveller should endeavour to guess what the means were, which were so effectual for preventing a general and acknowledged evil. It must, however, be admitted that the good man did not say this with a view to the Traveller's improvement, so much as to his own amusement; for nothing diverted him more than to prove the want of *reflection*, and neglect of reasoning power as applied to practical purposes, of his very scientific friend. He therefore desired to know, what the Traveller *supposed* was the reason, and what he would suggest as a remedy.

"The *reason*," said the Traveller, "is perfectly clear. There is no meat without a mixture of greasy matter. Broths and soups are made by the extraction of the gravy or the juices of meats, which is effected by their being immersed in water which, when heated to a certain point (unnecessary to particularize), and subjected to the long continued action of the fire, extracts what is called by the cooks 'Stock,' on the surface of which floats that nauseous material which, when hot, resembles oil, but which is peculiarly offensive to delicate digestions. I trust I have lucidly explained what you desire to know."

The Hermit bowed. " You have expressed yourself with a fluency truly admirable. But the *remedy* you would recommend has not been mentioned."

" There is but *one*," said the Traveller with a sigh, " that *I* have ever heard of, and that is of such difficult attainment that it bears a very high price, and consequently there is no hope of its being generally available. It is the possession of a *very clever* cook, who has an unfailing memory, a quick eye, a light and dexterous hand; and who, by the exercise of all these talents, combined with unceasing activity, can remove every particle of liquid fat, with the utensil invented for that purpose, by repeatedly skimming everything, under the process of boiling or stewing, at the precise moment when that operation can be performed without injury to the dish in progress. Hence the immense difference between one cook and another; hence the enormous wages paid by the rich for persons with this rare combination of qualifications; and hence the reason why no person of moderate means, still less those in very confined circumstances, can *ever* have a well-cooked dinner."

"And do you *really think so?*" said the Hermit, in an accent of well-feigned simplicity; "then *how can* you believe that a poor Anchorite, like myself, can impart to you any plan by which the poorest person *need never have an ill-cooked dinner*, (if they have food to cook), and still less need *ever* have a difficulty in obtaining the purest soup and broth, without a particle of fat to disturb his digestion, or to offend his eye?"

"I must plainly answer," said the Traveller, "that I had great doubts of your being able to suggest any radical cure for this widely extended evil; but yet, as a drowning man catches at straws, I naturally caught at *hope*, being myself a delicately organized invalid."

The Hermit then continued his Catechism a little further.   "You have said a great deal," said he, " about *hot fat ;* what becomes of the unskimmed fat when it is *cold ?* "

The Traveller was so deceived by the innocent tone in which this question was asked, that he thought, for a moment, that his host really wanted information ; and he replied, with some degree of self-sufficiency, that it always remained at the top, where it congealed.

" And did it never occur to you," said the Hermit, " that if you wanted soup on a Wednesday, you had only to make it on Tuesday ?— by which means you would be able, the morning you require it, to remove *every particle* of the objectionable ingredient with a sharp knife, when it can be taken off as a solid cake, and that your soup or broth, whether in jelly or liquid, would then be as pure, and as clear of all oily particles, as if it had been skimmed, and *re*-skimmed again and again, when in a boiling state, by the first cook in Europe."

The Traveller was, according to his custom, when suddenly enlightened by plain practice, very silent ; for he saw in a moment, that he had not demonstrated any extraordinary intelligence in not having discovered so simple a remedy for himself. He therefore only said, " I suppose that this is not generally known."

" Not generally reflected upon, if observed," said the Hermit, " or you most assuredly would never have to complain of impure soup ; but as a practical lesson is worth more than a hundred lectures, I will to-morrow show you *how soup ought to be made.*"

" You have, then," said the Traveller, " no doubt a stock-pot ; for although I see you have no great idea of my culinary knowledge, *I am aware,* that there *can be no good soup without a stock-pot.*"

" I don't possess one," said the Hermit ; " and *if* I did, I *would not use it.*"

The rest of the day was passed in the usual rambles ; but before they went out the Hermit showed his friend the bare bone of the leg of mutton they had had for dinner, the meat of which had been all taken off.* " I am going to weigh this," said he ; " observe, it weighs three quarters of a pound."

---

* See Appendix No. II.

One of the Welsh widows then took the hammer before mentioned, and broke the bone as small as she could, and put it into a very strong iron vessel, in the lid of which was a hole into which fitted very loosely an iron stopper.

"This," said the Hermit, "is called a '*Digester*;' * it may almost be considered a work of the last century, in which I believe its inventor (Pappin) was born : at all events, I can remember that my good aunt used it fifty years ago, and perhaps it may be well known to you, unless something much more effective has been discovered since that period."

The Traveller was not anxious to afford any information on this point, for, indeed, he had never heard of any "digester" made of iron, and did not know the use of it.

The Hermit added a pint and a quarter of water, and, after shutting it up, put it on his stove, where he allowed it to remain until he retired to rest, being a period of two or three hours, slow stewing, when he poured off the liquor, and, taking out the bones, broke them

---

* See Plate No. II.

again still smaller, put them back in the digester, added a pint of water, and let them stew two hours more in a very slow heat.

The next day he produced a small piece of brisket of beef,* which weighed six pounds; to every pound of meat the Welsh widows poured a quarter of a pint of water, in all a pint and a half: they then chopped very small, leeks, celery, carrots, and turnips, and having a measure which, when full, held exactly a pound of chopped vegetables, the Hermit put in a pound and a quarter. The proportions of vegetables were, four parts leeks to three parts of celery, three parts turnips, and one part carrots. He carefully spread the vegetables over the meat, then sprinkled a little salt over the vegetables, and then placed about a pound and a half of very pure fat on the top of the vegetables.

The tin vessel in which the meat was placed was then put into the iron vessel belonging to it, which contained boiling water, as before described; and both lids being put on, it was

---

* See Appendix No. III.

left to stew for twelve hours, the water on the outside being occasionally replenished as it boiled away.

The Hermit then proceeded to prepare the dinner of the day, which was hashed mutton and white soup,* as the Traveller had especially complained of the difficulty of having mutton cooked a second time to be eatable. The Hermit assured him there were two ways of hashing mutton, which were both excellent, and he would begin with the most difficult.

The Welsh widows then produced from an inner repository some firm brown jelly from the mutton bone, which he put into a saucepan (or double), surrounded, as before, by hot water. The widows then chopped, in careful proportions, onion, celery, and turnip ; the whole quantity together was about a quarter of a pound. These they fried in a small well-tinned iron saucepan (the Hermit did not approve of copper), with very fine fat, which he said had been taken off the stock of the stewed beef which the Traveller had eaten

* See Appendix Nos. IV. and V.

cold, and of which he had so much approved.
They stirred the chopped vegetables and the
fat rapidly round and round for ten minutes by
the clock; after which they shook in, with a
dredger, as much flour as was sufficient to form
the whole mass into a moderately stiff paste.
They stirred in the flour for five minutes more,
and then transferred the whole into the stock,
which by this time, from a jelly, had become
hot and liquid.   They again stirred the whole
briskly together, and left it to simmer for a
quarter of an hour.

He then asked the Traveller for his opinion.
He pronounced it to be like good brown thickened soup; after which he tasted it, and asked
his friend to do the same.   They both agreed
that a little more celery and sweet herbs would
render it a most excellent made gravy.

When finally flavoured, the widows put it
through a wire sieve, and the Hermit observed
that he had a great objection to the use of
tammies or horse-hair sieves, when it was
possible to avoid it.

The Welsh widows then returned the gravy

into the inside saucepan. The Hermit tasted it again, calling upon his friend to observe that it had lost a portion of the flavour which it before possessed.

" This," said the Hermit, " is always the case with everything that is passed through a sieve. The closer the sieve, the more the flavour is abstracted; and for that reason, a tammy is the most destructive to flavour of all the species of sieves, as it is, in fact, a very fine flannel, the threads of which are so minute that they not only hold back every particle of the vegetables, but it is necessary to work them so hard with a spoon, that all their flavour is absorbed and arrested by the tammy-cloth; and although they have used a coarse wire sieve for our present dish, you will perceive that it is somewhat diminished in flavour by the process of straining, and therefore it is necessary that I should *re*flavour."

For this purpose the Hermit selected a small sprig of orange thyme, a little savory and basil, twisting them together with a bit of thread, and then stirred the fragrant nosegay round two or three times, till it had imparted sufficient flavour to the sauce.

The Welsh widow (1st hand) then produced the cold mutton, and the Hermit requested the Traveller to cut it up for the hash, which he immediately began to do in straight long slices ; but on being told that *that* was not right, he cut it in thick dice, for which he was equally censured. The Hermit then took it in hand himself, and showed him that, for a hash, cold meat ought to be pointed at each end, the ends being as fine as possible, but the centre of each piece much thicker than the extremities, and all the skin and fat carefully removed.

The meat being thus prepared, was placed in the sauce, and after being well stirred was covered and left to simmer in the usual way, surrounded by hot water, for about half-an-hour. After which it was declared to be ready, and the Traveller again confessed that he had never eaten a better dish ; " for," said he, " it has the real flavour of the mutton, without being over done. It has not the slightest greasiness, and yet there is an agreeable com-

bination of herb and vegetable, which render
it, instead of a nauseous and unwholesome
preparation of cold meat warmed, a really
good and wholesome made dish."

"That," said the Hermit, "is what everything *should be*, that is dressed a second time.
It should be an *excellent variety*, instead of an
unwholesome and *disagreeable necessity*; but I
wish you to observe, that the principle of
making good sauces is exactly the same as that
of making good soups, and that I equally
repudiate the use of butter in both the one and
the other. The fat that you saw used to-day
for frying the vegetables was produced from
the stewed beef, of which you so highly
approved, and the preparation of which will be
my next lesson. The fat which I recommend
for soups and sauces is always better for that
purpose fresh and *un*clarified, just as it comes
off the stock when cold; but my widowed
handmaids always keep a stock of clarified
fat, which is perfectly pure and innoxious,
but which of course cannot impart the same
flavour of vegetables as the fresh fat which

is produced from meat stewed for many hours, with a large proportion of the latter ingredient unclarified."

The Traveller having honestly admitted his admiration of the hashed mutton, could not resist an attempt to puzzle the Hermit. " My venerable friend," said he, " there was one remark that you made, which I do not think is always borne out by facts, although I admit that it was correct in reference to our culinary experience of to-day. You said that straining through fine sieves always diminished flavour. If this is the case, how do you account for the flavour of sweet jellies?—since even my moderate acquaintance with the culinary art has taught me that jellies are strained through a flannel bag."

" Your question enables me to confirm my assertion," said the Hermit. " First of all, you must remember that a jelly, when hot, is a thin, clear liquid, the flavour of which is imparted by *other* clear liquids, and not, like soup, by *substances*, reduced to a pulp, which are retained by the sieve or flannel bag; but, if you doubt the correctness of my assertion, that everything that is strained through similar mediums loses a portion of its flavour in the process, you have only to taste a jelly *before* it is poured into the bag, and afterwards, and you will find that there *is* a loss of flavour which is abstracted by the bag; although, from the causes I have mentioned, it is so slight as not to be of much importance."

The following day's dinner was the long-promised stewed beef, which, it will be remembered, weighed six pounds; it had stewed slowly for some hours; the quantity of water put in was a pint and a half; the quantity of liquid stock taken out was nearly three pints!

The meat was put on in the inner saucepan; it was gently warmed with a portion of its own stock, and on the beef the widows put all the remaining fat, which had been taken off the stock when cold, and produced by the original stewing.

In another saucepan, the widows prepared a sauce with a portion of the same jelly stock of the beef flavouring it in a similar manner to

the sauce he had made for the hashed mutton,
with the exception of putting a larger proportion of carrots in the preparation of the chopped
vegetables. He also had carrots and turnips
cut into small balls, and put them to stew in
broth, in a separate double saucepan.

The beef, when thoroughly warmed through
(which process required about two hours), wa
served with the sauce made as described, into
which the balls of carrots and turnips, which
were tender and fully done, were removed before it was poured over the beef, which, having
been taken out of the stock in which it was
warmed, was not in the least greasy, although it
had a flavour and richness derived from its own
unadulterated fat, which had slowly filtered
through it in the process of warming.

"Some persons," said the Hermit, "would
place a thick slice of fat bacon on the top of
this beef, during the process of warming; but
I am a great enemy to marring the flavour of
one good thing by the addition of another,
which is not required. I have often known
a good dish spoilt by the addition of a quantity

of rusty or very salt ham or bacon, which was intended to improve its flavour. The only thing I ever use, except what you have seen (viz. its own fat), is a slice of moderately salted boiled pork, laid on the top of the beef when warming."

The Traveller declared he was so well satisfied with his dish, that he did not desire the slightest alteration or addition.

The next day, two basins of soup made their appearance at dinner. The soup was perfectly clear, and most delicately flavoured.

The Traveller reproached his friend with not having allowed him to see the preparation of this excellent soup; but he assured him that the only preparation was what he had witnessed when the beef was originally put down to stew, and this soup was the remains of that cookery. He said that all meat put down in a double vessel, with a proper proportion of water and vegetables, ought to produce gravy soup, perfectly well flavoured; which could be called vermicelli, macaroni, or rice soup, merely by the addition of those ingredients.

F

The Traveller inquired whether there was any particular process observed in making those additions.

The Hermit requested him to state how *he* would proceed, if he added macaroni or pearl-barley, &c. to his soup.

" Of course," replied his friend, with an air of conscious experience, " I should first of all boil the pearl-barley or rice in water. I should then, when fit to eat, put it into the soup."

" And do you suppose," said the Hermit, " that your soup will then be of the same strength as before ? "

" And why should it not ? " returned the other.

" That question will be easily answered," said the Hermit, " by reminding you of the quantity of water absorbed by rice or pearl-barley, &c. &c., before *they are* fit to eat; and therefore, if you wish to preserve the original strength of the soup, you should merely wash them in water, and then put them into a sufficient quantity of the broth, or stock, to swell and to absorb; and when soft, put them into the soup itself, which is destined for the table."

"And why not put them into the soup itself at the commencement?" said the Traveller.

"For the simple reason," answered the Hermit, "that it does not improve the flavour of soup to keep it on the fire, after it is made, for two or three hours; and therefore it is better to prepare the rice or pearl-barley in another vessel, with no more stock than is required for the purpose of cooking it."

Shortly after this conversation, the hashed mutton was eaten, and the Traveller reminded the Hermit, that as he had now taught him the most difficult way of hashing mutton, he hoped the next day he might learn the most easy method. *

The Hermit said he must excuse him for making the following day's dinner a repetition, which was generally bad management; but that the process was so simple, he could not fail to understand it by description. It was merely to cut the mutton in the same manner as he had

* See Appendix No. VI.

shown him, to lightly flour it on each side, turning it over and over with two forks; then to put it in a double saucepan, with a sufficient quantity of the jelly from the bones of mutton, flavoured with a little onion and herbs,—or, if more convenient, the clear gravy from a roast leg of mutton, without any fat, but which had been previously flavoured with onion, herbs, and salt. The meat should remain in this sauce or gravy in a gentle heat, being often well stirred, for about three-quarters of an hour, when it would be ready for the table.

It was afterwards agreed that the next day's dinner should be a mutton pie,* which, as it required previous preparation, was commenced that evening.

The Hermit's Welsh widows took a neck of Welsh mutton, and, cutting it into thin chops, weighed it, and put in a small double saucepan, with rather less than a quarter of a pint of water to the pound weight; they then chopped celery and onion, a little orange thyme, basil, and savory, and left it to stew, with the water slowly simmering round it, till it was perfectly

---

* See Appendix No. VII.

tender, but not over-done. They then strained
off the stock from the meat, and put it away to
cool; and when the fat had formed a hard cake
on the top they took it off; and to the surprise
of the Traveller, he saw underneath a firm jelly.

" I never knew," said the Traveller, " that
mutton made jelly."

" Perhaps you thought," said the Hermit,
" that mutton pies ought to be made by baking
raw meat. And, before I proceed further, I
must ask you to detail to me your experience
with regard to mutton pies."

" That is soon told," said the Traveller.
" They are, without exception, one of the
worst of the innumerable bad dishes which
have contributed to ruin my digestion :—the
meat is generally as hard as a stone, the gravy
is like melted fat; and either the pastry is
burned or the meat is not half done, but if the
meat *is done* the paste is scorched to a chip;
and in either case it is greasy and unwholesome.
The chops are frequently put in with all the
bone and fat, having been previously rolled in
pepper and salt until they would excoriate the

throat of a salamander; and the paste is greasy, and redolent of burnt butter."

The Hermit smiled.

" You will not have to complain," said he, " of these faults in my pie."

He then proceeded to give directions, in mountain Greek, to the widows, to cut the meat off the bone, taking off the skin and all the superfluous fat. They then put the mutton jelly, together with the prepared mouthfuls, into a basin, the pieces being about the size of half-a-crown, but of irregular shapes, the meat of each cutlet making about two pieces. They placed the basin over a saucepan of boiling water, covering it with a plate, upon which he put the lid of the saucepan, and in a very short time the jelly melted amongst the meat. When it was hot the Hermit tasted it, added a little salt, and had it put away all together, in the basin, in a cold place till the next day, explaining to the Traveller that, by leaving the meat and the jelly to cool together, the meat would imbibe the flavour of the stock, instead of becoming hard and dry, as would otherwise be the case if left exposed in the air all night.

The next day the Welsh widows, by the Hermit's order, took flour, and having placed it upon the board, put water on the fire with some of the cake of fat which had been taken from the surface of the mutton stock, and when boiling hot, added it to the flour by degrees, stirring in with a spoon, and thus made the paste, having previously filled the pie-dish with the mutton and mutton jelly prepared the day before. The widows took care in forming the little ornament which decorated the top of the pie to make a small stem, which fitted into a hole on the top of the pie-crust. They then filled a baking tin with cold water, which the Hermit explained was to prevent the meat from being overdone before the paste was baked. In less than three-quarters of an hour the paste was baked to perfection, and the widows placed the pie upon the table, when the Hermit, gently screwing out the ornament at the top, poured in with a small jug as much additional liquefied mutton jelly as the pie would hold, which jelly had been kept back and warmed in a double saucepan for the purpose. The ornament was replaced, and the Hermit explained that the heat of the oven produced an absorption of the liquefied stock, although the heat was diminished in some degree by the water in the baking tin, and consequently there was always room (after a pie was baked) for an addition of gravy reserved for the purpose.

The Traveller said, that of all the good dinners he had yet had in the Hermit's cell he thought this was the best; and he knew not which to praise most—the paste, the meat, or the gravy.

The Hermit then begged to know what other dishes the Traveller had the most unpleasant recollection of, under the ordinary mode of cookery; upon which his friend replied, that he had so often felt as if he was poisoned at dinner, it would be almost impossible, amidst the crowd of unpleasant reminiscences, to say which was the worst; but he didn't think anything could exceed a bad beefsteak, which, with mutton chops, appeared to form the whole bill of fare of an English inn; and that when they again had soup he would be very thankful for some instruction about *Pea-soup,** which was generally Pea gruel, or a greasy, unpalatable mixture.

The Hermit said, that with regard to the soup, he should have pleasure in showing him two ways of making it, both of which were equally good in their way, but the one was best suited for the economist, and the other to those whose means permitted extra luxury.

The peas for the soup he directed the widows immediately to place in a pan, which he ordered to be sunk in the well.

The Traveller, who had begun to imbibe some of the Hermit's habits of reflection and observation, thought to himself that the peas would float; but he perceived that the Hermit's widows took the precaution of pouring water upon them before they sunk the pan in the well; which being done carefully, only a *few* peas floated on the surface, which he took care to inform the Hermit was owing to their light, worthless quality; and his host was too well

---

* See Appendix Nos. VIII. and IX.

bred to tell him that he had before supposed that all the world was acquainted with the fact that light grain swam.

After the peas were put to soak, the remainder of the day was spent in the usual manner; and the next morning the peas were put on in a double vessel, with a little water and a certain quantity of top fat (from the stock of stewed beef). They stewed for some hours, and were then pressed through a colander, and then afterwards through a wire sieve; after which they had a proportion of mutton broth added to them, and a plate of onions and celery chopped fine, they were again put on the fire in a double vessel, and well stirred.

After having stewed some time, and the soup being perfectly smooth, the Hermit desired the Traveller's opinion of the taste, which was that it required more flavour. Upon this, powdered mint was added out of a bottle, and, after another tasting, the Hermit added some extra pieces of celery and onion, and a bunch of marjory, which were stirred round and round, until the necessary additional flavour was imparted, and the soup was pronounced to be excellent.

The Hermit remarked that this was winter pea-soup, and then made the following explanation of the reason for some of the proceedings which he thought the Traveller might not have understood. He said that he always delayed putting in the mint until the soup was made savoury and palatable without it, as the mint having a strong flavour, it was not so easy afterwards to apportion other ingredients. He also explained that his mint and other herbs were always gathered when in bud, as they should not be in flower or in seed when brought in for culinary preservation.

They were never hung up to dry, but, having been cut when in perfection, were put by the Welsh widows between two dishes in a moderately warm oven, or hot closet, where they dried quickly, preserving all their aroma as well as their green colour; they then pounded them in a mortar, and bottled them for use, carefully corking them; in which way they were much more convenient and effective for flavouring soups.

The Hermit said it was unnecessary to prepare a second portion of peas for the variety of
pea-soup that he had promised; and, as the
first preparation was the same, that the latter
part could be shown on the following day with
the soup left on the present occasion. The
beef-steak, he promised, would be good;
although he did not profess to give him a
broiled beef-steak, as he was not able to procure
beef which had hung the precise time to be
tender, and yet fresh; and that as this was a
very common case, he thought it would be
more useful to show him a way of preparing a
beef-steak which would always insure a good
dish, whether the beef was tender or not. He
said that the goodness of a plain broiled beef-
steak depended entirely upon the goodness of
the meat, and the manual dexterity of the
broiler, and the state of the fire—three things
which he was quite sure his friend, in common
with the greater part of the world, would
never learn, and consequently could not teach;
but he believed that the process his widows
were about to show might be learnt by any-

E.J.Fecit

Large Double.

body, and consequently taught without difficulty.

The beef-steak * was placed in a saucepan with
a little salt, and continually turned and stirred
round until it was brown on both sides; it
was then put into a "Double,"† with a small
quantity of hot water, in which had been previously scalded chopped onions, turnips, celery,
and sweet herbs. It was left to stew about
an hour, by which time it had become very
tender, although it retained the appearance and
a good deal of the taste of broiled meat. The
whole was then put into a small pan (narrow
at the bottom) to cool. The fat was carefully
taken off when congealed, and the gravy put
back into a double saucepan with the meat,
where, as soon as it was reheated, it was ready
to eat, and pronounced by the Traveller to be
wholesome and agreeable.

Nor must it be forgotten that the Hermit's
Welsh widows added balls cut out of raw
potatoes, which, after being delicately fried by

---

* See Appendix No. X.

† "A Double" is used to indicate the cooking utensil
which has an inner vessel.—See Plate IV.

them in the fat that had been taken off the beef-steak gravy after it had cooled, with a sufficient addition of a similar nature, were put into the gravy with the beef-steak.

The Traveller pronounced the beef-steak to be an admirable substitute for the generally *evil* dish of that name, but declared his preference for the plain good old-fashioned broiled beef-steak, of which he had a distinct recollection, though a rare experience.

The Hermit, with the candour which was so conspicuous a trait in his character, repeated still more strongly what he had before said, viz. that the old genuine beef-steak owed its celebrity to a combination he did not possess, and therefore would not pretend to teach, viz., fresh beef which had been hung to the hour before decomposition commences, and, secondly, upon a degree of practice in the art of broiling which his widows did not possess and could not acquire in his establishment, and which was necessary to avoid three evils—the steak being underdone within and burned outside, or the fat and gravy falling into the fire or on the hot stove during the process, which would produce a most dreadful smell, the fumes of which would give the meat a similar taste (upon the same principle as has formerly been explained in reference to roasting the leg of mutton); but the Hermit added that his object was to teach well what he practically understood, and that he did not believe there ever would be any certainty in the production of a good beef-steak unless by cooks who had been practised for months together, *all day long,* in some place where little else was ever eaten, for that beef-steaks well broiled required as much manual practice as rifle-shooting.

In the course of their walk after dinner, the Traveller remarked that there were many things relating to cookery without which it could not be good, but which were pre-liminaries to the art; for instance, the management of game and poultry, the salting of meat, &c. &c. In reference to the latter subject, he amused the Hermit with an account of having gone into a larder in a very large establishment, where there was a professed cook, and a housekeeper, and innumerable kitchen-maids : but it unfortunately happened that at the moment of his entrance the cook was suffering from the smart of a pin, which had run into her hand in feeling the plumpness of the breast of the chicken, which, having been torn in plucking, the skin had been fastened together with a pin ; * and that, on his expressing his horror at so dangerous a proceeding, the cook informed him it was not at all uncommon, when fowls were plucked at home, as the feathers being pulled the wrong way, the rents thereby occasioned were thus partially concealed ; and on his representing that death to the eater might be the consequence, he was coolly told that it was " very true ; " but she " supposed the pins were generally taken out before the fowl was sent to the table."

The Hermit could not resist on this occasion an ironical remark.

" I suppose," said he, " that this is a proof of the progress and improvement of the present age. I never heard of chickens being used

---

* A fact.

as pincushions in the last century, for by your
account this is a wilful practice, a risk of
murder voluntarily incurred *not* under the eyes
of the mistress, as it appears from your account
that mistresses in the nineteenth century have
neither eyes or understanding for the practical
and most necessary arts of life, but under the
eyes of that important functionary called the
'*Professed Cook,*'—a title which, I believe, has
come into use since I left the world. In my
time the cook was often called '*Cook-maid,*'
meaning the *handmaiden who cooked,* and you
will very much oblige me by explaining what
it means—because, in my humble opinion,
persons calling themselves cooks, and being
hired as cooks, thereby profess *to be* cooks.
What is the difference, therefore, between '*a
cook*' and '*a professed cook ?*'"

The Traveller was determined to show that
he was well able to answer *this question;* and
without any hesitation he said that a professed
cook was a cook who understood everything
appertaining to the culinary department; but
that a *cook* who did not lay claim to the

G

word "*professed*," only understood *part* of her business.

"Then," said the Hermit, "the professed cooks, of course, are accomplished in salting beef, tongues, pork, making bacon, &c. &c."

"By no means," said the Traveller. "Very few, if any of them, know how to salt a tongue. They are generally entirely ignorant of salting beef, and expect all those things to be done for them; but the plain cooks occasionally can undertake those matters."

"I think," said the Hermit, "I must take lessons anew in the English language, as from your explanation I am to conclude the *professor* is the cook who has the most limited knowledge of some of the most important branches appertaining to the art which she professes entirely to understand, while the *non*-professor is far less ignorant."

The Traveller was obliged to acknowledge that there was a good deal of truth in this remark, but still he maintained that a professed cook knew a great many things which he could not explain, but among which economy and good management, he *believed*, were *not* to be included.

The conversation then reverted to the pre-servation of poultry and game; and on their return to the cell, the Hermit took him into his larder in the rock, in which were iron hooks, from whence depended two fine fowls plucked without a scar, and *without* pins in their hearts! a hare, and two young rabbits.

The Traveller remarked that the birds were all hung head downwards, and that the last time he had noticed poultry and game in a larder, they had been hung by the head, the hook being forced through the upper and lower mandible of the bill.

The Hermit said that such a practice could not be defended by any sort of reason—that by wounding the head and throat the bird would sooner decay, the air get in, and flies would be attracted—that all birds ought to be hung up by the legs, and have a string tied tightly round the throat, as soon as they were brought in, by which means the weight of the interior pressed upon the neck, which being tightly tied excluded the air; and nothing more was needed than a small bit of charcoal to preserve the birds till they had hung long enough to be tender, and that poultry ought never to be drawn till they were cooked.

" But what do you do in hot weather," said the Traveller, " if you have more than you require to eat at once of poultry or game that will not keep ? "

" I always roast them off while they are good."

" *Half* roast them, I suppose you mean," said the Traveller, with a little air of conscious knowledge. " I have heard cooks talk of being obliged to *half roast all the meat* in hot weather."

" A very bad plan," said the Hermit, " or rather an impracticable attempt. No one can exactly tell when a bird or a joint is *half* roasted. It may be a quarter roasted, or *three parts* roasted, but is always believed to be *half* done; and then (when cold) it is put down again to the fire when required for the table, to receive the other half *supposed* to be due : but by this process the hardened outside will not imbibe moisture while basting, and becomes still more hard, and by the time it reaches the table, it is a flavourless tough morsel, like greasy leather on the outside, and without any moisture within. And the same with all other things treated in this way; whereas by *roasting completely*, but *not* over doing, and when wanted placing the bird or joint thus treated in a double vessel, with a little pure suet over it, and a small quantity of pure broth, sufficient to make a steam under it, and letting the water boil slowly round in the outside vessel, and then serving it with another pure gravy from roast meat (if possible of the same sort), it will be difficult to know that it was not roasted the day before; and I think," he added, " it would be difficult even for you, whose organ of taste I perceive is very acute, to pronounce whether it had been fresh roasted from the fire or not. At all events, it is the very best method of treating meat or poultry which require to be dressed a day or two beforehand. But I have another way of preserving game, &c. for a longer time, which I will give you in

writing;* and for these and other purposes the
gravy from roasting should be preserved in
separate basins, to have a supply when required
of kind to kind, instead of an abominable concoction of everything mixed together, the
colour of treacle, commonly called gravy."

The Traveller inquired what the contents
were of various pans of salt meat, and expressed
his surprise at the quantity of provision in the
cell of an anchorite.

The Hermit said, he must remember he was
not a monk, and that it was needless to assure
him that it could not be intended for his own
use; as, although he might be called a Hermit, inasmuch as he had no companions to live
with him, that he had a comfortable fortune
paid by the rents of his industrious Welsh
tenants; and he had also a rich, aged, and
benevolent neighbour, who, having ample
means at his disposal, requested him to expend
a certain sum every week in various sorts of
food, which he was to dispose of according to

---

* See Appendix No. XI.

his discretion, for the benefit of others, on condition that it was all prepared and cooked either by his own hands, or under his own personal superintendence; as his wealthy neighbour was aware that by this means it would produce much more food, and that the Hermit would thus never be unprovided with proper diet for the sick, who so often sought his aid, and, also, that all the assistants occasionally required by the widows would learn good cooking.

The Traveller said he could not understand how the Hermit could have *time* to attend to both species of cooking, as he had always understood that cookery for the sick was a separate branch altogether, which was scarcely ever professed, much less understood, excepting by nurses; and he had often heard it remarked that it was very little use for doctors to give lists of permissible articles of diet, which were generally called " *slops* "—a horrible name, the sound of which was enough alone to make people ill, while at the same time there was not one of these medical authorities that could tell,

or did tell, how such " *slops* " ought to be prepared, or to define the difference between bad
and good, wrong and right, although they
generally agreed that when the patient was
quite unable to take any more physic, his life
would depend upon his being able to take
properly prepared food. The Traveller could
not contain his exultation, as the idea struck
him that the Hermit had never heard of the
homœopathic system of medicine. And, as he
had greatly benefited by it, and had taken
some trouble to understand the principle on
which so many cures were effected under that
mode of treatment, and as he had visited the
hospitals in London, and those on the Continent,
where homœopathic treatment was pursued, he
dilated upon it, and gave the Hermit a good
deal of information on the subject, and he
rather anticipated the pleasure of an argument,
in which he thought he should come off vic-
torious. But as there was no battle, so there
could be no victory, for the Hermit became
unfeignedly interested in the history of homœ-
opathy, and only regretted it had not been dis-

covered sooner, for the sake of others; but for *himself*, he said, he had always had wonderfully natural good health, the preservation of which he attributed very much to abstinence from all fermented liquors, the excellence of the water, and abundance of air and exercise, by which means he had never had recourse to the druggists' shops, and had never administered to his poor patients any compounds, though he was able to do much good by the in-fusions of herbs given singly, of which the traditions of his countrymen had taught him the use.

"But to return," said he, "to the point from which we started—*cookery for the sick.* Do your homœopathic physicians understand the preparation of food *better* than their an-tagonists in the old system?"

"*Very little*, if at all," said the Traveller: "they know better *what is bad*, and prohibit deleterious ingredients; but I do not think that they are much more learned than the others with regard to the preparation of food for the sick, to *ensure* what is good. But again let me ask, How can you attend to both these schools of cookery ? "

" I maintain there is only *one*," said the Hermit. " Wherever there is a chicken boiled *properly*, in a double vessel, there must necessarily be the *best* chicken broth ; wherever veal is boiled, or stewed, there ought to be the purest veal broth, which is nearly as mild as chicken, and will be in a jelly that may be taken out like lumps of ice. The same with beef, &c. &c. And a boiled turkey will produce one of the most excellent stocks for white soup, without any destruction of the flesh, but it is too rich for an invalid, and not as light as the jelly from a boiled chicken."

The Traveller here interposed with a question, which was, how stocks which were always highly flavoured if they were prepared for soup stock, *could* be fit for invalids.

The Hermit told him that it was a common, though a great mistake, to suppose that all the flavour necessary for soup must be bestowed upon it in the first stewing, and that all sorts of meats must be stewed together ; that, on the contrary, he not only never mixed the meats together when stewing, but he took care with the more delicate, such as veal and chicken, &c., not to put any vegetable to them when stewing besides a small quantity of onion or leek and celery, as other flavours could be added as required, when made into white soup. For beef, he had explained before, he allowed a pound of finely chopped mixed vegetables to every five pounds of meat.

" This," said the Traveller, " would make a very different stock from *beef-tea,* which is generally ordered for invalids."

" Experience has taught me," said the Hermit, " that of all the so-called ' slops ' ordered for invalids, beef-tea is *the one* which consumes the greatest quantity of meat to produce the smallest results, and is the least liked, and of which the patient soonest becomes tired ; and I have never known a case of illness where the stomach could receive beef-tea more readily or with better effects than the pure broth from chicken jelly or veal jelly, which always, in my practice, is administered first ;

and when a change is wanted, I have always found that the stock from beef, prepared as we did it the other day, with all the fat removed when cold, agrees perfectly with a convalescent patient, previously restored by the pure stocks of white meats."

" I wish," said the Traveller, " I may be your guest, if I am again doomed to be unwell; for, whether it was the *manner* of preparation or the *kind* I know not, but, when last ill, I *longed* for something different to the brown fluid called beef-tea."

The Hermit assured him that he would be very glad if he *had* a slight indisposition, that he might prove the truth of his remarks, when he might have personal demonstration that sick cookery did *not* require a separate department, either in study or practice, to have proper broths always at hand, as the same principles of cookery which were so conducive to the preservation of health in the ordinary requirements of life were to be applied to the restoration of health during illness.

The Traveller said, that he was so anxious

to test his friend's skill in cookery for an invalid, that he could almost make up his mind
to travel from inn to inn for a fortnight, that
he might ensure being very unwell when he
sought the shelter of his friendly cell again.

The Hermit said, he believed an additional
great cause of indigestion was the confectionary usually eaten; for that, although it was
generally admitted, by those who had any
pretension to medical knowledge, that a fair
proportion of fruit, as well as vegetables
and farinaceous food, was requisite for a
healthy person, to nourish and support the
human frame, yet that, even before he retired
from the world, those dishes commonly called
" confectionary" were very often most unwholesome, although a goodly list of receipts
existed, of excellent and innoxious tarts and
puddings; and he inquired of the Traveller
whether there was any improvement in this
particular, or the reverse.

The Traveller said that he could not suppose
there was any *improvement*, inasmuch as he very
seldom met with a good tart; and when he did

find unobjectionable contents under the crust,
the quantity of fruit was so meagre, and the
paste itself was so full of butter and so indi-
gestible that he seldom attempted to eat it, and
that he had never seen a tart with paste the
least like what the Hermit had set before him,
and of which he had partaken without the
slightest subsequent suffering—that puddings
were better understood of farinaceous materials,
though generally they contained far too many
eggs, but that fruit puddings (the best of all)
were seldom seen, and that, when they were,
the paste was equally objectionable, and redolent of butter.

The Hermit said that, from all accounts, it
appeared there must be a complete *mania for
butter* in the present age, or an utter ignorance
of any other substitute, and that, although he
allowed the use of butter in moderation in
cakes and tarts, yet that he never allowed the
use of butter in a boiled fruit pudding, the
paste of which ought always to be made of
suet; and that he considered wholesome confectionary ought to consist for the most part of

puddings and tarts made of fresh fruits in summer, and of bottled fruits in the winter, preserved without sugar, or with as little as possible, so as to retain the greatest amount of their natural flavour when fresh, compatible with their keeping.

The Traveller said, that almost everything now was turned into syrup, or into sweetmeat, and that, instead of sugar being secondary, it was made the principal ingredient; that jellies, instead of being flavoured by fruit, were seldom anything but vehicles for wine, brandy, liqueurs, or other strong and objectionable cordials.

The Hermit promised that, on some future occasion, the Traveller should have a specimen of his lemon jelly, and should assist in making it. It was arranged that the next day's dinner should be a fillet of veal,* as the Traveller complained much of his recollections of that dish, and was anxious to know how the Hermit baked it.

The fillet having been stuffed by the widows in the usual manner, after the fillet was

---

* See Appendix No. XII.

weighed, and a little water added, it was placed in the iron vessel known in Wales as the Ffwrn fach (see No. I. Plate), but *without* an inner tin; on the top of the veal was placed a certain quantity of fresh mutton suet. The Hermit said, if they had had a sufficient quantity of the fat of *veal*, he would have preferred it; but not having a loin, the widows could not make use of that material, and that mutton or beef-suet would do exceedingly well. Over the suet they placed the rind from a piece of cold boiled pork. The lid was then shut down, and the Ffwrn fach put into an iron oven, which, having been heated, had had *all the fire taken out*, when the veal was put in. It remained there for three hours, and was then taken out, and put upon a hot dish, while the liquor was poured off into a pan, and left till the next day. The veal was served with a pure gravy, which had been preserved from a previous occasion.

The fillet of veal was accompanied by a tongue,* which had been boiled in a double

* See Appendix No. XIII.

vessel, and was peculiarly tender and well flavoured. The Traveller was anxious to know how it was salted; but the Hermit declined entering upon that department, until his guest knew more of fresh-meat cookery; but he promised that he would the next day teach him how to make root of tongue soup, as he expected a fresh tongue, the roots of which were very valuable for soup, and very injurious when salted with the tongue, as the roots often prevented the tongue from keeping.

This remark reminded the Traveller of another of his misfortunes, as he recollected that he had often met with an unpleasant taste in the salted root of a tongue, even when the lean part was good; which the Hermit said proceeded from the difficulty of making the kernels (which are the chief part of the root) imbibe salt effectually.

The Traveller also wished to know why the Hermit, who was such an adept in the art of roasting, allowed a fillet of veal to be baked? The Hermit said that he should not attempt to give a scientific reason, as he was not a scientific man, but a plain practitioner—that, generally

H

speaking, successful results in cooking were easily accounted for by a little common sense and intelligence—but that, on the present occasion, he could only answer him by fact without explanation. That a fillet of veal was an exception to the general rule, which was, that roasting produced superior results to baking; but that a fillet of veal *roasted*, was generally *hard* on the outside, and dry within; and that although very great care and incessant basting might obviate or modify these effects, yet that it was never so tender or so juicy as when baked in a slow heat, in the manner he had just witnessed, and that, in that way, it was impossible to detect the common *baked* taste, or the flavour of fat frizzled in an oven; the inside was juicy, the outside was brown, but not hard or scorched, and the gravy that proceeded from it was a very pure jelly, perfectly clear, and most useful for various purposes, for gravies or sauces, for made dishes, or as an addition to soup, or to eat as a savoury jelly for cold pies.*

The Traveller said that he thought a fillet

---

* The Hermit particularly objected to Aspic jelly, which he considered spoiled the flavour of the pie.

of veal must be often a very inconvenient dish, as in a small family there might not always be a tongue to dress at the same time, and a Ham had a very awkward and unwieldy appearance.

The Hermit perfectly agreed in this remark; but said that when he had not a *tongue,* the widows boiled a small Ham in the same manner, in a slow heat, and in a double vessel, which Ham would afterwards keep a considerable time, and which he used frequently for fried sandwiches, with veal, chickens, or rabbits.

The Traveller's countenance indicated that he had never heard of "a fried sandwich;" and, therefore, the Hermit, without waiting for inquiry, proceeded to tell him how they were made.—He first of all said, that he had pieces of bread cut in the form and size of sandwiches, which he placed in pure *cold broth,* until they had absorbed as much of the liquid as they could well take up without being too soft; he then had chopped herbs sprinkled on each side of the bread, and placing very thin slices of Ham between two pieces, covered the whole with batter, and had it fried of a golden brown. These sandwiches were to be served round the meat with which they were to be eaten.

The Traveller asked the Hermit *à propos* of white meats, what he considered the best method of dressing rabbits?

He replied, that tastes were so various, *he* could only answer for himself; but that he thought a rabbit fricassee an excellent white *made* dish, and it was arranged to have fricasseed rabbits for the next day;* preparatory to which two rabbits were cut up limb from limb—the heads being left whole — and, having been weighed, water was added, a small quantity of chopped onions, ditto celery, and a little salt, and being put down in the inner tin of the Ffwrn fach, both lids were put on, and they were left to stew slowly for some hours, when they were put away in a cold place, meat and gravy altogether.

The Traveller was surprised, the next day, to find the gravy from the rabbits was firm, clear,

---

* See Appendix No. XIV.

well flavoured, savoury jelly, a portion of which
the widows took, and put on the stove in a double
vessel. When melted, and hot, they added
such herbs and vegetables as they considered
were required for flavouring, after adding some
fresh cream; and, when that process was completed, they put in the two rabbits, cut up,
and let it stew slowly all together, frequently
stirring; and, before it was served, chopped
parsley was sprinkled plentifully.

This fricassee fully justified the Hermit's predilection. He informed his friend that the
rabbits might be floured before the pieces were
put in, which would make the sauce thicker,
but would decidedly diminish the flavour; and
therefore, if it was desired to produce a thicker
sauce, the object should be effected by frying
finely chopped onions, celery, and a little
potato, together with some fine top fat, for
ten minutes, and then making it into a paste
by stirring in a little flour for five more
minutes, in the same manner as soup—that
this vegetable and farinaceous paste would
thicken the rabbit jelly and the milk, or cream,

without diminishing the savoury flavour, but rather *adding to it*, though, for his own individual taste, he preferred it in the present simpler mode, as preserving in greater perfection the pure flavour of the rabbits.

When their dinner was concluded, the Traveller expressed his hope that the Hermit would let him receive some further instruction in soups, which was promised for the following day—the Hermit observing that it was particularly convenient, as the remains of the fricassee would make an excellent white soup. It was also agreed that they were to have in addition, for dinner, a boiled shoulder of Welsh mutton with onion sauce.

The next day, the proceedings were as follows :—The Shoulder of mutton was put in a double vessel, with chopped onions and celery, and some water, and simmered slowly for three hours. The remaining rabbit jelly, which was not used for the fricassee, and the jelly from the fillet of veal, was put on in a double saucepan ; and, while heating, the widows chopped (*finely*) onions, celery, and potatoes, with a small quantity of carrot. This was stirred for ten minutes with fresh top fat; then as much flour shaken in as made a stiff paste, and, by rapid stirring over a steady heat five minutes more, in a single saucepan, the whole of the fat was soon absorbed by the flour, and the entire mass was flavoured by the vegetables, and transferred to the hot rabbit and veal stock in a double saucepan, where, after being well stirred, it was left to stew; after which it was passed through a wire sieve, and returned into the inner saucepan, when two or three tea-spoonfuls of cream were added, a nosegay of sweet herbs was stirred round, and all the rabbit meat left from the fricassee was then put in (but deprived of the bones). The pieces were reduced to the size and form of pulled chicken, which being stirred, and stewed for about a quarter of an hour, were ready for the table. The shoulder of mutton being also ready, onion sauce * was poured over it, the recipe for which the Traveller wrote down.

The Traveller said it would be impossible to

* See Appendix No. XV.

believe that the Hermit's Welsh shoulder of mutton came from the same species of animal called " a sheep " in London, or that two rabbits could have produced such a fricassee, and afterwards such a soup.

The Hermit promised that the next day he should have the mutton-broth, (produced by the process of boiling the shoulder of mutton they had just eaten,) with the cold fillet of veal, which he said, in his opinion, would be much better cold than hot, and would also better demonstrate the tenderness produced by his method of baking the veal ; but to make amends for a cold dinner, he promised hot sausages.*

The Traveller had by this time become so convinced of the practical culinary knowledge of the Hermit, that he was fearful of asking any question that might seem to be dictated by impertinent curiosity ; but as he had not seen or heard of any pork for making sausages, he wondered what his host would do.

The following day the Hermit called his

* See Appendix No. XVI.

attention to the surface of pure and solid fat on the mutton-broth, round which the senior widow dexterously passed a knife, and taking it up, displayed it entire, like a round cake. He then asked him to taste the broth (cold as it was), and the Traveller was surprised to find that it was palatable as well as pure, that he could have taken more with pleasure, even without its being warmed.

The second widow then put it on the stove in a double saucepan, and gave a little additional flavour, by stirring round pieces of celery and onion, and a bunch of sweet herbs, which, when the right medium of flavour was obtained, she took out. She then, with a three-pronged fork, mashed some previously boiled carrots, which were added to the broth, and had the appearance of marygold leaves, but not being in season, he could not obtain marygolds, which otherwise he would have preferred. She then cut the lean that remained on the shoulder of mutton, into rather thick but pointed mouthfuls, and added them to the broth. She also added two or three spoonfuls of pearl-barley, which had for some time previously been swelling to its utmost limits in broth, in a double saucepan, surrounded by hot water; the last finish being a sprinkling of fresh chopped parsley.

The Hermit apologized for having a species of cold meat, which was decidedly not light of digestion, but the Traveller begged he would not distress himself on that account, as his digestion had been so wonderfully strengthened by a long series of well-cooked dinners, that it would be a *feast* to him to be enabled again to eat cold veal, which he was sure he could now venture to do without any danger of bad effects.

The Hermit's sausages were made of some of his stewed beef, chopped very fine, with a little tongue, and then pounded with a certain proportion of beef suet, seasoned with pepper and salt, and flavoured well with powdered sage and onion; they were about half an inch in diameter, and three inches long, rolled in yolk of egg and crumbs, and fried of a golden colour, and, when perfectly dry, served with mashed potatoes.

The Traveller was particularly well satisfied with the veal, the tenderness of which was remarkable, though he was at a loss to account for its being so juicy, which the Hermit attributed to the addition of the suet, which the slow heat had distilled equally through the naturally dry meat, while at the same time its own juices were preserved unimpaired in flavour.

The sausages also occasioned various remarks, as the Traveller had no idea that sausages could be made of anything but pork.

The Hermit said, that *he* considered pork was a meat that ought never to be eaten except by those in perfect health; but that it was very possible, as he had just proved, to have excellent sausages made of beef, which was more digestible; in fact, that veal, mutton, beef, or any meat would make sausages, if properly flavoured with sage, &c., and, well fried, would be as palatable as if made of pork, and lighter of digestion. In addition to which, in a small establishment, not more than one or two pigs were killed in a year, and, consequently, sausages, if only made of pork, would be very seldom tasted.

The dinner was declared by the Traveller to be so good, that he and the Hermit were rather afraid they would not have a sufficient quantity of the fillet of veal left to make a cold veal pie, in the mysteries of which he was very anxious to instruct his friend. But his fears were groundless, and he had the pleasure of displaying one of the most complicated achievements, in which he had instructed the intelligent Welsh widows Marged and Gwenllian.*

Having taken away all the skin, and any remaining stuffing, they cut up the veal very small, and then pounded it in a mortar, with as much of the jelly stock produced by the baking of the fillet as rendered it moderately moist; they added as much pounded tongue as was required to give it a proper degree of saltness, and then flavoured it with a very little pounded lemon-peel, a little basil, and a very little pepper. He said, it was difficult to give an exact recipe in writing for this pie, because its

---

* See Appendix No. XVII.

excellence would depend upon the flavouring, as well as the thorough amalgamation and trituration of all the ingredients; and the proportion of those ingredients must depend on the quantity of cold veal left and appropriated to the pie, and *that*, again, must, of course, depend on the quantity previously eaten, a point to which he should not have thought of referring before dinner.

The Traveller assured him that if he had had an *idea* that the remainder of the fillet of veal would form the basis of so interesting a lesson, he would not have indulged himself with eating so much; and that, in truth, any reasonable mortal might have been satisfied with a dinner of such admirable mutton broth, and such excellent sausages.

When the veal and the other ingredients had assumed the consistency of damp clay, and the Hermit and his friend were satisfied the flavour could not be improved, the Hermit's senior widow made a paste with flour and the pure fat which he had removed from the jelly stock of the baked veal. She then took a pie-dish,

and after slightly brushin   the inside over with
the white of an egg, she put small pieces of
vermicelli all over it; she then lined the dish
with paste, and put the veal into it, pressing it
down with a spoon, so as to form a solid mass
without hollows : when quite full and perfectly
level, she covered the top with a piece of the
same paste reserved for the purpose.   She then
placed the pie in the baking tin, which she
filled with cold water, and as soon as the top
crust was done, she pronounced it finished, and
put it away in a cold place.   The following
morning she produced it at breakfast, and
turning it upside down, it dropped out of the
pie-dish, which was put away, and the bottom
formed the top, covered all over with the vermicelli, which had a very pretty appearance.

The Hermit cut the end straight off, and the
meat which adhered to it was one firm solid
mass, and was attached to the crust, and cut in
slices like cheese.

The Traveller was delighted with the result,
and the Hermit then informed him that when
he went on long expeditions into the moun-

tains, he often provided himself with sandwiches, made of one of these pies, which in his opinion were far preferable to slices of cold meat, and at all events made an agreeable variety. When not provided with a pie, he said he often had the remains of his boiled chicken, pounded, with the cold jelly produced from its broth or bones, and only flavoured with a little salt.

" And what do you do," said the Traveller, " when you have only the remains of a *roast* chicken, and you take these peregrinations ? "

" I am seldom at a loss," said the wise man, " for you must remember, that although roast chicken does not produce *broth*—which, when cold, is a fine jelly, yet that the *bones*, after the meat is eaten, will produce very substantial jelly, which is more than enough for my sandwiches, although it has not so much flavour as the jelly produced by the boiling of the chicken itself."

The following day the widowed handmaids produced a salt duck,* which the Traveller had

* See Appendix No. XVIII.

seen in a soup plate, being carefully rubbed
night and morning with salt for three days.
The duck was put on in a double vessel, in
the same manner as a boiled fowl, and was
slowly done until it was quite tender.   It was
then served with onion sauce, made in a similar
way to that previously described.   The Hermit
had also pea-soup,* which, being the remains of
what they had had on a previous occasion, was
varied in the following manner :—the Hermit's
widows having already heated the pea-soup in
a double saucepan, they prepared, under his
directions, in another double vessel, a pint of
pure veal stock, extracted from the bone of a
boiled shoulder of veal, after the meat had been
eaten.   This was flavoured with chopped leeks,
celery, and sweet herbs, and, when properly
flavoured, the hot pea-soup was added to it,
and the whole left to stew together for three-
quarters of an hour, when, the vegetables being
strained out, three spoonfuls of cream were
added, and, when thoroughly mixed, the diminution of flavour was restored by some addi-

* See Appendix No. XIX.

tional pieces of fresh onion and celery, being left in as long as was necessary, after which the soup was ready for the table.

The Hermit said he sometimes added rice, which had been previously boiled in milk. This cream pea-soup was what the Hermit considered a luxurious dish, but wholesome, as an occasional variety, for those in health who could afford it. The Hermit informed him that, if the cream was added before the soup was strained, there might be no necessity for any additional flavour, the only objection to which was, that the cream was somewhat diminished by adhering to the strained vegetables.

"What do you do," said the Traveller, "with the strained vegetables?"

"They are added," replied his host, "to the broth of the widow cooks' suppers, or to the broth for the poor. They are excellent."

The Traveller then asked the Hermit if he would excuse the liberty he took in asking where he had met with the receipt for this last soup.

"I can assure you," said the good man, "I never met with such a receipt, but the natural course of circumstances, in domestic management, has taught me such an immense variety of soups as would, if written down, form a volume in itself; but if you and your friends would only follow my advice, after learning the proper mode of extracting, instead of destroying, the juices of flesh, fowl, and vegetables, you would never require a book of receipts to enable you to have good soups, as the varieties are endless which one's own intelligence daily invents, according to the materials at hand, from the accidental provision of meat boiled or stewed necessary for the maintenance of an establishment more or less numerous."

The Traveller said, he was not sufficiently advanced in culinary knowledge to comprehend the possibility of the mere possession of materials producing invention without actual receipts.

The Hermit assured him that he should consider the time spent in his cell as half thrown away, if he did not succeed in making him understand the truth of his assertion, by enabling him individually to exemplify it; and if he was not too proud to submit occasionally to a culinary catechism, he thought it would very much assist his progress in the practical knowledge of the culinary art, as well as impress on his mind what he had seen, with a view to his own information or the instruction of others.

The Traveller assured him that, although he knew much more since he had had the benefit of the Hermit's instructions than he had ever known before, that he was infinitely more humble than he had previously been, because he daily felt how much more he ought to know; and how many years he had been wandering about the world, grumbling and complaining, without calling into action the powers of intellect and observation, which are more or less bestowed upon all mankind, and which must improve by exercise, and tend to increase general as well as individual good.

The Hermit, finding his friend and pupil in so excellent a frame of mind, thought that he had better begin at once, lest he should change his opinion, and he announced his intention of continuing the same plan whenever opportunity permitted.

The Traveller repeated his readiness to do his best; but obtained the Hermit's promise to instruct him afresh, wherever he found he was deficient, which he feared would very often be the case.

The Hermit then commenced with the following question :—

" From what you have seen since you have resided in my cell, what do you consider the first objects to be attained by cookery? or, rather, what are the principles that every rational being, who has authority over the preparation of food, ought to understand and be able to have carried out? State also the reasons which ought to induce all persons to promote the practical application of such principles."

The Traveller looked as if he thought that the examination was likely to be more serious than he had anticipated, but he was ashamed, after all the trouble that his venerable host had taken, to appear to shrink from the ordeal; and, conquering his natural indolence, he determined to do his best.

"I suppose," said he, "that the first object to be obtained is a well-cooked dinner; and the *reasons* which ought to induce all persons to promote good dinners are, without a doubt, the promotion of health as much as the gratification of the palate; and, in *my* opinion, a large proportion of those distressing sufferings called 'dyspepsia,' to which I have been a martyr for years, are to be attributed to the unwholesome food which is given to us poor mortals through the grievous ignorance that prevails in the science of cookery, which renders what ought to be our nourishment our poison, without the satisfaction which some people derive from physic, in the belief that the more nauseous it is, and the more they suffer from it, the better they will be at some future time of unknown date."

The Hermit could not repress a smile at the characteristic answer of his guest, as he had long perceived that his attendance upon the scientific lectures, of which he was so proud, had not taught him combination, and in the answers which he now received it appeared that he had lost sight of all objects excepting the gratification of his palate and the benefit of his health; he however thanked him for his reply, but added that his own objects (in the attention he had given to cookery) had been much more extensive than those just mentioned, and that his own tastes were so very simple that the gratification of the palate alone would never have induced him to make a practical study of cookery, that he could not say with truth that he had ever suffered to any great extent from those dreadful concoctions described by the Traveller (the result of the idleness and ignorance of teachers or artificers) so as to be compelled, on the score of health, to devote his time to practical cookery: his own first great object had been to ascertain the best method for prevention of waste, which he considered a very great sin, as everything that was wasted was a robbery of the poor, and that great fact could not be too strongly inculcated upon the minds of all young people from the

first dawn of reason. He knew that in pro-
secuting his experiments to prevent waste, he
had day by day become more enlightened as
to the fact that the better the cookery the
less the waste—by *better* he did not mean the
common very vulgar notion that by increasing
the quantity of expensive materials a dish must
necessarily be improved, but he meant that
the taste of a dish was *not* improved, but
the contrary, by the utter *destruction* of any
material, and that its reduction (viz. boiling
away) in the process of preparation for soup
did not improve the taste, and was not only
totally unnecessary, but in many cases rendered
good food unwholesome and unpalatable.

The Traveller here interposed, and begged
to know if the Hermit *really* meant to assert
that if he was obliged to superintend a banquet
where he would desire to obtain the very best
results, as far as the palate was concerned, that
he would not *then* consider it necessary to
destroy a considerable quantity of meat for the
production of soups and gravies, as he recollected when a boy being shown in triumph by

a cook an *immense lump* of solid stuff that looked like a compressed mass of wet brown cotton, or thin pack-thread, which he was informed had once been the best meat, veal and beef, which had been reduced to the state above described to make soup for a great dinner-party; that not being able to believe such a metamorphosis could have taken place, he (school-boy like) asked to *taste it,* when to his astonishment he found that there was no more resemblance to meat than a bit of soaked paper, and he was informed that even dogs and cats would not touch it, as there was not a particle of nourishment or flavour left, and he asked the Hermit whether such an immense sacrifice of food could really have been made without any advantage?

The Hermit assured him that it was not only without benefit to man or beast, but that the soup would not be at all better, probably not near as good as what he could himself make any day from meat which was only stewed in a double vessel sufficiently to be wholesome food for eating afterwards; that the miserable material which he had well described as resembling wet cotton or paper was destroyed, for no one justifiable or desirable result, that the first and best part of the distillation had been entirely injured by boiling away, and that the meat had been destroyed to produce a sufficient quantity for use in consequence of the wilful sacrifice of more than half the produce by continued boiling away in a single vessel.

This reply seemed to make the Traveller very melancholy, and he afterwards confessed that he could not help thinking how much people had to answer for who thus unnecessarily permitted the wholesale destruction of food, of which so many were in want.

The Hermit could not resist clapping his hands with delight at this avowal. "My dear friend," said he, "have I succeeded in convincing you of the truth of what you have just uttered? But how is it possible you have been so many years without thinking of this before?"

"Because," rejoined the other, "I *never* was taught *to think,* and I did not take to it naturally. I have thought more since I have been in your cell than I ever did before in my whole life. I used to listen to lectures upon abstruse subjects, which to tell you the truth I felt were exceedingly dull, because I did not understand half that was said, and they did not relate to any matter of importance or interest in my own sphere of life; but from seeing so many others similarly circumstanced who appeared satisfied that their hours were very well spent when listening to what would never be of the least use to them in their practical life, I supposed that I must be a much *wiser* man by thus spending my time, and I plumed myself not a little in recording in my diary, and repeating to my acquaintance, the numbers of lectures on chemistry and electricity I had attended, although I cannot deny that I never had the slightest turn for those studies. I was, therefore, not a more informing companion from having been so patient though inattentive a listener. I now see that I might have done more good in my generation if I had made use of my powers of observation, in connection

with the powers of reasoning, which would
have assisted me to some practical results beneficial to myself or others."

The Hermit then reminded his friend that he
had not answered the *second* question of his
catechism, for that day, viz., " the reasons
which ought to induce all persons to promote
the practical application of such principles."

The Traveller did himself more credit by
his answer on this occasion than on the former
one, and replied without hesitation, " Those
reasons are the prevention of waste, on the
principle that bad cookery not only robs the
poor, but injures the health of all classes."

The Hermit was well satisfied with this
answer, and arrangements were made for the
next day's practical instruction, when the dinner
was to consist of root of tongue soup,* which
the Welsh widows immediately began to prepare, and a roast chicken.

The roots of tongue having been washed
and immersed in spring-water, were placed in
the inner tin of the Ffwrn fach, which being

---

* See Appendix No. XX.

of very thick iron the Hermit said he always preferred, to obtain a slower heat.   A little salt was added, and chopped herbs—celery and turnip, with a little carrot, was added, and the whole left to stew very slowly for three or four hours; it was then strained off to cool, and the roots of tongue put in a dish in a cold place.

The next day the Hermit's senior widow removed, as on former occasions, a cake of fat from the top of the stock (which was a fine clear jelly), and the Hermit requested the Traveller to remember that in the case of roots of tongue he seldom allowed any water, the reason of which was that they required a great deal of soaking and washing, during which process they imbibed water; consequently, if they had the proportion of water allowed to other meat which was *not* thus washed and soaked, the product would be broth instead of jelly; and that it was some time before he had discovered the reason that he was so frequently disappointed in the jelly that he expected for his root of tongue soup.   After the root of tongue jelly had melted in a double vessel, it was flavoured with the extra celery and herbs required. The chicken was roasted on a hook suspended to the woollen yarn in the usual way, the same system being pursued as that adopted with the leg of mutton.

The Hermit pointed out that it was particularly necessary to have the most delicate fat for basting fowls and turkeys, as the skin of a well-roasted bird of that description ought (if properly dressed) to be one of the best parts to eat, and an indispensable accompaniment to the white meat.

The Traveller inquired whether *butter* would not be better than fat for this purpose; but he was assured that it would not, as there was a peculiar rancid or sickly flavour in butter, when acted on by fire, which could almost always be detected in savoury cookery, if a sufficient quantity was used to saturate the roasting meat, and where a sufficient quantity of fat was not produced by the bird or beast to be roasted—viz. chickens, pheasants, hares, rabbits, &c. &c. —pure suet was the best material to select, next to the fat of veal; but that no one need

complain of a chicken roasted with the fat from
the stock of stewed beef, which was what he
had used that day.

The Traveller said that he had frequently
been offended with the strong taste of the
roasted chicken skin, and he wished to know
what the Hermit supposed the cause to be.

His reply was, that no doubt what was
commonly called dripping, (viz. the fat from
the gravy produced by roasting brown meat,)
being commonly employed for the purpose,
which had probably been frying in the dripping-pan for hours, instead of being raised into
an earthen pan each time the meat was basted,
as might be remembered with his leg of mutton,
and which plan he had pursued with everything
else; but that he never used the dripping,
even thus carefully preserved, for fowls and
game, lest it should impart a flavour of roasted
butcher's meat; though, if he should ever be
so circumstanced as to have nothing else to use,
he should order one or more *extra* clarifications
for the purpose.

The Traveller said the Hermit had not

given him any instruction yet about "*clarifi-cation,*" and begged to be enlightened.

He was informed that fat properly clarified was melted over the fire in a double vessel, and, when in a liquid state, poured into a large pan of boiling water, and then well stirred with a large stick, and, being left to cool, the impurities sunk to the bottom, or adhered to the lower surface of the cake, whence they were easily removed with a knife; and this process of clarification * might be repeated two or three times if desirable. The Hermit said it was a process indispensable to good manage-ment, as there are very few, if any, households, where there is not more fat than is required for the consumption of the family, although its consumption is greatly increased where it is properly used and kept separately, and where butter is entirely repudiated for savoury cookery. The Hermit then promised his friend a sight of the clarified stores of this valuable, but generally despised and neglected, material, which could not then be inspected,

* See Appendix No. XXI.

as the senior widow announced that the fowl was beautifully frothed, and the roots of tongue, previously stewed, having been cut into moderate-sized squares, after being deprived of fat, skin, and sinews, were about to be put into the soup made from them.

The Traveller was again well satisfied with his dinner, especially with the bread sauce,* which the Hermit allowed him to write down as a regular receipt, where it will no doubt be found with other receipts by the reader in due course of time.

The next day the Hermit introduced the Traveller to a very cool recess in his larder, which had been hollowed out of the rock into the form of a cupboard, with shelves of the same material, on which were arranged little red and yellow pans, which held two and three pounds each. They had each a piece of paper or white calico over the top, with a small piece of flat wood which fitted closely within the rim. The Hermit's widows uncovered several of the pans, and each of them appeared to be filled

---

* See Appendix No. XXII.

with an ivory-like material, of which the only difference was, that some were whiter, and some of a yellower tint than others.

The Hermit explained that the whitest was from mutton, and clarified dripping; the yellowest was beef fat and marrow, not only the marrow taken out of the tube of the bones of beef called by that name, but was also produced from the bones themselves, broken up and stewed in water, after all the solid marrow had been taken out of the tubes.* The Hermit took this opportunity of recounting to the Traveller the result of his practical experience with regard to the production of marrow from bones which appeared to be entirely bare and completely hollow, but which, when broken up and subjected to slow heat in a digester, yielded a large proportion of marrow to the weight of bones.

The Traveller inquired to what use he appropriated these various stores.

The Hermit informed him that the marrow was equal to butter for tart paste, and superior

---

* See Appendix No. XXIII.

K

to it for the paste of mince-pies, and that the widows always were instructed to keep a good stock of these different sorts of fat in hand, not only for basting, but for other processes which the Traveller had, or would witness ; but that every month the senior widow disposed of the superfluous stock while it was good, and that none might be kept to be so old as to be deteriorated. He also reminded his friend that he gave a great deal to the poor, but that clarified fat (and none was ever put away *un*-clarified) was *not* one of those things that he gave away, and that he considered it was of greater benefit to allow them to buy it; but when the demand of his poorer immediate neighbours was not equal to the supplies, he sent it by the senior widow to a small town, some miles distant, with an ass and cart, where she also purchased his groceries, disposing of the fat to be spared at from 3*d.* and 5*d.* to 6*d.* per pound, according to its quality. That fat which had been used for frying ought to be clarified three times over, and this, he believed, was used for candles, and it bore the lowest price, as it was of inferior quality, and did not recover its natural colour, from having been so often subjected to the fierce action of the fire; whilst the other kinds, from not having been thus exposed to burning heat, were perfectly good for culinary uses.

The Traveller said he knew that where perquisites were allowed, fat was taken by the cooks, and sold for their own benefit.

The Hermit simply remarked, that those who permitted this to be done, were guilty of two sins; the first, wilful extravagance in housekeeping, and thereby robbery of the poor; the second, tempting a servant to dishonesty, by allowing a direct advantage to result from the neglecting of the first duty of her office, which was to make the most of everything under her care, for the benefit of her employers, or the good of her fellow-creatures; and having discovered that the Traveller was a good arithmetician, he gave him a small account to cast up, of the number of pounds of fat, which in the course of twelve months the Welsh widow had sold for him; by which his friend discovered to his surprise, that he had had not merely shillings, but many pounds' value, with which to assist the poor in other ways.

The Traveller said that it appeared to him that the Hermit was practically charitable, and that he evidently himself saved to give; but that as he was also the dispenser of charity for another benevolent individual, and that he would esteem it a favour, as he was now becoming more alive to the requirements of others, if he would let him see the soup made for the poor, about which he had seen him engaged in superintending the widows twice each week, at which times he had purposely withdrawn himself from the recollection that their compact did not entitle him to pry into *that* department.

The Hermit expressed his satisfaction that such a desire had been enkindled in his mind, and assured him that he had purposely refrained from inviting his companionship and assistance, from the belief that he would not take any interest in what did not immediately concern himself personally.

The Traveller coloured, from the consciousness that such would have been the case a short
time before, and the next morning he engaged
himself to be the Hermit's scholar in preparing
soup for the poor.*

It has already been stated that the Hermit
had a very extensive and well-stored garden;
containing vegetables of all descriptions—such
a kitchen-garden as is to be met with in the
general average of gentlemen's houses. The
host and the visitor were followed by the
widows, provided with baskets; the Hermit
filled the baskets with the stalks and leaves of
celery, carrots, onions, leeks, parsnips, and a
few potatoes, and cabbage-leaves. On their
return, these were all washed and chopped
very small, while the water which had boiled
half a round of beef the day before was being
warmed in a large double vessel, The Hermit
informed his friend that he never kept his half-
rounds of beef in salt more than six days, and
sometimes not more than five, by which means
the flavour of the beef was very superior, and

---

* See Appendix No. XXIV.

the water in which it was boiled was not salted like brine, but retained some flavour of the meat, and was consequently more nutritious.

The widows then fried several soup-plates full of all the vegetables they had chopped, in a single saucepan, for ten minutes, with clarified fat; they then added oatmeal, and stirred it rapidly for five minutes more, and put the whole mass into the hot beef liquor, which, after stewing for some time in its double vessel, was converted into a very savoury soup; the oatmeal and vegetables having given flavour, and consistency, and counterbalanced any overplus of salt in the beef liquor; moreover, it was not the least greasy, because the fat that had been used had been previously entirely absorbed by the vegetables and oatmeal, and the Hermit called his friend's attention to the undeniable amount of additional nourishment, produced by this method of incorporating a certain quantity of pure fat in the manner which had been just exemplified.

The Traveller inquired what the Hermit

gave the poor when he did not boil half a round of beef.

" On some occasions," said he, " I have peas soaked as you have seen in the well, and then stewed, with as much fat as they would absorb without being greasy; a small quantity of finely-chopped onions are then fried, and stirred round with flour or oatmeal, in the same manner as the other vegetables, which being added to the pea-soup, imparts a savoury flavour, completed by powdered or chopped mint. Another broth for the poor is made from two sheep's heads,* which are stewed a considerable time in a double vessel, with the proportion of a pint of water to the pound weight. The meat is then taken from the bones, the broth put away till the next day, and the bones broken small, and put down in the digester for some hours. The liquor is then poured off, the bones rebroken, and subjected to the same process, with fresh water; the liquor is again strained off, and when cold, both the first and second extract produces a good jelly; the

* See Appendix No. XXV.

sheep's broth having itself an excellent flavour,
is not thickened with fried vegetables and oatmeal, but a few chopped leek leaves and roots are
put into it, and when served out, the meat from
the sheep's head being cold, and cut in mouthfuls, is put into the bottom of each jug before
it is filled, which is a better plan than letting it
be overdone, by stewing longer in the broth.
The third material which I have for soup for
the poor," said the Hermit, " is the jelly which
is produced in considerable quantities by my
faithful ancient British widows, with the aid of
those valuable iron vessels, ' *the digesters ;* ' they
carefully collect every spare bone, and day by
day break them small, and stew them down till
the goodness is all extracted ; there is not any
sort of bone that does not produce a first and
second jelly, and veal bones will produce jelly
after a third time's stewing. These jellies are
as nutritious as any delicacy that can be invented ; they only require the flavouring of
vegetables, and they may be adapted for clear
broth or thickened soup, and when there are
any bits of dressed meat to spare, they are of

course put into it. In my secluded life, there is
seldom anything left upon plates which is fit for
this purpose; but in houses, where many guests
are received, it is certain that some of them very
improperly take upon their plate a great deal
more than they can eat, and it has always been
my rule that every substance left in plates, should
be put apart on a dish before they are washed,
and if in the contents of this dish there are any
good pieces of meat, they are neatly cut into
dice, and put away to add to the next soup, as
I consider one of the precepts most necessary to
inculcate, is everything to its proper use, and I
do not think that the proper use of *meat*, any
more than *milk*, is *to feed pigs !* "

The Traveller, on hearing this, said that he
had been surprised, when in London, at seeing
daily a cart come to the opposite house, accompanied by two persons, with a bag and a tub, or
vessel of some kind. These individuals used
to go down the area, and regularly return with
a loaded bag, of such an apparent weight, that
it excited his curiosity to know with what it
could be filled; and that it had just struck him

that the contents must have been the remains of bread and meat, given or sold for pigs, which, after being aware of what might be done for the poor by care and economy, now really appeared to him a great sin.

The Hermit said, that as he had not been in London for more than half a century, he was the last person who could explain what the Traveller had observed, but that he might depend upon it, that where food was not preserved for a legitimate or moral use, it would be disposed of for very bad purposes. " I have," said he, " now given you an outline of the broths that I have most frequently made for the poor; but in large households, where there is a considerable consumption of roast, and boiled, and stewed meat, there is so large a quantity of bones, that quarts of jelly ought to be made every day, and gallons every week; and this ought to be a considerable proportion of the soup given to the poor, together with the boilings of salt beef and pork, which, however, if salted too heavily, or left too long in pickle, are not only de-

teriorated in flavour, and become hard instead
of tender, whilst the water in which they are
boiled is mere brine, and it is cruelty, instead
of charity, to give it to the poor."

The Hermit became animated upon this
topic, and his eyes sparkled with indignation
as he recounted a visit that he had paid to a
Welsh cottage, where the mother of the family
was very ill, and required the best pure jelly
broth that could be produced. Knowing her
condition, he had ordered the Welsh widows
to send some chicken jelly in the morning.
The boy who was sent for it had fallen down
and broken the jug when out of sight of the
trusty Gwenllian, and, being afraid to acknowledge his offence, he had not returned at all.
The Hermit had also ordered a large supply
of fresh made beef broth to be sent for the
use of the children, of whom there was a large
family, who, from the poverty of their parents,
were really often in want of food.

When he arrived at the cottage, he was
surprised to find that the chicken broth had
not been received, and he waited in expectation

until the little girl returned who had been sent
for the beef broth, which was always mixed
with other ingredients to make it more palatable.   By the time it arrived, the poor woman
was so exhausted that she begged to have some
for herself; but said the good Hermit, " Where
an invalid is concerned, I never miss an opportunity of tasting the food myself, when it is
possible," and, to my astonishment, I found that
the soup, which, (with the best preparation,)
could not have been well adapted for her state,
was *so salt*, that it could only be compared to
sea-water, and I dared not give it her, and was
shocked to see the poor children devour their dry
bread soaked in this dreadful brine, and I must
confess, that nothing but my regard for the
sick mother's nerves, would have prevented my
exploding with violent passion; but I checked
myself, and thus I soliloquised, (though not
aloud) :—" Weak mortal ! the erring widows,
who are the objects of your wrath, cannot be
profited by your anger at two miles' distance !
Think of the present moment !   Here is the
wretched woman dying for want of sustenance,

your duty is to assist her." But my good angel seemed to forsake me. What could I do? There was nothing in the house but a crust of bread, or in the garden but a bed of leeks; and although the leek is a most wonderful herb for nutritive, as well as for medical purposes, it did not suit the present case. Suddenly a thought struck me. There was an old woman not a field's distance, who had a hen and chickens. I did not feel the ground under my feet till I arrived at her door, and, quickly explaining my distress, I begged she would sell one of the brood. To this she objected, on the true plea that, for the purpose I required them, they were too young to be of any use; but said she, "I have a troublesome cock of last year, who fights with his uncle, and I should be willing to kill him for the sake of peace in his family; but were he my *best* fowl, I would kill him at your request, and for the benefit of my neighbour."

I begged her to follow me with the cock, while I returned on the wings of the wind, to discover what utensil I could find to cook the fowl, when I had got it,* without waste.

The cottage only produced an iron pot, some jugs, cups and saucers, one or two pans, and some basins. In a few minutes the pot was on the fire, with water to boil, and a jug was selected which would contain the chicken when cut limb from limb, which is always the best way of dressing a chicken, if it is intended solely for an invalid, because it can be frequently stirred, and is not only cooked much quicker, but the flavour is more perfectly extracted, and each part is more thoroughly done; and in three-quarters of an hour, by keeping the water briskly boiling round the jug, with a saucer on the top, I was enabled to administer a cup of chicken broth, which, though weak, was pure and of excellent flavour. I then added more water to the chicken in the jug, as more water may always be allowed when it is cut up. It then stewed an hour and a half longer, very slowly, after which it was poured off for future use;

---

* See Appendix No. XXVI.

but as there was no digester there with which
to extract the jelly from the bones, I taught
one of the little girls how to take all the
meat off, and, putting the bones into a basin,
ordered them to be brought down to the
widow Gwenllian, who, I promised, should
perform this office, and send the produce back
another day.

On my return home, I felt that it was not
only a satisfaction, but a duty, most severely
to reprimand my hand-matrons; and, after
minute investigations, it appeared that Gwenllian, (the first in command,) had trusted Cattws,
the third under her, to fetch the half round of
salt beef, and had instructed her how to put it
on to boil, without detecting any error; but
the fact was, that the piece then boiled had
been *forgotten* the week before, and had lain
a fortnight in pickle, the result of which was
the brine I have described, and you may be
sure that the delinquent did not escape severe
censure, although I attributed more blame to
the first in command, who ought not, *first of
all,* to have *forgotten* this beef, or have trusted

the most inexperienced of her assistants to select the meat without supervision, and she ought not to have allowed anything to be given away without herself flavouring and tasting it.

"I think," said the Traveller, "my good friend, that you have been a little unjust, according to your own narration. Why should you have censured severely the inexperienced Cattws, when it appears to me that she performed a service in taking that unfortunate meat to be boiled, which had she not done, might have remained a third week in pickle."

"I was *not* unjust," replied the Hermit. "Cattws has been under instruction so short a time, that her sole duty was implicit obedience. She was told to go to the second pan from the door, instead of which she went to the third; had she gone to the second, the beef would have been exactly in a proper state for boiling, and for broth for the poor, and those poor children would not have been injured by salt water; whilst the forgotten beef in the third pan would not have been much the worse for

eating by the next morning, which was the
day for my making personal inspection of the
salted provisions, when the negligence would
have been detected, the beef would have been
boiled, and the water would have been thrown
away."

" As," said the Traveller, " you have so
kindly recounted to me this little domestic
history, allow me to ask how long you consider
an intelligent female would be, or ought to be,
in learning, under such instruction (as is to be
found here), a sufficient knowledge of the real
principles of cookery, to enable her to roast,
to boil, and to stew well, and to make good
and wholesome broth and soups ? "

The Hermit shook his head. " It is impossible for me," said he, " to compute *how
much* sense and activity are required to make
' *one intelligent female.*' I can, therefore, only
say, that in my experience, a sharp and attentive
girl of fifteen would learn each of the processes
you mention, and be able to make two or three
good soups in four months; but unfortunately,
at that early age, ' *sharpness* ' *and* ' *giddiness* '

are more generally combined than sharpness and *attention*."

"I should never dream," said the Traveller, "of a cook of *fifteen*. What could put such an idea into your head? Of course, at that age, no girl could be trusted with such a charge as must always devolve upon a cook—I mean, an intelligent female of five or six and twenty, or two or three and thirty."

The Hermit again shook his head. "At that age," said he, "if females are really intelligent, they have had some practice in endeavouring to do something for themselves or their families, either in or out of service, by which means they have been long convinced that they know a great deal, and therefore I should reckon an additional year of learning for every additional year of age after twenty, and, before that period, I should give a year or two *more* to instruct the girl of twenty, than I would to the girl of fifteen or sixteen. No one but those who have tried the experiment, can imagine the difficulty of making any one in the kitchen department *un*learn or *leave off bad habits* once acquired."

"Am I then to understand," said the Traveller, " that these well-aged matrons have been in your service since they were fifteen ? "

" *No*," said the Hermit, " for although I was approaching my grand climacteric when I retired from the world, I had too much regard for the propriety of appearances ; and being a bachelor, I selected Gwenllian, who was *then* of a very sedate age, but in addition of a most teachable disposition, with extraordinary activity, and great steadiness, and as she never had been a cook in her life, she knew no more of the culinary art than the ordinary life of a Welsh peasant had taught her. She was then a widow, and she did *not suppose* that she understood anything about cookery. She was cleanliness itself in her habits, as many Welsh peasants are, whose houses vie with the Dutch in neatness and comfort, but she had no supposititious knowledge of cooking, and her mind was therefore as open to instruction as a child's ; whilst her activity, and general habits of cleanliness, rendered her invaluable in that service, where, of all others, cleanliness is most indis-

pensable. My second widow, Bettws, was
much the same sort of person, and sufficiently
Gwenllian's junior to be under her control.
The other widows have been added, and are
each of them considerably younger, and will,
I hope, by degrees, become props to the elder
matrons, who, it must be expected, sooner or
later may require more efficient aid, though,
I trust, they will never be superseded."

The Traveller expressed his acknowledgments for the details he had received ; but said
that he " did not see how the information now
afforded would assist himself or others, who
had *not* the advantage of living within reach of
Welsh widows, or, if they did, would not be
able to instruct them ? "

The Hermit said that his efforts for some
weeks had been directed unceasingly to the instruction of his guest in the first principles of
cookery, and that he thought it impossible that
his friend would not, within a reasonable period,
have attained sufficient knowledge to impart
a good deal of it to some intelligent gentlewoman, in his own class of life, who might,

perhaps, find somebody who *knew nothing.*
The only difficulty would be, to find one who
was not so *proud* of *knowing nothing,* that they
would disdain to be taught anything, but that
of course instructions could be much better
given by ladies than by gentlemen, and that he
also supposed that there were, in England, old
maids as well as widows, who might be found
willing to be taught, and capable of learning.

" Do you not think," said the Traveller,
" that *schools for cookery* ought to be very
good things ? There are places in London that
are called schools for this purpose, and friends
of mine have taken cooks who have been instructed in them, and have sent cooks to be
taught in some establishments of the kind—but
I have never heard of any satisfactory result."

" I cannot judge," said the Hermit, " of
what such schools may be, but I have *no faith*
in schools for teaching any of the practical arts
of life. The best school for those arts is *home ;*
the best teacher is the *mother* or *mistress* of a
family, and her first scholars ought to be her
own daughters or younger sisters. When once

this principle is again acted upon, there will
be *no scarcity* of good servants, and much more
comfort, and abundance of proper liberality
and true charity in every class that has anything to give, whilst the number of those who
lack charity will be greatly diminished."

The Traveller replied, that although he
believed there was no country in the world
where there were so many charitable institu-
tions as Great Britain, yet that since he had
begun to reflect, he recollected many circumstances which convinced him that there was
a great want of discretion, as well as practical
experience, in the present age ; that the Hermit had demonstrated clearly how much more
ought to be made for the maintenance of the
body, by the proper preparation of food, and
that he was quite sure that *souls* would be
more benefited, if all those who, with the best
intentions, devoted their time to visiting and
religious instruction, had more consideration for
bodily wants, and rather more discretion as to
the time of day which they selected for their
readings, as it was impossible to expect a starving

penitent to pay attention to religious instruction when very hungry or in the middle of a wash.*

This remark led to a long conversation between the Hermit and the Traveller on the evil effect of the Poor Laws, as at present constituted, of which the Hermit could not be in total ignorance, from his intimate acquaintance with his poor neighbours, although happily, from their primitive habits of domestic industry, and the comparatively small population, he had not known many cases where parish relief was needed ; but he had known enough to inquire anxiously whether there was no hope of any philanthropic individuals devoting themselves to the task of collecting and publishing statistics, which would easily prove that the present Poor Laws were productive of serious evils, that their effects were most undeniably demoralizing, and that their amendment was most necessary.

The next day, the Hermit reminded his friend that it was time he should put him through his catechism again, and that, with

---

* See Anecdote in Traveller's Note Book.

his approbation, the next examination should be upon soups, which was a subject especially interesting.

" I will," said the Hermit, " put a few questions to you after dinner; and in the meantime you shall see the preparation for minced veal; * previous to which I will take the liberty of asking you how *you* would instruct a cook to make it ? "

The Traveller had by this time become sufficiently humble to answer with *some diffidence*, although he felt great confidence in doing himself credit by his reply—" I should have the veal chopped up," said he.

" May I ask," said the Hermit, " what instrument you would use for 'chopping ? ' "

" I mean," said the Traveller, " reducing the veal into little bits, with a thing called a chopper—a piece of steel in a handle."

" *That*," said the Hermit, " would make a very inferior dish. Observe how Gwenllian proceeds."

Gwenllian, having placed a white board on

----

* See Appendix No. XXVII.

the table, cut slices from a cold baked fillet of
veal, of the proper thickness. She then cut
each slice into small square dice, having carefully removed every particle of fat.

The Traveller looked on with attention for
some time, and then said that he really thought
chopping, instead of cutting, would have saved
a great deal of time and trouble.

" It would," said the Hermit, " have saved
both ; but, unfortunately, it would not have
produced the desired result of a good dish of
minced veal, and you will allow that there is
no economy in being a *short time* in making a
bad thing ; but after you have tasted the present
preparation, I will explain, as well as I can,
why ' *chopping* ' veal spoils the dish ; but
whether my explanation is satisfactory or not,
is of very little consequence, as such is the
practical fact."

After the veal had been thus prepared, it was
slightly floured and salted, and, after being
turned over and over with two forks, was left
in a basin for an hour. Meantime, some pure
veal jelly, made from boiling a shoulder of veal

in a double vessel, was put into the inner tin
of the Ffwrn fach.   When liquefied, it was
flavoured with pieces of celery and onion, and
a nosegay of sweet herbs, composed of margery,
orange thyme, and basil.   These were stirred
round and round until the proper flavour was
obtained, when some cream was added, and
stirred with the same ingredient, until the
whole had a most agreeable flavour.   The
vegetables and herbs were then taken out, and
the floured veal, cut in dice, was put in, and
well stirred for some minutes, after which the
whole was covered with two lids, and the veal
left to infuse, in a slow heat, for about half an
hour, by which time the flour had thickened
the sauce, and the veal had communicated its
own flavour to the whole, and the Traveller
pronounced his dinner to be as good as he
ever desired to taste.

The Hermit informed him that this was the
simple way of making minced veal, but that a
richer dish might be made by frying finely-
chopped vegetables with the pure top fat from
soup stock, and adding it to the veal jelly in

the same manner that had been shown from
hashed mutton; but that he considered the
present plan produced a purer taste, and was
more agreeable to his palate.

The Hermit then commenced his queries
about soups, and informed the Traveller what
the materials were which were then in the
larder—viz a small quantity of veal jelly stock
(not sufficient for soup for two); there was
also a small quantity of beef jelly stock, and
a small quantity of pease stewed and pulped
ready for soup. He asked what soup his
friend considered had better be ordered for
the morrow, considering the materials at
command.

The Traveller said that it appeared to him,
that, although there was a great variety, there
was not sufficient of anything for the purpose
required; and therefore that the only plan was
to mix the veal jelly and the beef jelly together,
which he now knew enough to be aware would
make a very good soup.

The Hermit said he was so far correct;
but, as they had had gravy soup the day before,

it would prove a great lack of contrivance
to have the same sort of soup the day following.

The Traveller said he did not know what
else to suggest, unless the pease could be made
available.

To this the Hermit replied that the pease
were insufficient in quantity to do more than
make pea broth, which, though a very good
thing, was not the best thing that could be
devised under present circumstances.

In vain the Traveller "racked his brains"
to invent any other sort of soup; he was fairly
puzzled, and the Hermit was obliged to come to
his assistance, and to inform him that a certain
portion of finely-chopped vegetables, prepared
as he had before seen, and then mixed with
the veal and beef jelly, passed through a wire
sieve, and returned into the double, would be
the first process he should direct. The next
would be the addition of the minced veal left
at dinner, with an extra spoonful of cream,
previously flavoured with herbs and vegetables;
and that the whole mixture would make a

most excellent extemporary soup, although the various stocks thus mixed together were not combined from any recipe, but simply from the knowledge which experience had produced from former experiments, with the same materials at hand ; and the following day the practical results verified the Hermit's prognostications, previous to which the catechism was continued a little further.

" Supposing," said the Hermit, " that I had only the pease and some mutton broth, what would you advise ? "

" I would make pea broth," said the Traveller, " as you say it is so good, by putting the pease into the mutton broth."

" That," said the Hermit, " could be easily managed, certainly ; but how would you make it appear like pea soup, the quantity of pease being insufficient for that purpose ? "

" I would make a paste with vegetables," said the Traveller, " in the same way that I have now so often seen that process performed by Gwenllian."

" You are improving," said the Hermit.

"You would not have hit upon that expedient a week ago. But there is a better plan than that for mock pea soup, although yours would not be by any means bad, and indeed your plan is in part what I should do, with the addition of oatmeal * instead of flour to make the vegetable paste, which will assimilate with the pease, and produce a better imitation of the flavour of pea soup; in fact, a very good mock pea soup may be made with *oatmeal*, without any pease, after being well incorporated with the vegetable paste with which the stock is thickened. I will now ask you," said the Hermit, "how you would produce soup or broth, supposing you have *no* jelly stock in the house, excepting the jelly of mutton bones, and the remains of a mutton pie?"

The Traveller, who had become much more inventive than on previous occasions, said that he would put the contents of the mutton pie into the jelly of the mutton bones, and thus make broth.

The Hermit reminded him that the jelly of

* See Oatmeal in Traveller's Note Book.

the mutton bones would have very little, if any, flavour, and that consequently they would diminish the flavour of the contents of the mutton pie, without imparting any additional taste.

The Traveller then, without much difficulty, discovered that the mutton bone jelly could be flavoured with vegetables and herbs so as to make it very palatable mutton broth, which, when added to the contents of the pie, would produce altogether an excellent mutton broth, the meat of the pie being in the best possible state for being eaten in the broth.

The Traveller became so much interested with the soup examination, that he desired to prolong it; but the Hermit, having a great objection to overloading his pupil, declined to put any further interrogations till a future day.

The next day a harrico of mutton * was the selected dish, of which the Traveller said he had never tasted but one good in his life, and then he had never inquired how it was prepared.

The Hermit desired that he would state the particular faults of which he had to complain.

* See Appendix No. XXVIII.

He replied that they might be comprised under two heads—being greasy, and having a very strong burnt flavour, very much like the odour of which they had before spoken, of cinders falling into the dripping-pan.

Gwenllian and her attendant handmaids were hastened by the Hermit, and their proceedings were as follows :—The cutlets were taken from a neck of Welsh mutton, they were neatly cut (in the form of pears), but none of the fat was taken off the bones, which the Hermit said was a very great error in making a harrico. They were then placed in a well-tinned iron saucepan, where they were stirred and turned round and round, the saucepan being on the hottest part of the hot plate, until they were thoroughly heated through without burning, and had begun to brown without being at all dried, when they were immediately transferred into an inner tin saucepan, which stood ready surrounded by boiling water, and a little boiling water poured upon them, in which button onions had just been scalded ; the scalded onions were put aside, while some raw onions,

finely chopped, with celery, a little turnip and
carrot, and a nosegay of orange thyme, basil,
and savory, with a sprinkling of salt, the
whole being covered with two lids, were left
to stew till tender, though not overdone; and
their gravy, being extracted to some extent,
had produced, with the onion water, and other
vegetables, a savoury sauce, which was strained
into a basin, while the cutlets were drawn off
to a cooler place. The basin of gravy having
been plunged in a pan of cold water, the fat
soon congealed on the surface; and as soon as
it could be taken off, the gravy was poured
back upon the cutlets, and they were replaced
in the outer saucepan as before. During this
time, small pieces of carrots and turnips, neatly
cut, had been stewing in another double saucepan, in some beef jelly stock, the attentive
widows having taken care to anticipate the
Hermit's inquiry as to whether the carrots
had been put in half an hour previous to the
turnips, as otherwise the turnips would be
over-done, or the carrots half-cooked. These
carrots and turnips, therefore, being quite

M

tender at the same time, were added to the cutlets, and in about ten minutes the harrico was ready for the table; and the Traveller pronounced that it was well flavoured, without the slightest taste of what he had before complained, and he particularly admired the clearness of the fat of each cutlet, at the same time that the gravy was so completely free from grease; while the vegetables were as savoury as the meat, in consequence of not having been stewed in water.

The Traveller then claimed the Hermit's promise of telling him what in general occasioned harricos to be so very bad. The cause was explained as follows: that the cutlets are generally done in a frying-pan, and are not only burnt, but, from the intense heat and the narrow sides of the frying-pan, the fat often flies into the fire, or on the hot plate, and produces a dreadful odour, the taste of which is, through the vapour, communicated to and absorbed by the cutlets; in addition to this, onions are often cut up and fried with the cutlets, and it is hardly possible to produce

a more unconquerable flavour than that of
onions and fat burned together. This once
done, the Hermit said, no cook in the world
could afterwards make a well-flavoured harrico;
and that, probably, little, if any, portion of the
fat was removed from the gravy, if the same
gravy was used, but that it was probable that
the best essence of the mutton was thrown
out of the frying-pan as useless, and that some
nauseous concoction of butter and flour was
used for gravy, mixed with bought ready-made
sauce, and the whole, well peppered and filled
up with carrots and turnips boiled in water,
were served with the cutlets, which, having
lòst all their own essence and flavour, were
smothered in a liquid made of other materials.

The Traveller then requested the Hermit to
question him, that he might see whether he
really improved in culinary knowledge.

" I shall confine myself," said the Hermit,
" on this occasion, especially to matters of
general daily economy in domestic management. Supposing that we have a small quantity of beef jelly stock, but not enough for the

quantity of soup we require; that we have half
a pint of onion sauce, left from a boiled shoulder
of mutton or boiled rabbits, and a small quantity of the remains of minced veal, with a pint
of chicken jelly stock.   Having those materials
only, what would you propose to do?"

The Traveller said, that, having seen how
each of the above-named sauces and made
dishes had been prepared singly, he should not
be afraid to mix them all together; but in what
order he did not know, or which to begin
with.

The Hermit said, that the first thing was to
warm the beef stock in a double saucepan,
then to add the chicken stock to it; then to
flavour both with celery, onion, and a bunch
of sweet herbs, until they obtained the proper
flavour for gravy soup; the onion sauce should
next be stirred in, and then the remains of the
minced veal, with its sauce, and more vegetables
to flavour, if needed.   " The above mixture
will make an excellent soup," said he, " which
incidental circumstances alone taught me to
invent, but for which a guest would very pro-

bably request the recipe. And, after all,"
added the Hermit, " it is not so very extraordinary that it should be good; for, if you
consider the ingredients of each, you find that
they will all assimilate and improve, without
counteracting or superseding the flavour of
each other. Veal, chicken, and beef stock
will always go together. Onion sauce is made
of new milk and flour, flavoured with scalded
onions; the sauce of minced veal is made from
the jelly of the same meat, flavoured with
vegetables and enriched by cream. In this
way, by understanding how to combine the
materials accidentally in hand, there never
ought to be a difficulty in procuring soup
where meat is cooked for other purposes; and
it is generally a great improvement to soups,
for those who are in health, and able to take
sufficient exercise to obtain a sharp appetite,
occasionally to have solid morsels in their soup,
provided those morsels are good. The remains
of fricassees are a great improvement to white
soup, if there is no butter in the fricassee."

The Traveller said, that he should like to

know something about the preparation of fish, of which he had as yet seen and heard nothing.

The Hermit said, he could not give him much instruction upon that head, as he was too far inland for sea fish to reach him often; and that of fresh-water fish he saw little except salmon, the preparation of which he thoroughly understood, and would give him a specimen of it the following day, if a salmon was brought in, but that a lobster did occasionally find its way to his wealthy neighbour, across the mountains, from the coast, and that he had been particularly successful in teaching the Welsh widows to make lobster sauce.*

The Traveller clapped his hands, declaring that he had once had an illness of three weeks' duration, from lobster sauce, which certainly had not improved in the present century, and that it was, without exception, one of the most dreadful specimens of modern cookery as generally prepared.

The Hermit said, that although he had never had the opportunity of perfecting his culinary

* See Appendix No. XXIX.

knowledge by experiments in cooking many sorts of fish, that he had done enough to know that the same principles would be well applied, and he specified shrimp sauce.*

" Of all things," said the Traveller, " it is one of the worst made sauces, next to lobster sauce."

" And yet, " said the Hermit, " it is one of the most easy to prepare, if only done the right way. The shells of the shrimps ought to be pounded slightly, and stewed with a very little water in a double vessel. The essence thus made from them, strained off, should be used instead of plain water, exactly in the same proportion as for the melted butter with which the parsley sauce was made on the day of our first dinner; and when the melted butter is thus made with the shrimp-shell water, nothing more is required than to put in the shrimps, and, after stirring them well, let them stew in a double saucepan for a quarter of an hour. The lobster sauce is on the same principle; the shell ought to be pounded and stewed down with a

* See Appendix No. XXX.

little water in a digester; and, when cold, it is a
lobster jelly, of which as much is taken as is
required, instead of water, to add to the melted
butter for the sauce. The lobster itself, in my
opinion, always requires vinegar; and being
pulled into moderate sized pieces, I have it
soaked in vinegar for an hour or two before
it is wanted. It is then drained from the
vinegar, and put into the lobster jelly melted
butter."

The next day a salmon* was brought in,
which had been very properly crimped, as soon
as it was killed. The Hermit ordered it to
be put into a stone reservoir, supplied from a
famous well, the stream of which ran through
his larder, in which the widows plunged
various pans of jelly stocks, in the summer,
the moment they were taken off the fire, for
the purpose of the quicker congelation of the
fat, which the Hermit was very particular, in
hot weather, in having immediately removed
as soon as cold, although, in cold weather, its
being left upon the jelly tended to preserve it

* See Appendix No. XXXI.

longer.* After the salmon had remained in spring water for an hour, it was prepared in the usual manner for boiling, having been previously divided into three or four parts, and placed in a fish kettle of cold spring water with a little salt, and as much vinegar as made the water very slightly acid. The moment the water was scalding hot the strainer was taken up, with the fish upon it, and the water in which it had been scalded was poured into a pan, and removed to a cold place, where the strainer with the fish was placed across the pan, so that the fish and the fish water might gradually cool together; during which process the fish imbibed its own flavour from the steam of the water in which it was scalded.

The Traveller, who had viewed the above-named process with great attention, now looked at his watch, and was alarmed to find that it was half-past twelve o'clock, and the dinner hour was one o'clock. "My excellent friend," said he, "there is only half an hour before dinner,—now, how long do you propose that

---

* See Appendix No. XXXII.

this salmon should remain here? for it is not fully boiled I know, and the time is short."

"Trust me, my good sir," said the Hermit, "our dinner will be on the table precisely at one o'clock; but as the proper preparation of a salmon brooks no delay, I gave directions to the widow Gwenllian to proceed with the preparations for our frugal meal."

The Traveller turned pale, and then red; he looked at his host, and then looked at the salmon. "I thought," said he, in a plaintive tone, "that we were to have this salmon for dinner?"

"I never promised *that*," said the Hermit. "I promised instruction in the preparation; but I never gave the date for eating it: and although, had it come in earlier, it might, of course, have been cooked and eaten on the same day, it will be infinitely better on the second day."

Bettws having announced that dinner was on the table, the Traveller hastened, impelled by hunger and curiosity, to see what Gwenllian had been able to effect with her handmaidens alone. The dinner consisted of delicate Welsh mutton chops,* broiled upon a gridiron, with their own unadulterated gravy; they were tender, savoury, and neither scorched nor dried. In addition to which were two boiled Bantam eggs, and two larger eggs, with baked apple dumplings.

The Traveller requested the Hermit to tell him why he had boiled eggs for dinner,† instead of poached eggs; as he was very well aware that nothing was done in his house without a reason.

"My reason," said the Hermit, "was, to have a text for your catechism of to-day; and if you will take a small egg, I will take a large one, or *vice versá*."

The Traveller complied. Both the small and the large egg were equally well boiled; and the moment the shells were removed, both disclosed the milk, which is the criterion of a well-dressed egg.

When dinner was concluded, the Hermit

* See Appendix No. XXXIII.
† See Appendix No. XXXIV.

asked the Traveller if he had any fault to find with his egg?

He said it could not be better. " And how very odd it is," said he, " that an egg is so seldom boiled properly."

" How would you instruct your cook to boil an egg?" said the Hermit.

" I can reply to that without difficulty," said his friend. " Three minutes, by the watch, an egg must boil. If it is a very small egg, like the Bantam's, it must not boil more than two minutes, or two and a half."

" You must have a priceless cook," said the Hermit, " if you can find one that, for two days running, would stand with a watch in her hand over the saucepan of eggs, or would be able to keep one eye on the clock, and the other on the saucepan—to keep exactly to three minutes, or exactly two and a half; besides which, eggs vary as much as the human countenance. It is not merely a big egg, and a little egg, but there are all the medium sizes; and the weight and size of eggs differ as much as the hens that lay them, and there is not one of these Welsh widows that would not tell me, by the look of my eggs, to which hen each egg belongs. Consequently, if the Bantam takes two minutes, and the Dorking takes three minutes, there must be other subdivisions for Cochin China, and Hamburghs, and Spanish fowls, &c."

The Traveller could not deny the justice of this remark, but confessed that he could not suggest any remedy for the difficulty.

The Hermit said there was a very simple one, which he would teach him; which was, always to put eggs into cold water, instead of boiling water, and the moment the water boiled each egg was done, whether large or small.

The Traveller could not understand the reason of this; and the Hermit, after an innocent joke upon his want of science, said that the reason was very clear to his practical perception—viz. that a gradual advance to the boiling point was the degree of heat required to cook an egg in perfection, and that needed neither clock nor watch. The cook had only to let the fire and water do their work, which would be completed at different periods of time, according to the thickness and quantity of shells which had to be heated through.

The Traveller, after this simple explanation, particularly inquired whether the gridiron used by the Welsh widows was on the common construction, which he had often seen in iron-mongers' shops—viz. iron bars in a square frame, with a handle, and a little iron trough at one end.

The Hermit showed him a gridiron, which was exactly what he described, and said he was very much surprised to hear that such a grid-iron was still in common use ; for that, although he did not boast of any mechanical talent, he considered that it was a very awkward utensil for its required purpose, and great practice and much dexterity were necessary to enable a cook to dress mutton chops as well as they had been done that day, from the difficulty, not only of saving the gravy, but of preventing its being spilt upon the hot stove, and producing those intolerable fumes which equally offended and affected the nose and the palate.

The Traveller said that these remarks brought

to his recollection the gridiron that he had seen in the kitchen of the great hotel at Turin, when on his travels through Italy, the construction of which had only then struck him as being unusual, but which, he was now convinced, was very superior to the gridiron he saw before him for the purpose of preserving the gravy of broiled meat; and the Hermit regretted that he had not introduced the improvement into Great Britain.

The apple dumplings * were the next topic of inquiry; and the Traveller was informed that the paste was made of flour and clarified marrow, baked lightly, glazed with white of egg and white sugar, and served with or without cream, according to taste.

The next day the salmon was to be eaten; and it was found, when cold, to be firmly fixed to the strainer by its own jelly. The fish-kettle was put on, with the water in which the fish had been scalded, and over which it had cooled, and in which it was again placed on the strainer; and when again heated through, it was com-

---

* See Appendix No. XXXV.

pletely done, and of course, by this slow process and double infusion in its own liquor, it had a much greater richness of flavour than it otherwise could have retained.

The sauce served with it, in the opinion of the Traveller, surpassed anything of the kind that he had ever tasted, and he earnestly requested the recipe; which the Hermit told him he really could not give, as it had been hereditary and traditional in his family, and handed from mother to daughter; but that his mother had taught the grandmother of Gwenllian, whose mother had taught her, by his particular desire; and that it was a recipe that had never been clearly written down, but that, if, when his friend was further advanced in ordinary knowledge, he chose to learn to make it *himself*, he should have every opportunity of doing so, and then he might write it down; * but that it was one of the few things practised in his primitive establishment which was extremely complicated, and very difficult to make twice alike, and which depended, more than

* See Appendix No. XXXVI.

anything else which he had ever met with,
upon acute taste. He said that Gwenllian
could not herself ever succeed in having it
exactly right as to proportions of flavour, unless
she prepared it the day before, when he always
tasted it himself before it was finished off.

The Traveller asked if it would suit every
sort of fish?

The Hermit said that it did so, and that one
reason for its being so relishing, and yet so
mild, was that there was no addition or admix-
ture of any sort of ready-made bought sauce,
which he considered very unnecessary, where
such an accompaniment to fish could be made
in the house.

After this, the Hermit made several remarks
upon meagre cookery, such as he recollected it
when in the world.

The Traveller said that it was not the least
improved, and that he did not at all wonder
that Roman Catholics were frequently troubled
by weak digestions.

The Hermit said, that he was an old-
fashioned Protestant, and there were only two

days in the year that, unless unable to eat meat,
he entirely abstained from it—Ash Wednesday and Good Friday; but that he firmly
believed, at least half the gastric disorders and
weak digestions, from which no doubt Catholics
suffered to a great extent, was more frequently
owing to the dreadful concoctions of made
dishes with butter, eggs, and ollapodridas of vegetables, stewed in butter, and superstructures of
sweetmeats, and luscious confectionery, than it
was from excess of abstinence from meat; that
there was no doubt that many Catholics, with
good motives, though weak understandings,
seriously injured their health by fasting, and
might thereby lay the foundation for many
diseases, just as there were many Protestants,
who, under the idea that the more they could
swallow the better they must be, gorged themselves with meat to such a degree, that they
could not digest it, and instead of nourishment
it became poison, by overtasking and overloading the digestion; but that he really wished, for
the sake of humanity, that a rational system of
meagre cooking could be taught, for the benefit

of Roman Catholics, on those days when they consider it right, when in perfect health, to abstain from meat. He said that he had most vivid recollections of the dishes that he had seen served upon those occasions, half a century ago, and begged the Traveller would tell him what *he* had beheld in these days, that he might judge whether it was better or worse.*

The Traveller gave him the following bill of fare, of a meagre dinner of which he had partaken—meagre soup, made with butter and flour, yolks of eggs, and cream, with chopped herbs.

The Hermit here interrupted, and said he thought nothing further would be required for the rest of the day !

The Traveller proceeded — salt fish, fried, and fresh fish, swimming in butter, and with melted butter mixed with anchovy sauce over it, buttered eggs, an omelet of eggs and herbs, a mould of jaune mange, jam tart, and cream cheese, with a variety of wines, which are frequently drunk on these occasions, to make the

---

* See Traveller's Note Book.

N 2

food more palatable, and which of course are an additional trial to the digestive organs.

The Hermit said that he supposed the science of meagre cookery in Great Britain was much as he remembered it, but that in former days they had fewer dishes, though equally unwholesome compounds.

The Traveller inquired what he would recommend for an abstinence or fasting dinner.

"I should advise," said the Hermit, "a plain poached egg, on toast, *without* butter; a vegetable soup,* made of the jelly of bare boiled bones, without eggs, and with new milk instead of cream, and *no butter*. Meagre soups can be made with well-chopped and fried vegetables, provided they are fried in delicate top fat (which *is* allowed) *instead* of butter, so as to be both palatable and wholesome. A plain fruit tart, with skim milk, and a plain rice pudding, needs no contrivance; and those who cannot eat simple stewed fruit alone, will find that it agrees perfectly well if mixed with skim or new milk and eaten with bread; but

---

* See Appendix No. XXXVII.

plain boiled or fried fish, with anchovy sauce, the melted butter part of which is prepared in the same way as the parsley sauce melted butter, is simple and innocent, for those who can take any sauce at all, but there are many persons with whom melted butter disagrees, however carefully prepared, and they should avoid it, and eat their fish with only a little salt or a little vinegar. Plain bread and cheese, bread and cold fresh butter where it agrees, water from the spring, with hard biscuits, would make a far better dinner alone, and be more conducive to health, than any of the compound meagre dishes which you have mentioned, which are positively deleterious; and it surpasses my comprehension how anybody can partake of any one of the compounds of eggs and butter that you have named, far less of three or four of them. The two great obstacles to the preservation of a good digestion are too long intervals between meals, and then a too plentiful or an unwholesome meal; or a continued system of repletion by what is called ' *nourishing diet*,' which, when taken in excess, either drives the patient into an atrophy, from his inability to extract nourishment from the large quantities he takes, or produces that most distressing disorder—a ' Wolf in the stomach ' —a constant craving. And the effect of the ill-usage to which the poor stomach is subjected by its owners may be described by a parody on the ' Curse of Kehama : '—

> " With a pain in thy heart,
> And a fire in thy brain,
> While sleep shall desert thee
> And visit thee never,
> And the *Curse of Repletion*
> Be on thee for ever."

The Hermit then said that he wished the Traveller would give him an idea of the opposite side of the question ; and having heard of a meagre dinner, he would be much gratified by knowing something about the diet of a person in his rank in life, in the habit of dining out in London, or pursuing a similar system in the country.

The Traveller said that there were, unfortunately, so many country houses in England where the excessive luxury of London tables was maintained, that it would be just the same thing if he took an example from one of those establishments, which would give a better idea of the repletion system than it was in his power to afford from London, where he never went out to breakfast : but that in the country he would give him an account of diet, which would include the whole day from morning till night; and he would begin with the ladies, as they had different habits, in some respects, from the gentlemen. At the same time, he begged the Hermit to believe that his report, though not the least exaggerated, was not universal, and that there were exceptions to the following routine :—At half-past seven, or, at the latest, eight o'clock in the morning, tea and bread-and-butter was taken to the lady *in bed*, who, at ten o'clock, breakfasts a second time, downstairs, on coffee, followed by tea and cold meat, in addition to, or instead of, an egg, honey mixed with butter, or raspberry jam, and hot rolls, or dry toast, and sometimes buttered cake; then, at one or two o'clock, they eat roast mutton or chicken, often pre-

ceded by a made dish, and succeeded by confectionery of various sorts, accompanied by
wine. At four or five o'clock, tea, bread-and-
butter, cake, &c. ; at seven or eight o'clock,
fish, soup, made dishes of all sorts, followed
by roast, or boiled, or stewed meat, followed
again by game and poultry, and áll kinds of confectionery, and lobster salads, with varieties of
wine, cheese, butter, and dessert. At half-past
nine o'clock, tea and coffee, biscuits, and cakes.

By this time the Hermit groaned aloud, and
begged that he would go no further, if he had
anything to say, for that (as it was) he feared
an attack of nightmare! and with arithmetical
precision the venerable man counted on his
fingers the number of hours and the number of
meals, exclaiming that six meals in little more
than thirteen hours would only leave an average
of two hours between each meal for the process of digestion, and that he hoped that the
gentlemen did not follow the same system.

The Traveller said he thought their system
was quite as bad, though not exactly the
same. He did not believe they breakfasted in

bed, at least, not many of them, or breakfasted at all before they appeared downstairs; but that, not content with plain cold meat, or no meat at all, they frequently ate a complete hot dinner of dressed meat the first thing in the morning. They also often followed this up with honey and butter, and sweetmeats. That the greater number professed not to eat " *luncheon*," * although they *all* declared that it *was* the " natural and proper time of day to eat," and that they had often an appetite at that time, but that the *fear* of *eating less* at seven or eight o'clock, induced them to refrain from food when they required it. Gentlemen, the Traveller added, did not *generally* take tea at five o'clock, but they were naturally often glad of it after fasting from half-past nine or ten o'clock; and if they had not had anything, they were *ravenous* by seven or eight o'clock, and consequently ate a great deal more at one time than was necessary for their sustenance, or good for their health, and laid the foundation for gout and dyspepsia, and all sorts of future miseries, to say nothing of corpulence or

* See Traveller's Note Book.

emaciation from defective digestion; and that they generally took tea and coffee afterwards, which was far better avoided when not required as a meal in itself, but superadded after an over-plentiful dinner, or, more properly, supper.

The Hermit inquired what sort of health those persons had who lived in this way systematically?

The Traveller replied that it was very rare to meet with an instance of a gentleman past fifty, and many much earlier, who had not some ailment connected with the digestive organs, and others who at that age were not martyrs to gout, or rheumatism, or continual invalids in some way or other, scarcely any retaining the clear complexion and colour of health which is so frequently seen even in very advanced life in temperate specimens of the rural population, especially mountaineers, who have spent their lives labouring in the open air, who have only three meals a day at regular intervals, and never eat more than they really require. But that, unless really alarmed by serious illness, the men in the higher classes would go on without observing that, little by little, they become less and less able to exert long before advanced years rendered repose absolutely necessary. " In fact," said the Traveller, " there is no doubt that a large portion of mankind in these islands are premature invalids from over-feeding and unwholesome cookery from infancy to age, and a still larger proportion are in want of food with which they might be amply supplied if the tons of nourishment were bestowed upon them which is wasted from ignorance and carelessness, and by the want of proper domestic management in the culinary department, and which would be to spare, in *additionally* enormous quantities, if those who now take so much more than is good for them, only ate what nature requires." *

Although the Traveller willingly gave the Hermit the above information, and was mightily diverted by the horror and indignation he excited, yet he now thought it time to let his host have a turn in answering questions, by which he hoped he might, in his turn, gain a little advantage over him.

* See Traveller's Note Book.

" May I ask my venerable friend," said he,
" whether the aristocracy of the last century
did not indulge in most unwholesome dishes?
I have some idea that, in looking over old
cookery books, the quantities and the compounds struck me as being particularly unwholesome."

The Hermit replied that he was correct in
his impressions; that in the last century they
certainly made use of excessive quantities of
eggs, butter, and cream; " but," added he, "the
bad effects of this error were more than counterbalanced by the superior simplicity of their
every-day fare. Their roasting was admirable:
a joint badly roasted reflected discredit on the
mistress of the house, as, although in the higher
ranks of life they did not, as in Germany, remain in the kitchen to see the meat roasted
themselves, servants were then judged by
their masters; and although accidents might
occur, yet habitual bad cooking, as connected
with roasting and boiling, which were then
the principal part of every country gentleman's
dinner, would have reflected disgrace or dis-

credit on the mistress of the family. Baking, also, was *well* understood. There was no gentleman's house where good bread and cakes were not the especial pride of the ladies of the family : thus two of the principal materials for sustenance were well prepared, and it was only on gala days that the extravagant compounds took place, of which butter and eggs were the principal ingredients ; and whatever bad effects might have resulted to those who ate them, they were very light as well as temporary in comparison with the destruction of health consequent upon a daily round of made dishes, which are now only the precursors of what formerly used to be the dinner."

The Traveller remarked that he believed our ancestors had much better health, on the whole, than is now enjoyed; that they did not often require sofas to recline upon, were much upon their legs, and yet spine complaints were seldom heard of; "and," added he, with a malicious smile, " we all know, my good friend, that gentlemen of the last generation were not remarkable for sobriety, but dyspepsia is not often alluded to in old memoirs, and yet one might suppose that it was well deserved."

The Traveller was, however, disappointed at not having succeeded in making the Hermit angry. He was too rational, and really too anxious to discover cause and effect, to enter upon an angry argument, or to try to make out that the incontrovertible fact of drinking mentioned was limited to the minority.

The Hermit, therefore, only mildly replied that he did not think it difficult to account for the superior health and strength of the grandfathers and great-grandfathers of the present generation; that they kept *very early* hours, and morning and night were a great deal in the open air; they had a much larger proportion of wholesome food, better cooked, and a minor proportion of unwholesome food; and they had *three* meals a day, instead of six or seven. And although he admitted that the habits of the country gentlemen of that day, in taking wine to excess, was most degrading and reprehensible, yet here again there was not that mixture of all sorts of fermented liquors which were now the fashion; and though not taken in a degree to obscure the intellect, they were yet taken sufficiently, and in such variety as, to interfere constantly with the digestive powers. That our ancestors also took very considerable exercise, which, with the early hours that they kept, counteracted, in a great measure, the ill-effects of occasional excess; but that, in the present day, according to the Traveller's account, "*the candle was lighted at both ends;*" and it was, therefore, not wonderful if health was consumed in half the time.

The Hermit said he could produce other reasons, drawn from the Traveller's own communications with respect to nursery management in the present age—as he had favoured him with an account of the system pursued in the families of some of his friends,—which was so very different from his own experience more than eighty years ago, of which he had a perfect recollection, as well as his good mother's and grandmother's conversation on the subject; so that he did not at all wonder that, in the course of two or three generations, there was a gradual and regular decline of the strength of constitution.

"To what do you particularly allude?" said the Traveller; "for I have related many things to you."

"I allude," said the Hermit, "to the description you gave me of the manner in which your nephews and nieces were reared, which certainly was very different to the system pursued with my brothers and sister."

"Had you any brothers and a sister?" said the Traveller. "I always fancied you were the only one of your race."

"I had one sister and two brothers," rejoined the Hermit, "all younger than myself; but, unhappily, my two brothers were killed in the wars, about fifty years ago, and my sister was drowned, the ship being lost in a storm at sea, returning from Ireland, after the death of her husband."

"Which part of the system did you consider so very different, which I related to you," said the Traveller, "from the customs of the last century?"

" The especial points," said the Hermit,
" which I consider would have an increasingly
bad influence on the health of each succeeding
generation, are as follows :—1st. According to
your account, children are now (though supposed to be under the eye and direction of their
mother) in reality under the entire management
of the nurse, they live the greater part of their
time in the nursery, are taken out, at stated
hours, for formal walks, but know not what it
is to wet their feet, the girls being always in
half-boots and hoops,* which, in a high wind,
must make them as awkward and uncomfortable as a hen in a storm. We, on the contrary, though probably less expensively, were
less awkwardly attired, and, deprived of many
of the luxuries you describe, were nursed in
cottages, which, of course, were selected as
belonging to the most cleanly and respectable

---

* Since these pages were written those dangerous and absurd
inventions have nearly disappeared in good society, but are
still to be seen on children ; and trains have increased, and are
perilous to those who wear them and those who tread upon
them.

o

tenants on the estate; in fact, in those days, a
great part of the cottage or farm tenants were
old servants. In these cottages we had air and
exercise, and freedom of limb; and although
our parents visited us constantly, and we were
also brought to the house to see them, we remained till three or four years old, without a
thought or a care beyond the interests of the
poultry and other animals that surrounded us,
being constantly in the open air, and clad accordingly; by which means a store of health
was laid in, instead of a store of ailments, long
before we knew there was such a thing in the
world as an alphabet. And from the time we
returned to be inmates of the paternal roof, our
brains were not oppressed by learning, and by
very slow degrees we were taught to read,
write, and spell, while the habits, acquired in
the cottage, of activity and out-door amusement continued; the great change in our
existence being the necessity for learning draw-
ing-room behaviour, and being in full-dress on
certain occasions, when we were under very
strict drill. But how is it possible for children

to be generally healthy, and enjoy vigour in youth, health in middle life, or retain any energy in old age, if their first years are spent chiefly in a nursery upstairs, and their exercise taken in half-boots and hoops?"

"What is your objection to boots?" said the Traveller. "Hoops, and all their kindred crinolines, are universally condemned, though still continued, but I thought boots for females were considered very useful for strengthening the ancles."

"What is the proof of strong ancles?" said the Hermit.

The Traveller perfectly well knew what to answer, but he would not commit himself, that he might not hasten his own defeat.

The Hermit was therefore obliged to reply for himself. "Walking," said he, "is the use for which feet and ancles were made. Are the ladies of the present day particularly good walkers?"

"Particularly the reverse," said the Traveller. "There are, of course, exceptions everywhere, but, on the whole, the women of the present day in Great Britain walk remarkably ill, which I have attributed to their dreadful iron hoops, or cages, or crinolines, which are now so common, that they have positively become a public offence, and ought, in my opinion, to be put down by Act of Parliament as nuisances. Deaths are constantly occurring by fire, as well as broken legs, from these most senseless articles of apparel, and there is no doubt that the art of walking (if art it be), viz. the power of action and movement by carrying the body onward with convenience and comfort to the individual, and with grace to the beholder, is at present unknown, except in some remote, happy, and secluded corners, where there are peasants who still carry baskets and pails on their heads, and where this most miserable mania has not been adopted; but I do not myself see any objection to children being always in half-boots, which are said to strengthen the ancles."

"Many things are '*said*,'" replied the Hermit, "which a little sensible investigation would prove to be unfounded. Only for one moment, I pray you, *use your own understanding,* and you will see that it is impossible that boots *can* strengthen the ancles, although they may supply the place of bone and muscle, when it is wanting, owing to some natural defect, or unfortunate accident. What would any rational person say to a proposal to enclose the arms of children or young people in a tightly-laced sleeve of hard materials, whenever the hands and arms were required to be in full action? Exactly the same principle applies to the ancles, which, to be strong and capable of their work, ought *not* to be bound up by ligatures, which prevent the supple actions of the muscles, retard circulation, and often occasion habitual cold feet; they also render the footing un-steady, as the ancle is prevented from bearing its proper share in the movement of the body, and you may depend upon it that the bad walking you complain of as being so general, commenced before the cages—hoops—and crinolines, which you say are of compara-tively recent date, and the ladies of the last century were remarkable for their graceful carriage in walking, and their firm and elastic step."

" I wish one of them would *re*-appear," said the Traveller, " to show the present generation what good walking means ; for though I well know what it is, I could not describe it in words."

" My grandmother's definition of good walking," said the Hermit, " and what my sister was always told to aim at, was, that her body should be erect, and move forward like a column on wheels, the feet carrying it on in such a manner, that those who met or followed should not be able to perceive the slightest approach to that waddling gait, which is so exactly exemplified by *the duck*."

" It appears to me," said the Traveller, " that the ducks are the models of the female walkers of the present day, or *vice versâ*, excepting that the good duck would be much maligned if she were accused of taking pattern by them, as, however waddling her gait, she never soils her feathers by sweeping the ground ; while the majority of females of the nineteenth century sweep up the dirty ground behind, while they brush the hedges on both sides at once : but let me ask you, whether your grandmother did not wear a hoop ? "

" She certainly did," said the Hermit, " when in full dress, but her active morning avocations were never incommoded by that inconvenient attire ; and it was the rule of her house that no female servant should ever wear a hoop, which was considered a dress of cere- mony, inconvenient and objectionable, very pro- perly confined to a certain class, and only worn by them at certain times and seasons of formal appearance. It must also be remembered, that petticoats were never in those days lower than the ancle, and consequently neither endangered the safety of the wearer, nor entangled the legs of others." *

During the following evening ramble, the Traveller expressed his surprise at seeing a woman milking the Hermit's Welsh ewes,

---

* And when not borne in ceremony by pages on court fes- tivals, were looped up, or drawn through the pocket-hole, or carried over the arm.

which were all black. He asked whether all Welsh sheep were black, and was informed that there were many more white than black, but that the mutton of each was equally fine, and the milk equally good for cheese, though, in consequence of the non-encouragement, or rather the discouragement, of the old native Welsh cloth, and of hand-knit stockings, black wool was now sold in some places at a lower price than white; whereas, formerly black (very justly) always bore a higher price, in consequence of its superior value for stockings, and home-spun cloth, which, requiring no dye, was much more durable, and the tint of which could be made less intense, where desired, by mixing white wool with it.

The Traveller had never heard of milking sheep in England, and when the Hermit had said, soon after his arrival, that the excellent cheese they had at dinner owed its superiority to a considerable proportion of sheep's milk mixed with that of the cows, his guest did not believe him, and really thought, as he afterwards related, he was playing the same trick that he recollected had been played by a mischievous young Irish lady, who persuaded an old woman that in Ireland they milked Cats, which, she being credulous enough to believe, was laughed at to the end of her life.

On the present occasion, the Hermit was too well bred to comment on his guest's evidently continued incredulity, with respect to the purpose to which his sheep's milk was applied, although he saw a fine pail of milk carried away, the produce of the beautiful flock of ewes.

It appeared to the Traveller very strange, that if the cheese was so superior, a practice so easy of imitation should not be generally known and adopted in England. They afterwards visited a Welsh weaver, where the wool of the Hermit's flock was woven. This Welsh mountain weaver had a water-wheel to work his spinning-jenny and wove with his loom: the manufacture is almost indestructible, and although not of a romantic turn of mind, the Traveller could not help saying to himself, he hoped the evils of large manufactories might long be averted from that happy region, where a troop of thriving merry children repaired to the weaver's, from the neighbouring cottages, to pick wool in a healthy atmosphere, for their daily wages ; and, after an agreeable walk, returned in the evening, through pure air and fine scenery, as merry and happy as they went.

They afterwards visited the Hermit's pigs. The Traveller was again much surprised, to find them so thin ; not that they appeared at all starved, but had thin figures, such as are occasionally seen in pigs belonging to cottagers that range the high roads. A conversation ensued on this subject. The Hermit's ideas were so completely contrary to those of the present day, that his guest did not subscribe to them, and they returned home mutually dissatisfied with each other.

The Hermit had a very large yard for his pigs to range in, and never allowed them to be shut up in a sty, or regularly fatted for killing ; and he actually shuddered when the Traveller described the pigs, and other animals, that he had seen blind from fat, which are common at agricultural shows, and said, that to give prizes for excess of fat, and to produce blindness in pigs, by cramming, and privation of air and exercise, was, in his opinion, a sign of the decline of the human intellect, and a proof of barbarism or insanity, rather than of intelligence.

Although indignant at the Hermit's obstinate refusal to admit that the excessive feeding of animals was a wonderful art, and that the cultivation of *any art* must prove the *progress* of the human mind; the Traveller, at length, however, admitted that it was to be regretted that agricultural shows afforded every encouragement to cramming, and consequently those who could afford to cram obtained the greater number of premiums.

The Hermit maintained that the best breeds for symmetry ought to be encouraged, *without any artificial fatting*, and prizes given to preserve or restore all those races which are specially and variously adapted for different localities, different climates, and, consequently, different pastures.

The Traveller, at length, admitted to his host, that the flesh of many prize animals was of a very inferior quality, and actually yellow, from the quantity of oil-cake used to produce unnatural and unwholesome obesity;* and that, although real Welsh mutton was admitted by all epicures, and by medical men, to be the very finest for flavour, and the lightest of digestion of all the breeds of sheep known in Great Britain, very few prizes were ever given for the encouragement and preservation of so invaluable a breed of animals; and that even at Welsh inns, during his last absence, he had been *sickened* by large coarse mutton, though within a mile of mountains, where the best Welsh sheep were to be had, and could alone live and flourish. He added that, at private houses, the same complaint may often be made in Wales as well as in London, from whence the rich, nevertheless, send abroad for all sorts of foreign luxuries for their table, on which the best Welsh mutton is seldom or ever found.

These facts furnished the Hermit with an additional argument to prove that the Agricul-

* See Traveller's Note Book.

tural Shows, which his guest maintained were one of the greatest improvements in the last half-century, were, by his own account, not conducted altogether on principles to corroborate the correctness of his allegation; and that some of the best native breeds in Great Britain, both cattle and sheep, were suffered to exist without notice or encouragement, and in some instances to become almost extinct from the same cause.*

The Hermit's dairy was visited, and he took great pride in showing some of the best breeds of cows in the Principality.† There were the

---

* N.B. These pages were written before the outburst of the Cattle Plague.

† The Pembroke, or Castle-Martin breed, *is admirable* for beef, and they are excellent milkers. The old Pembroke breed, white, with black ears, and remarkably handsome, are becoming extinct, and those that remain are wild from *want of care.*

The Glamorgan cows are magnificent animals,—black, with a white strpie down the tail; excellent milkers.

The Caermarthen cattle are black, very much like the Pembroke; also good for milk.

In the counties of Brecon and Radnor, the landowners have generally introduced Herefords and Shorthorns, which are inferior, in many respects, to various breeds of the Welsh

small and beautifully formed natives of "Mona;"
the larger but *very valuable* cow of Glamorgan
(which is fast becoming extinct); the black
cows of Pembroke and Caermarthen, very different in form, but each having qualities worthy
of note.

They then visited the Hermit's arable land,
of which he cultivated the quantity necessary
to grow roots to support his cattle, his flocks,
and his pigs through the winter, and corn
enough for his two mountain ponies, his
poultry, and all his wild birds, which he
described as a beautiful sight in hard weather,
when rooks, and wood pigeons, and quantities
of small birds came with confidence to receive

---

cattle.   Merioneth has a small breed which, if well kept,
would prove valuable.

In North Wales the Mona breed (Isle of Anglesea) is the
best, and is equal, if not superior, by various *combined excel-
lences*, to the larger breeds in Wales, and, like other Welsh
cattle, are very hardy.   It is remarkable for its small size, with
great symmetry, mild temper, large supply of rich milk, and
ability to feed and do well on short pasture, and also to fat
with the greatest ease, and for beef it cannot be surpassed.

Brittany cows are also excellent, and thrive as well in Wales
as their British kinsmen who are natives of the Principality.

their expected meal, and all fed together, and repaid him, in summer, by their songs and their destruction of insects.

The Traveller was surprised to see oxen ploughing, which used to be a very common sight, but is now rare. The Hermit said, that he considered oxen by far the best animals for the tillage of land—that when an ox was old it could be killed for food, not so a horse—that their keep was much less expensive, their price much lower, consequently their loss by illness or accident less serious.

An argument followed from the Traveller, who spoke with ridicule of cows and heifers drawing light carts, in various parts of Germany, and often bringing the weekly produce of small farmers to market. His host took the part of the Germans vehemently on this point—said there was much practical good sense in the custom, and that he should not be afraid to lay a wager, that a cow, trained from a heifer to draught,—not tasked beyond her strength, but only used to go a moderate distance, with a very light vehicle, walking her natural pace, and having food taken with her, could perform light tasks for the benefit of her owner, without the slightest detriment to herself, or diminution of her milk, and provided she was not worked when " in milking " above three hours in the day, which he contended would be an immense boon to a poor and industrious man, who could not afford to keep both a horse and a cow. The Hermit was much interested with the account given by his guest of the manner in which the German cattle in certain districts drew by the *head* instead of the *neck*, as he said, it had often distressed him to watch his own oxen working in their yokes, as it was evident that the *strength* of an ox was in its *head*, and that the *neck* of an ox was ill-adapted for draught ; which remark caused the Traveller, for the *first time*, to wonder why that mode of harnessing oxen was not adopted in England ? and why the practice of ploughing with oxen was so much disused, as the advantages for those who had limited means to provide animals for draught were so very evident.

The Traveller could not, however, throw any

light upon this subject, but remained convinced
that agricultural associations must act solely from
experience of practical success, though he could
not give any reason for this belief. His host
continued of his previous opinion, and repeated
that the system of education of the present age
must be very defective, as there was scarcely a
topic in which the facts mentioned by his friend
did not prove that great evils were incurred,
and even encouraged, from the want of common
reflection—in fact, from the want of observation, with cultivation of the reasoning powers.

The Traveller, though very much provoked
at the pertinacity of his host, and stoutly deny-
ing the correctness of many of his opinions, yet
did not confute them, nor could he disprove that
it was very much the custom to ridicule *everything* not understood *unless* introduced by a
great name, and as often blindly to extol what
was *not* any better understood, and which, in
some instances, was *very inferior* to what it was
allowed to supersede, and he fully admitted
that some of the most valuable breeds of cattle
and sheep, best suited to the climate mentioned

P

by the Hermit, and to the short but sweet pastures of many parts of Wales and which would also suit various parts of England, are wilfully ignored if not entirely unknown in agricultural exhibitions

The Traveller did not defend the unnatural and unwholesome system of fattening cattle for shows, involving farmers in great expense, often deteriorating the meat by rendering the animals diseased, and, in fact, raising a barrier against the exhibition of animals in a natural and wholesome condition; but he did not like to admit that the Scotch aristocracy were the *only* magnates who, *as a body*, made it a rule to preserve and encourage annually, by a number of very liberal prizes, the preservation and encouragement of the native breeds of Great Britain, (as far as they were especially identified with Scotland,) having an Agricultural Society in which the above national object is always especially supported.*

* The Highland and Agricultural Society of Scotland give prizes for the pure breeds of Ayrshire, Galloway, Angus, Aberdeen, and Highland cattle, as well as for Highland ponies.

On a later occasion, the Hermit and his guest visited the Hermit's Welsh ponies, which were grazing in the shade near a picturesque brake, in the centre of a verdant piece of pasture land, surrounded by a fine hedge, a great part of which was composed of hollies, birch, and hazels, as well as thorns and beautiful bushes of elder, here and there covered with fine clusters of cream-coloured flowers. In each *corner* of the field, the Hermit had planted sycamores and beech, which produced a charming shade, being about forty years old, under which his cows were lying down, protected from the heat of the sun. There were also some other trees of more ancient date, oaks, limes, and horse chestnuts.

The Traveller was surprised to hear the distances these little ponies were in the habit of going, *with and for* the Hermit, among his poor neighbours in the mountains. He said they never had any corn except when they took a *very long* journey, and then the quantity was small, but they were never restricted in bran. They were always turned out when not used, excepting in the very cold and wet weather, when they could not benefit themselves by grazing, but they were allowed a comfortable shed to run into.

The Hermit was much shocked at the Traveller's account of clipping horses, who in vain tried to convince him that it was humane, and that it tended to prevent their catching cold, because they would otherwise have a thick coat saturated with perspiration when standing in the cold air, but his host only became more indignant, and said, that whoever clipped a horse, could never have studied its natural history; that nature had provided a very fine undergrowth of fur, as winter approached, to protect him from the inclemency of the cold season, and that to clip that coat off, close to the skin, was really barbarous.

In vain the Traveller urged that by depriving the horse of his coat, he was much quicker dried, when coming home in a great heat, but he was unable to refute the Hermit's arguments, which were to the effect that those persons who choose to keep horses in the highest state

of artificial condition, are only the wealthy, to
whom expense is of no consequence, and who,
therefore, have certainly no need of clipping ;
because a horse that is kept up day and night,
clothed from the end of August, or the beginning of September, to the following May or
June, will never have any winter coat to clip,
as nature has so provided that continual warmth
brings off the extra hair as fast as it comes on ;
that, with regard to such horses, there is therefore no question of such an operation, but for
the animals which are kept in a more natural,
and therefore more healthy manner, it is much
more dangerous to cut off their natural winter
clothes, and leave them exposed to every blast,
when they are out of doors, than to fear the
chance of their catching cold in a stable, by the
negligence or idleness of those who ought to
rub them down well when they come in hot.
The Hermit moreover declared that he had
more pleasure in looking at the soft long hair
of a healthy horse, in a good winter coat, well
cleaned, than he should have in contemplating
the finest and most shining skin of a *furless*

hunter or racer, artificially produced in mid-winter, and that he would undertake, that if statistics were correctly kept, it would be found that *un*clipped horses had, on an average, much better health than clipped horses, and were much less liable to cold; that, in his day, post-boys, in riding long stages, if violent rain came on, which was likely to continue, always allowed themselves to be wet through, *before* they put on their great coats, which had the effect of a comfortable steam bath; also that with horses, if they were in a sweat in the under-coat, it was a very long time before it reached the upper-coat, and when it did come in contact with the air, it formed a sort of thick *paste*, which preserved the warmth underneath, and was a great protection against the inward chill of cold atmosphere,—so that, when a horse was brought into a stable in this state, if there was no one at hand, ready or willing to rub him down as they ought to do, yet, by throwing a rug over him, he would be much less likely to take a cold, than the poor creature who, shorn and divested of his natural covering, all at once, at the very time he most requires it, was obliged to work in the piercing wind, or the chilling rain, whether in a sweat or out of it, without any protection against the effects of the elements.*

The conversation then turned upon a very pretty glade in a hollow in the centre of the field, composed of hazels, thorns, and hollies, alders and elders, in the midst of which there was a spring.

The Hermit could not forbear asking the Traveller if he did not think it was a beautiful scene?

" I admit," said his friend, " it is beautiful; but the agriculturists of the present day would not, I am afraid, admit that it is beautiful."

" Why not?" said the Hermit. " Does agriculture destroy all taste? and is it incompatible for any man with the eye of an artist, or who admires the beauties of nature, to be an agriculturist?"

" The question was never propounded to me before," said the Traveller. " My experience

---

* See Traveller's Note Book.

is not very extensive, nor have I studied the
subject minutely ; but I should certainly say
either that agriculture *is* an antidote to all perception of the beauties of nature, *or else* that
all those to whom Providence has denied the
power of perceiving what is beautiful become
agriculturists, for I have often mourned over
the unnecessary destruction of wood which
really causes some of the finest parts of England
(or, rather, those parts that used to be considered
the most picturesque) now to appear quite bare,
burnt up in summer, shelterless in winter, without a sprig that a passing horseman could gather
from the hedges to put in the bridle of his steed
large enough to frighten the flies! without a
tree, or only one solitary tree in the centre of a
field, mourning for its companions ; and whenever a glade like that before us existed in all its
verdant beauty, it has been, to use a common
expression, ' *grubbed up* ' by the roots, the
hazels of the growth of centuries are chopped
up into fire-wood, the beautiful crab trees, the
greatest ornament to woodland scenery in
spring, the flowers of which are also a feast

for the bees, are undermined by the pickaxes employed by remorseless agriculturists, who cannot bear to see anything growing in a field in the shape of a tree, bush, or shrub, whether it is arable, or whether it is pasture. The wearied creatures wander in vain over acres of unvaried grass, or still more cheerless furrows bounded by miles of *so-called* hedges, which look more like temporary basket-work than the natural and varied growth of native trees and bushes, which are the natural and legitimate charm of the roadsides of the United Kingdom wherever they are still to be found." *

---

* The hedges at Eastbourne in Sussex are an honourable exception to the evils above complained of, as well as the banks on which they grow, which are neither pared away nor undermined, so as not to leave any soil from which they can derive sustenance, but are really what banks ought to be, viz., *buttresses* on each side of the road, a natural and solid foundation of soil and stones, furnishing abundant nourishment for the luxuriant growth of the hedges which surmount them, and which exemplify, in the most undeniable manner, that where good and substantial banks are preserved, hedges *will flourish,* and form a fence, so thick and close that no quadruped can make its way through it, whether the wood of which it is composed is hawthorn, hazel, beech, or other varieties of indigenous growth ; and those persons to whom the care of those highways is consigned, have not only done credit to them

The Hermit said he deeply regretted to hear of such frightful innovations, which he thanked Heaven had not found their way into his own happy and secluded corner of the Island of Britain. " It is melancholy indeed," resumed the Hermit, " to think that mankind

---

selves, and benefited their district by the discreet preservation of the hedges, but they deserve the thanks of the visitors, as well as the inhabitants of the locality, for the ornament and comfort derived by pedestrians and equestrians, for the shelter thus afforded from the winter winds and from the summer sun. At the same time that the *observant* public in general must derive advantage from the practical demonstration of a truth which is, unfortunately, so little regarded in many other parts of the United Kingdom, where miles and miles are rendered shelterless and frightful wastes, from the mistaken notion that good roads require the destruction of roadside timber and the levelling of hedges, until they are a mere apology for a fence, and that *air cannot pass between leaves*, although there is no obstacle to a current overhead, as must always be the case when the lateral branches are clipped to admit of the free passage of vehicles on the Queen's highway. Such is the case at Eastbourne in Sussex, where trees by the roadside and hedges *properly so called*, appear to be really valued as they deserve, and where it is impossible to desire better roads. It is also worthy of note, that even where walls have there recently been built along the side of the road, a circuit has been made, or a gap has been left, to preserve the beautiful trees which grow in the line, and trees are also carefully preserved in the streets, and give the town a most picturesque appearance.

can be so led away by want of reflection as
to suppose that any sweeping destruction
of the beautiful and bountiful provisions of
Providence can possibly be necessary or desirable, and I should much suspect that many
evils are incurred which are as yet unnoticed, in
consequence of the strange influence of fashion,
from the *mania* for novelty, the prevalence
of imitation *without thought*, with the still
greater absence of observation on many important things which might be injuriously affected
by the wholesale devastation which you say is
now so prevalent. I am thankful that no duty
obliges me to travel and to witness these melancholy changes in the aspect of other parts of
Great Britain. To what do you attribute the
origin of this destructive mania ? "

" I am sorry to say," said the Traveller, " as
I have a great respect for Scotland, and as I am
proud of a little Scotch blood in my veins,
that I believe we owe the barren appearances
I mention to Scotch example,—not that the
Scotch are to blame, but it is possible that
the wholesale imitation of the Scotch low-land

farming has been the cause of this great change
for the worse in the aspect of some parts of
England if not of Wales? The Scotch, no
doubt, are a most painstaking and industrious
race; they farm in a manner which suits their
soil and their climate. It is the nature of some
parts of their country to be woodless, and they
have large tracts well suited for corn, where
wood does not naturally grow, but the English,
not satisfied with adopting their system of
agriculture where suitable to the locality,
have, in the spirit of close imitation, ploughed
up good pastures and destroyed a great deal of
valuable wood of native growth, which was,
without question, the principal charm of land-
scape scenery," and which he wished the
Hermit could find agricultural arguments for
retaining.

The Hermit begged to be excused from any
argument on the subject, but he said that, from
the information given by the Traveller, there
was little doubt that, sooner or later, the good
people of the nineteenth century would discover that (to quote the old proverb) they had

been " robbing Peter to pay Paul." " It does not
become me," said he, " who have not seen the
frightful disfigurement of which you complain,
to enter particularly upon the evils which must
thereby be incurred, but I will, with pleasure,
tell you the positive benefits which I derive
from the system you see here, which is not
only conducive to beauty, but also is productive
of various advantages. It is very *bad economy,* as
well as *cruelty,* not to provide shade for cattle,
and especially for sheep, in the summer-time,
and shelter is often as much required in
heavy summer rains as in autumn's storms ; but
there is another benefit derived from the preservation of trees and glades of native growth,
in pasture as well as arable land, where there
are streams, as the roots and the fibres of trees
act as conductors for moisture, and are of
great service to the contiguous pasture—the
roots of even one tree will often run a distance
of incredible extent—the tree not only deriving
nourishment itself from what it imbibes, but
conveying a vast amount of superabundant
moisture, tending to the nourishment of the

herbage far and near. On the same principle, alders and every species of brushwood
ought to be preserved and encouraged on the
sides of all rivulets, and, if not of native
growth, they *ought* to *be planted there*—in the
first place, to act as conduits or feeders to the
pasture land ; secondly, as a protection to the
edges of streams, which would otherwise be
more liable to burst their banks, as well as to
become slippery and unsightly by the continual
treading of cattle along their whole length. In
this locality, wherever there is a glade or a
wood, there is almost invariably a fine spring ;
this of itself always creates a stream, and I
suppose that water is as precious in other parts
of Great Britain as it is in this, where its value
was never more felt than in the last summer,
when the absence of rain would have rendered
the drought much more serious but for the
blessing of our numerous springs, rills, and
rivulets, many of which, though low, continued
their valuable supply during the whole period."

The Traveller, in answer to subsequent
questions, said he " scarcely knew whether he

should be correct in asserting that water *was much valued* in England or *not*, that the present conversation called to his recollection many circumstances which were apparently so contradictory, that if he stated in a court of justice that water was 'very much valued,' and that his cause depended upon the proofs of his veracity, facts might be adduced which would *prove exactly the reverse ;* although, on the other hand, he would state other facts which were equally true, but which certainly went far to prove that there was no country in the world where water was so *little valued*, so *little* turned to account, and so constantly *made away with without end or aim.*"

The Hermit said that he had often thought his friend spoke in riddles, and that he had frequently had great difficulty in comprehending his narrations relative to the present time ; but that, of all the riddles he had yet heard, the present was the most difficult to understand or to reconcile with assertions of the " *marvellous progress* " which had been made in human intelligence in the last fifty years.

The Traveller remarked he had had too many discomfitures to venture upon a defence, but that he would relate to the Hermit the facts which appeared so contradictory, and he might then judge for himself. " First of all," said he, " to prove how much water is valued, London is supplied by water companies,* and every house pays for every drop that it consumes." The price of water is enormous ; and, consequently, he could truly say that water *was highly valued*, as not only good, but bad water was *paid for ;* but, to judge by the scarcity of fountains, or any visible supply of running water for the passers-by in the streets, it might be supposed that England was a desert, without springs or rivers, and that the only supplies of water the inhabitants could procure must be brought in pipes through the sea from France ! So dear, so scarce, and often so bad was that element, (generally supplied by Heaven in quantities commensurate with the wants of all created beings,) that, very recently, philanthropic individuals had become painfully aware of the

---

* See Traveller's Note Book.

sufferings of a large part of the population of London, and other great towns, from the impossibility of obtaining a cup of cold water to drink, in the course of transit through the streets during the heat and toil of the day, and many thousand pounds had been charitably subscribed towards fountains in some of the most populous parts of London, and that benevolent and wealthy persons had recently erected fountains at their own expense in some other towns ; that of course every drop was a boon to men, women, and children dying of thirst, and thousands of whom, without that natural refreshment, had been, and still were, *forced* into public houses, whilst it was admitted, on all sides, that the curse of Great Britain was drinking, which was, to a great extent, caused as well as perpetuated by the want of convenient supplies of good water always at hand ;—that the lower classes in London hardly knew what good water was, and the charitable free fountains, though better than nothing, were seldom, if ever, of any benefit to the poor cattle and horses, which, instead of being able (as on the Conti-

nent) to drink out of large stone basins from
running water, to be found in every square and
the corner of every street, were entirely de-
pendent on the mercy (or the cruelty) of their
drivers, who either did not, or could not, supply
them in buckets from pumps, which were frequently far apart, and often shut up because the
water was considered absolutely poisonous.

The Hermit inquired why those humane
persons who erected fountains did not also add
a basin for passing animals? and the Traveller
had some difficulty in making him understand
that the supply of these (so called) fountains
was, in the majority of instances, only a minute
stream, the thickness of a quill, under which
poor little boys might often be seen patiently
holding a cup to be filled by this little dribbling
spout, while others were as patiently waiting
for their turn to obtain a few drops of that
precious, but slow and scanty supply, although
large sums are paid by the fountain donors for
this meagre boon, which could certainly not
afford any share for quadrupeds, unless a stray
dog sometimes by chance might benefit by a

few spare drops, and thus be prevented from going mad.

" So far," said the Traveller, " I have proved that water is dearly *priced*, if not *prized* sufficiently to arouse such an expression of public opinion as would compel the supply to be equal to the requirements of the population; but," added he, " I will now proceed to give you an account which you will have some difficulty in believing relates to the same subject. The ' *great progress of agriculture* ' has destroyed so many springs, that various parts of the kingdom suffer seriously for want of water, which formerly were well supplied."

" Destroy springs! " said the Hermit. " How can human beings destroy springs? Man has no more power to forbid water to flow than he has to create a spring."

" I may have used a wrong expression," said the Traveller, " by the word ' destroy ; ' but yet *it is destruction*, as far as the results are concerned, and the benefit of man or beast is involved. I allude to *draining*—I know tracts of land which used formerly to be too wet, but which, notwithstanding, produced a large amount of pasture, and have, from excess of draining, become so parched that, in a dry summer, there is scarcely a blade of grass upon them; and in other places, from overlooking the course which the springs previously took before the land was drained, the greatest distress has been occasioned by the supply of water suddenly ceasing in localities at some distance lower down, where the source of the water had ever been unknown and unnoticed, though enjoyed time out of mind."

The Hermit said it appeared to him that the evils now recounted were simply caused by total want of reflection and observation, and, he must add, of intelligence; that, where such a precious necessary of life as *water* was concerned, no person ought to be permitted totally and entirely to bury it in underground drains, the very courses of which are soon forgotten; that, wherever land is drained, and springs thereby concealed, a pool or reservoir of some kind ought to be a *matter of law*, and compulsory upon all drainers, whether landlords or tenants, so that access might always at once be had to water; and that no degree of drainage should ever involve the total concealment, and consequent entire loss, of that invaluable element in any locality whether wet or dry.

The Traveller said, that "the loss sustained by excessive and indiscreet drainage was also much felt by man and beast on the roadside; and that, although it might have been untidy, and sometimes inconvenient in wet weather, to leave little rivulets, so common in past times, to overflow and intrude upon the turnpike, or bye roads, yet that it was infinitely preferable to the total absence of water, which was *now* the characteristic of the Queen's highway, where poor horses, cattle, pigs, sheep, and dogs were obliged to travel miles without a single spout, stone trough, or streamlet, where they could quench their thirst, although beer-houses, on an average of two or three, or six or eight to every mile, were ready to supply their drovers with the perpetual means of intoxication!"

The Hermit, as was his wont, became sad and silent when he heard facts which appeared to his mind to indicate the diminution, if not absolute decay, of human intelligence ; he, therefore, contented himself with a deep sigh, while he ejaculated,—

" Is it possible that there can be any common sense left in the world, if men employ their ingenuity in burying water out of sight, because they have a superabundance of that precious fluid, while, at the same time, the very least drop is charged in London as if it was an expensive and artificial production, instead of a free gift to all from Heaven ? " He then proposed to the Traveller to return home by another way, which he selected, for the purpose of showing the comfort as well as picturesque beauty of several spouts of clear water, which filled stone wells, or basins, formed in the banks by the wayside, and equally adapted for the refreshment of man or beast, by each of which were large stones, where one or two laborers were seated under the verdant shade of a spreading hazel.

The Hermit remarked that one of these rustic figures reminded him of the beautiful

vignettes in Bewick's " British Birds," the
earlier edition of which, he recollected, was
printed at Alnwick in the last century; and
that, in engravings of that date, it was common
in rural subjects to see a peasant drinking out of
his hand or his hat by the roadside, or kneeling
down over a well.

" Alas ! " said the Traveller, " the poor way-
farers *now* would not find sufficient water by
the roadside to fill their hand, although they
would find intoxicating liquors manufactured
enough to drown themselves, and enough to
destroy both body and soul. With regard to
poor animals coming from fairs and markets,
the tortures they now suffer are dreadful to
think of; and, instead of these delightful
umbrageous hedges, which afford both shade
and shelter, everything is cut and shorn for
miles, until there is not shade for a snail
without a shell, where verdure used to
abound."

The Hermit asked what could be the plea
for such wanton destruction, as he did not suppose that it was really an epidemic or a lunacy ;

that some reason must be alleged, whether well or ill founded?

The Traveller said that any idea carried to an excess which *produced evil* might be denominated a *mania*, and that one of the manias of the present day was about roads; that he admitted roads should have air enough to dry them after rain, and that the hedges should not be allowed to extend their boughs in such a manner over roads as to impede the progress of passing vehicles, but that the degree of pruning which would answer for one purpose would answer equally well for the other, and that the excessive cutting down and exhaustive laying to which hedges were now subjected in many places was a twofold evil, as, by cutting hedges so low, travellers were cut to pieces by wind, or scorched by sun, and by laying hedges in the way generally practised, viz. cutting the live wood nearly (or quite) to the under bark, the quick (or whatever species of shrub was subjected to this treatment) became exhausted by loss of sap, and was thrown back for two or three years, and often killed. When the system of laying was pursued, each bough ought to be split or notched as *little* as possible, just enough and no more than would suffice to enable the hedger to bend it to its place ; that the tops of hedges ought never to be cut flat like a turnpike road, as was frequently the case, which often caused the quicks to die down several inches, from the snow lying on the top of the hedge and freezing into the young shoots ; that hedges ought to be allowed to grow up in single spikes, by which means the snow would slip off on the slightest thaw, instead of freezing and thawing, and *re*-freezing on the whole flat surface of the top of the hedge ; and that by cutting hedges so low, the possessor of the land lost all shade or shelter for his animals on the field side, and animals frequently broke over into the road, or seeing some of their own kind passing, galloped along exciting the horses of travellers to become restive, or run away.*

The Hermit expressed surprise and pleasure

---

* A most unpleasant result of hedges *not* being *fences*, and one which often occurs.

at the evident reflection which now accompanied the Traveller's *recollections* before he could have so clearly traced cause to effect, to which his guest replied with great candour, that before he had been led to reflect, he could only have stated what offended *his eye ;* but since he had been in the habit of observing, he had found that he was gradually becoming better able to judge of those things for which he could not previously have assigned any good reason either for censure or for commendation.

The Hermit asked him to name any other matters connected with the management of hedges which struck him, and the Traveller expatiated especially on the barbarous destruction of hollies in hedges, which he said were really treated as if they were the most pernicious weeds, instead of the most valuable of all live fences. The holly produced shade and shelter all the year round, and was, from its prickly leaf, quite impassable when properly treated, as well as one of the most ornamental of evergreens from its berries in winter; and,

indeed, profitable on that account in the neighbourhood of large towns, where the custom of
decorating with holly at Christmas was still
universal from the poorest to the richest, and
consequently the holly, the mistletoe, and ivy *
were sold in towns to an immense extent. But,
instead of the holly being carefully preserved in
hedges, it was often gashed and laid like the common quick, although, to use the language of the
gardener, " Hollies *would not stand the knife* "
with impunity, and soon bled to death if laid ;
and any one who noticed a holly hedge laid,
would find that it was not only thrown back
for years, but that a great portion of the hollies
frequently died down to the root, while the
boughs of holly cut off were of all wood the
worst for mending hedges, as they the soonest
perished ; that hollies ought never to be *topped*,
but left to grow up as high as possible, carefully shortening their boughs where they pro-
jected over the road, and where they could
not be twisted in and worked through the

* See Traveller's Note Book.

hedge, which, wherever it could be done, was
the best and strongest of fences; and as no
holly bore berries except on the ends of the
sprays, this was a cogent reason for not topping
them.   He also said, that, as in the case of all
other trees, the snow acted injuriously if it lay
and froze on the cut tops of the sprays; that a
good holly hedge on the farmer's side was the
most valuable shade and shelter for his sheep
and cattle, and on the traveller's side was of
similar benefit, whilst by keeping it clipped
or twisted back, no sort of injury could be in-
flicted on the highway—that hollies were very
slow in growing, but everlasting when once
well rooted, if not killed by the extraordinary
passion for destruction of the present age, or
the entire want of knowledge and reflection
so perpetually manifested in its treatment, but
he thought want of reflection was even more
palpable in the treatment of the banks upon
which hedges grew, whether natural or artificial.   When artificial, much labour must, of
course, be expended in raising the bank on
which to plant the hedge which was to form

the fence, and yet, in many districts that he had seen, the banks were not only so perseveringly pared on the roadside, that the roots of whatever formed the hedge were often seen to protrude horizontally through the soil, and were consequently dried up, and perished by the summer's sun and the winter's frost, but the banks were often undermined to such an extent that they gave way above ; and where *this* did *not* occur, instead of being green in summer with a luxuriant abundance of leaves, their sickly, exhausted state was evident from the privation of the nourishment continually abstracted by paring away the bank next the road or excavating under it.

The Traveller said he recollected that a friend of his had told him he had discovered, in his own locality, the *cause* of this annual destruction, to the injury of the road as regarded a good fence, and still more to the injury of the farmer, who would be *compelled* to be at the expense of making a dead hedge if he could not keep up a live one, and that all these evils were entirely occasioned by want of observation and reflection on the part of both parties most interested.*

The Traveller had become so warm on this subject, that he would have gone on longer upon the same topic; but the Hermit interrupted him, and, looking at his hour-glass, found it was getting late; he had turned it down at ten o'clock, and now it was past eleven. And he said, that although the principal study in which they were engaged (the culinary art) was agreeably and usefully diversified by "*various remarks on many things, past and present,*" yet the main point must not be forgotten—viz. the progress of his guest in learning how to provide for the pressing requirements of every day's food.

"I remember," said the Hermit, "that you asked me to give some information on the subject of salting meat. I do not profess to preserve meat for voyages, but if you still wish to know how meat ought to be salted for domestic use, where it can be procured fresh every week, I shall be very happy to enter upon the subject,

---

* See Traveller's Note Book.

as I have perceived so many indications of the improvement of your powers of observation and reflection, that I am not afraid of overpowering you by commencing on another branch of domestic economy which ought to be well understood in every house in the United Kingdom, where salt meat is ever eaten."

The Traveller expressed his acknowledgments for being at last permitted to enter upon this new department of knowledge; and the Hermit commenced his instructions by a few interrogatories, after taking him into an apartment he had never seen before, in the centre of which was a very large stone table, with a groove all round it, and a small channel cut out at one corner. On this table was a round of beef, weighing fifty pounds;* it was curled up in the usual form of a round of beef, though not skewered. The senior widow was standing by it with a large sharp knife in her hand.

" Now," said the Hermit to his friend, " that round of beef is to be salted. It came in this morning, and Gwenllian well knows that I

---

* See Appendix No. XXXVIII.

have reason to find fault with the manner in which it is placed upon the table."

Whether the excellent female to whom he alluded understood the English words he uttered, the Traveller did not know, as his host always made a point of speaking Welsh to all the widows, and was never addressed by them in any other language, but it did not require words to interpret the angry glance that lighted upon the unfortunate Gwenllian, who certainly comprehended its meaning, as she instantly seized the beef, uncoiled it, and laid it out full length, with the *outside next* the stone.

" Now," said the Hermit, " I will take advantage of the *un*usual forgetfulness of which Gwenllian has been guilty, to begin your examination from an earlier stage in the management of beef than I had intended. First of all, can you tell me why I was so much displeased at seeing the beef coiled up and placed in the shape it ought to be when boiled, instead of as it now is laid ? "

The Traveller was very much annoyed by this question, for he had hoped and expected to have distinguished himself by his answers, as he felt a certain degree of confidence, not arising (as formerly) from the *conceit* of *ignorance*, but from the consciousness of a certain degree of ability, obtained by the recent practical exercise of his faculties; but he was so completely puzzled by the present query, that he felt he had better confess at once that he could not divine any reason for the Hermit's preference for one position to another with respect to the beef.

His host next asked him what he would do with the beef, if obliged to direct the salting?

" I would mix salt and water together," replied his friend, " in a tub, and put the beef into it."

" What proportions of salt to the water ? " asked the Hermit.

" I do not know," said the Traveller ; " but I suppose I could tell by tasting it, and if it tasted like sea-water, it would be salt enough."

" I see," said the Hermit, " that you know nothing at all about the matter, and therefore it is no use to ask you any more questions until

R

you are a little better informed upon this subject, and I will proceed to explain my own
reasons. If the beef had been left curled up
long upon the stone, it would have become
tainted on the part touching the stone, and the
inside, being also so much excluded from any
draught of air, and more liable to corrupt,
would soon have begun to putrefy. I always
have the rounds divided into two parts, as they
are much easier to salt, and are quite large
enough for any ordinary table. Will you do
me the favour to show me how you would cut
this round in two ? ''

" With the greatest pleasure," said the Traveller ; and, seizing the knife from Gwenllian,
he was about to draw it across the middle of
the beef, when the Hermit seized his arm in
undisguised alarm.

" You will ruin it," said he, " if you cut it
in that way."

The Traveller was rather offended, and said
that it was the Hermit's fault, for telling him
that he always had the rounds of beef cut in two.

" But," said the Hermit, " I never told you

there was but *one* way of dividing beef into two parts.—Now give the knife back, if you please, to Gwenllian; and *if* she has recovered her powers of memory, you will see how she proceeds, and I will explain the reasons for each process."

Gwenllian then made an incision in the centre of the thin end of the beef, and split it the whole way through, thus obtaining two smaller rounds of equal length. She then laid one out, with the fleshy part uppermost, and the skin next the stone, where she left it, while, after having placed the other in the same position, she made sundry gashes across the thickest part, taking care not to cut it through. She then put her knife under the thin end of the inside of the beef, and, going on regularly, took off all sinews and slimy particles, wiping the meat *thoroughly dry* with a clean cloth as she proceeded, till she had gone from one end to the other. In the course of this process, she found one or two round substances imbedded in the meat, which she cut out and had buried.

These, the Hermit said, were known by the

name of " kernels ; " and if they were not removed, no meat would ever keep, however well
salted, but would begin to corrupt in the place
where the kernel lay, and would gradually
spread, till the whole of the meat became
tainted. He believed these kernels were much
more numerous in stall-fed and over-fed animals than others, and doubted if any round
of beef was entirely free from them, but, not
being a surgeon, he could not tell what these
kernels were, or of what they were composed;
about six pounds of ragged pieces of lean were
also cut off for pies.

Gwenllian having completed this first process, which she finished by cutting the thin
end of the flap into a tapering point, she took
a soup-plate, which held a pound of finely
powdered salt, which had been in an oven or
hot closet until quite warm ; she first of all
carefully sprinkled salt into all the gashes and
interstices of the meat, and then rubbed in
more salt with her hand, until every bit of the
meat had acquired a greyish-blue tint, instead
of being blood-red. She then did the same to

the other half-round, using half a pound of salt to each half-round. She then so disposed of the beef with reference to the groove in the table, and the channel in the corner, that the liquor which exuded from them should be received in a pan which stood under the corner. A quarter of a pound of hot salt was again rubbed into each round at night, another quarter the following morning, another the following evening, and the third morning another quarter of a pound was bestowed upon each of the halves, making in all a pound and a half to each half-round. On the third afternoon, they were placed in a large pan, with a sufficient quantity of brine to cover them, composed of a gallon of cold water to a pound of salt. In this they were turned about and rubbed in the evening; and the next morning the pickle, being quite bloody, was thrown away; and the rounds were then placed in a fresh pickle of the same strength, the only difference being that it had been previously boiled, and, having stood all night, was quite cold, and ready for use. In this fresh pickle the beef was turned, night and morning; and whenever it became muddy or bloody, fresh boiled pickle was exchanged for it, until the beef was boiled, at the end of five or six days.

The Hermit said, that the number of times the pickle required to be changed depended upon the difference of the meat itself containing more or less blood, and the heat of the weather, but that whenever it was bloody or muddy it ought to be changed; and that he found from six to seven days quite long enough for beef to be in salt before it was boiled, and after that time the meat continually lost flavour, and became a mere vehicle for salt, the water in which it was boiled being useless for poor people, as he had before observed.

The Traveller asked why he put unboiled salt and water the first time, and not afterwards?

The Hermit replied that he did so to save time, as, whether the pickle was boiled or unboiled, it would become so bloody after the first immersion of the beef as to require changing within twenty-four hours; and that there was, therefore, no advantage in boiling it the first time, as the boiled pickle was intended for longer keeping.

Gwenllians next proceeding was to attend to two ox tongues, which had also been brought in that morning; and, after cutting off all the roots and well washing the tongues, she rubbed them well with salt, and put them on a dish on the stone table. The further proceedings with the tongues were, day by day, inspected by the Traveller, and finally written down.*

The Traveller, having been rather disconcerted, from his inability to prove that he could devise anything with reference to salting beef, thought that he would venture upon a suggestion with respect to tongues, and he said: " I should think it would save a great deal of time if the tongues, after being well salted, were hung up to dry, instead of the trouble of re-boiling or renewing the pickle until the tongues are eaten."

The Hermit replied shortly, that as he never bought dried tongues he could not tell whether they ever were equal to those pickled and

---

* See Appendix No. XXXIX.

*un*dried, but that he *never* had succeeded in drying a tongue to be at all equal to those eaten fresh out of the pickle, that those dried were generally tainted on the under side, and he had always remarked the same difference and the same effects with regard to dried chines, which invariably became rusty.

The Traveller then led the conversation to bacon and hams, and commenced by asking what the Hermit considered the best food for fattening pigs?

" If," replied his host, " you could tell me the best food for keeping pigs *thin* without starving them, I should esteem it very valuable, and I never allow my pigs to be regularly fatted. The porkers are allowed to range in a very large yard, and take a great deal of exercise in the autumn when turned out in the acorn season."

" I thought pigs turned up the ground," said the Traveller.

" Not if they have rings in their noses," said his host. " But to proceed with what I was saying,—notwithstanding the advantages my porkers enjoy of air and exercise, they are *always too fat*, though never shut up in a stye to be fatted."

" What objection is there to their being fat ? " said the Traveller.

" There are two," replied the Hermit. " The first, that if very fat there is often great waste, if the meat is dressed when fresh, as all the fat *cannot* be consumed with the lean ; secondly, if salted, although a larger portion of fat can be eaten thus prepared, it is objectionable to have a great deal more fat than lean, the proper proportion for eating being two parts lean to one part fat."

" I am surprised," said the Traveller, " that, with your inventive talents, you have not discovered some mode of curing or mitigating this evil."

" The cure," said the Hermit, " is out of my power; although I know very well that if pigs could only range about in fields like sheep and cattle, eating grass and taking exercise, and having only two very moderate meals a day, and were killed without being put up, they would not have more than the natural proper accompaniment of fat, and the pork would be *much more wholesome* as well as better flavoured : but as I have no forests or warrens in which to turn them loose, and as, when they have no acorns to engage their attention, they have a peculiar delight in making their way through hedges or under gates into my neighbour's land, and as I find that labour is now too dear for me to afford a man for a swineherd, and my attempts at educating little girls or boys for that office have always ended in the pigs doing everything that they ought not to do, and the children making the holes in the hedges larger by creeping through the apertures the pigs had made, I have been obliged to content myself with abstracting the overplus of fat, and thus preventing waste, as, in spite of all my efforts, and all their running about the yard, my pigs are always fatter than I approve for domestic consumption ; but as there is nothing like a practical lesson, you shall see the second widow on duty preparing a porker in the next compartment."

The Hermit then led the way into his pork larder, where Marged had spread before her on another stone table two legs, two loins, two necks, and two shoulders of a porker killed the day before. The head was divided into two parts, and, with the tongue, ears, tail, and pettitoes, were put into a pan of cold salt and water, which had already been changed once. Although the joints of pork were not to be compared, as to the thickness of fat, to the pork the Traveller had seen in butchers' shops, yet he could easily believe that a great part of it could not be eaten if roasted with the lean, and he quickly understood the sense of the exploit he saw Marged perform. She dexterously cut off, in one thick piece, the whole of the rind, leaving only attached to the meat a sufficient quantity of fat for consumption when roasted. When this had been done to the necks and loins, a considerable quantity of fine lard was thereby saved from waste, which was again cut off from the rind, and, being reduced into small pieces, was thrown into a pan of spring water with sprigs of rosemary. The rind was placed on a dish by itself, and the Hermit informed him that it was very useful to place over beef when stewing, or over a baked fillet of veal; and after it has been used for these purposes, the remains could finally be finished for making glaze.

The Traveller was very anxious to know what the Hermit intended to do with the joints from which a portion of the fat had been taken, and those which had not been touched.

The Hermit informed him that he did not deprive the shoulders of fat or rind, as they had seldom anything to spare; but that the necks and loins were destined for roasting, for cutlets, for pork pies, and sausages.* The shoulders would be salted on the stone for two or three days, and then put into pickle made in the same way as for the beef; that the hams † would be cured with salt and treacle, and dried, and the pig's head and pettitoes were, according to circumstances, either boiled fresh out of pickle (being treated the same as the

* See Appendix No. XL.
† See Appendix No. XLI.

beef), or made into brawn.* The Hermit impressed upon his guest, that the same principles which he had endeavoured to instil into his mind with respect to the cookery of fresh meat equally applied to salted meat, and that a large quantity of very nutritious jelly, which assisted in making soup for the poor, was produced by boiling the pig's head and pettitoes in a *double* vessel, and also most savoury jelly stock was obtained by preparing the fresh pork for pies, well flavoured with vegetables, in the same manner.

The Traveller inquired how long the Hermit considered bacon could be kept, if properly cured?

His host informed him that he did not believe that any bacon could be kept beyond a year without being rusty, and that it was the very worst economy to keep bacon long; and there could be no necessity for so doing, as those who made their own bacon must kill their pigs once a year, unless they were very bad managers; and, of course, the longer it was kept the less nourishment, and consequently

---

* See Appendix No. XLII.

the worse food, it would produce after it had dried sufficiently to be eaten.

The Traveller said the Hermit had not mentioned his treatment of bacon pigs; to which he replied that the principle was exactly the same as the system for porkers, but that the diet of the porkers was rather different, the bacon pigs having more solid food, and having a stye and a yard to sleep in.

The Traveller inquired why the bacon pigs slept in an apartment by themselves, shut up from the others; and was informed that the porkers had an open, though warm shed, but that it was found from experience that the bacon pigs, being always more or less fat and unwieldy, were liable to be injured by the porkers, who, either in play or ill-temper, often bruised the bacon pigs, and were bitten by them in return, but the bacon pigs had as much liberty during the day as the porkers.

After this conversation the days passed rapidly, and the Traveller constantly cultivated his *recovered* powers of observation, and made evident progress in the art of reflection. He and the Hermit took a walk one day to some corn-fields. It had been unusually wet for four previous weeks, and the Traveller had expressed his fear that all the corn cut, but not carried, when the weather changed, would be saturated with wet, and not fit for use.

On the first fine day after these remarks, his host proposed that they should make a personal inspection of the state of the corn. The Traveller had never before paid the slightest attention to the different modes of harvesting, but he was now sufficiently advanced in intelligence to reason upon what he then saw, or recollected having seen; and he quickly noticed that there were some fields, which belonged to separate farms, in which the sheaves of corn were quite different to all the others. The exception reminded him of the sheaves he had seen in England, for, although he had never before thought upon the subject, the form was familiar to him, whilst the others were a complete work of art, and so constructed that they formed a point, and the straw attached to the corn was so placed and turned downwards, that the straw formed a complete protection against the drenching showers which had saturated the grain of the first-mentioned sheaves, but had had no effect whatever upon the others.

The Traveller made a sketch of these different modes of harvesting, and hardly needed the Hermit's explanation to prove the great superiority of the Welsh mode to that of the English. The Hermit assured him that he had known corn belonging to Welsh farmers *un-injured*, after having been out three weeks in wet weather, and which, after the cessation of rain, had reached the barn in good order.

The Traveller then examined the grains of some of the ears of wheat which were exposed according to the usual plan of English harvesting. He found that they had begun to sprout, whilst the grains he examined from the Welsh stacks were dry and hard, although the outer straw was wet; but that, the Hermit informed him, would very soon dry, with a little wind or sun. He said that these small Welsh stacks were called by the natives *bwch*,* and

* See Plate No. V.

Ang: Llanover fecit

Bwch.
Welsh Wheat Stack.

Ang: Llanover fecit

Geifr

Welsh Barley Sheaf.

Aug: Hanover fecit

English Wheat Sheaves.

when made of barley, *geifr* ; * and that there was a great deal of practical science, art, ingenuity, and good sense in their construction, and they needed no eulogium from him, as the state of the same grain, cut at the same time, but treated in so different a manner, required no further comment to prove which was the good system, and which was the bad one.

The Traveller could not at all comprehend why the English did not adopt the Welsh plan, as it was practically proved to be so much the best.

His host replied that he could not assist him in solving *that problem,* but he would simply inform him that the owner of the spoiled stacks had come into the country five years before, and had had every opportunity of seeing the benefit of the plan adopted by the natives, but, notwithstanding this, he preferred the continuance of the three sheaves plan placed with all their ears upwards,✝ so that each grain might imbibe the whole benefit of every

---

* See Plate No. VI.
✝ See Plate No. VII.

shower, by which means he had already *reapea*
the benefit by having damaged corn three times
in five years!

The Hermit was much diverted by the Traveller's credulity, and his sanguine belief that
his sketch would produce the slightest alteration in the English plan of arranging the
sheaves so that the wheat might be protected
from the rain, instead of being so contrived as
to receive the descending showers without the
loss of a drop of water! and the Hermit gave
a sketch of the manner in which the sheaves of
barley were made (called *geifr* in Wales), and
which was also good and adapted for throwing
off the rain, though not nearly equal to the
*bychod.**

In the course of conversation, on the way
home, the Traveller reverted again to the
culinary department, in which he took a deeper
interest every day, and informed the Hermit
that, as the time was approaching when business would compel him to go to London, and
afterwards to visit some relations in the country,

* Plural for Bwch.

he must ask him two more favours—the one, he was afraid, might meet with a refusal, if answered hastily, but it was a matter which he had so much at heart, that, being aware that his proposal would require reflection, he entreated his kind friend not to reply for a week, but to give it his best and most indulgent consideration; that his next request, though second in importance, he would mention first, as he was in hopes of receiving an immediate and favourable reply. " It is," he added, " that you will select an extra assistant for the widows for a day or two, or even for a few hours, and that you will allow me to be a witness of the instruction she receives, that I may have some idea of the method of teaching, as well as of the sort of mistakes which may be expected from a novice."

The Hermit replied that he would certainly comply with his wishes, but that he was very much afraid that the widows, however cleverly they executed what they had been taught, would not be able to teach without he himself superintended the first lessons.

The Traveller said he could not understand how it was possible for persons to know so well how to execute without being able to teach, and that (without any teaching) if their pupil was allowed to watch them, he believed that she might learn.

The Hermit smiled significantly, and said he could not compliment his guest with regard to his own memory. "For," said he, "what trouble have I not had to make you understand the reason of *anything* that you have seen, and for some time it was necessary for me to find *outward* eyes for you as well as *inward* understanding, before you could learn to observe and afterwards to reason."

The Traveller was in rather a contradictory humour on this occasion, and he fell back into his old habit of pertness, and answered rather tartly, that it "was a very different thing to teach cooking to an English gentleman and a Welsh kitchen-maid."

"Indeed *it is*," said the Hermit, "and I would sooner teach the latter than the former, because she would sooner learn!"

This speech exasperated the Traveller still more, and he exclaimed that he had no doubt that he would have learned much quicker if it had not been for the Hermit's obstinacy in always speaking Welsh to the widows, although they could understand English enough to obey the few directions that they required, and that indeed he did not believe that they required anything more than *a look !*

The Hermit generally became particularly good-tempered when the Traveller was very much the reverse ; and he replied, with the greatest good-humour, that he considered that every *soul* had as absolute a right to the use of his own language as the beasts and birds, and that if he had not been the countryman of his servants, he would still be proud to speak as much of their language as he was able to acquire; but that he knew well that the Welsh diminished in value (*as human beings*) in exact proportion as they became indifferent to their own land, which indifference was always produced more or less by the abandonment of their own native tongue, and that he would never promote the deterioration of intellectual beings any more than the adulteration of food ; that it was absurd and barbarous to suppose that different nations on the face of the earth, created by the Almighty with various talents and various tongues, could be improved by the extinction of any noble language (also the *work* of the *same* Creator) which suited the expression of their thoughts and feelings, and the accents of which called forth all the best impulses and sentiments of their nature. It would be as rational to argue that any of the best grains or roots bestowed by Providence for the bodily sustenance of man and beast, had for their benefit better be exterminated. The Hermit added that he spoke Welsh to the Welsh as a duty as well as a pleasure, and in so doing he only followed the example of every continental nation. The Breton nobility spoke Breton to their Breton dependants, whether they could speak French or not, the Belgians and the Dutch did the same, although they were equally fluent in French, and although, in the higher ranks, the Russians and the Danes, the Swedes and the Poles, *were* excellent French scholars, they carefully preserved their own languages. The English language was not, and never could be, so universally spoken by foreigners as the French; any man would be considered insane *out* of these islands, if he convened meetings to propose that all nations should not only agree to learn one common language, but that each should abandon its own tongue *for the purpose* of the *better* cultivation of the human intellect, the preservation and diffusion of literature, and the maintenance of that nationality which is the mainstay of religion and morality, and the support of the throne! " But," said he, "*you* have no reason to complain, for I have never given a direction about cookery in Welsh that I have not explained to you much more at length in English."

The Traveller by this time had repented his little ebullition, and was fully aware that he had been guilty of undeniable ill-breeding and of great ingratitude. He recollected that he had been hospitably entertained, and had

received food, information, and instruction
without fee or reward; that he was eating
Welsh bread in a Welsh habitation, that he had
a Welsh host, and was served by Welsh hands,
and yet that he (the Stranger), whose language
was courteously spoken to himself by his host,
had virtually questioned the right of that host and
of his native servants to the use of the tongue
of their own land, which he had first visited *un-*
invited, but where " hospitality had greeted
him," and " courtesy had taken him prisoner," *
although he could not utter a word of the
tongue which had been spoken by the ancient
Britons from time immemorial, whose earliest
literature was one of the most interesting in
existence, and whose modern literature included
every subject most conducive to the interest
of religion and the cultivation of the human
mind, and which has been kept up entirely,
both in prose and poetry, by the genuine sons
of Cambria, who are the authors, the readers,

---

* Translation from the Welsh :—

"Os Dieithr Lletteugarwch a'th erys
Os Gelyn, addfwynder a'th garchara."

the printers, and the publishers of Welsh books. Having a kind heart and a refined mind, the Traveller was really grieved when he thus reflected, and expressed deep sorrow for what he had said ; and believing in his sincerity, the Hermit was quickly pacified and changed the conversation by promising that he would grant his first request, and begging to know what the other favour was, which he mentioned as being *second* in order though *first* in importance.

The good man at last extracted from his friend that he wanted him to promise to accompany him to *London !*

The astonishment of the Hermit surpassed description, and it would require too much time and space to recount the animated discussion which took place before he yielded. The argument which at last induced him to consent was, that the Traveller expressed his apprehension that he should relapse into indolence and indifference if he returned to London without his venerable companion, and if again plunged *alone* into a world so different to that in which

the Hermit existed, that he should forget how
to see or how to observe.

This was all very true, but nevertheless the
Traveller was actuated by an additional motive
which he dared not name, but he certainly
anticipated far more amusement from the effect
of modern London upon the Hermit than expected improvement to himself by his friend's
society. It was, however, finally agreed that
they should together shortly proceed to London, where the Traveller was obliged to go on
account of his own affairs on leaving the cell
of his hospitable entertainer, and to exchange
the simple but elevating influences of a practically useful life in a secluded corner of the
Principality of Wales, for the tumult and dis-
tractions of the Metropolis.

Let not the reader, however, expect that he
will find in this volume full details of their
journey, or the history of the Welsh Hermit in
London. If the Traveller should hereafter be
able to prove the acquirement of sufficient industry to have written a journal containing the
observations made by his Centenarian friend

during that period of his life, they will probably be sufficiently numerous to make another book, which *may* or *may not* ever be published.

The next proceeding in the Hermit's cell was teaching a novice. A willing (but previously uninstructed) Welsh girl of the age of eighteen having been sent for, the Hermit desired the widows to show her how to make a tapioca pudding and a rice pudding fit for an invalid,* premising that he should not give a single direction himself, as they perfectly well knew how to make these puddings, and that the Traveller himself should stand by in silence, while they executed the above orders and explained what was necessary to their new pupil. It is *un*necessary to detail the particulars of what took place : it is sufficient to say that the Traveller was well amused by seeing the puddings made ; the Hermit was more amused by anticipating the probable results on the following day, and the pupil was highly delighted with the idea that on the morrow she would exhibit her new learning in the shape of two

* See Appendix No. XLIII.

more similar puddings, which she had not the slightest doubt she would make to perfection after one lesson. The next day was appointed for the trial of her newly acquired skill. The Welsh widows were desired to show the girl everything that they did, and the Traveller was inwardly gratified by the belief that, if the new scholar was at fault, *he* would be able to direct without the Hermit's assistance, from having only looked on the day before. The Hermit commenced by asking the scholar how much tapioca she required for her pudding. She said "a little bit." The Hermit upon this gave her a teaspoonful. She said she "had had it in a teacup before." He then put the teaspoonful into a teacup; she said she thought that it was too little.

"Was it not weighed or measured?" said the Hermit.

"No," replied the girl; "Gwenllian took it out in a teacup."

"How much was it?"

"It was a teacupful." The teacup she held

out was accordingly filled, and she then proceeded to ask for milk.

" How much milk ? " said the Hermit.

" A pint," was the answer.

A pint was given. In due time the milk
and the tapioca were put together to " cree,"
in a double saucepan. The girl was asked
if she wanted anything else for that pudding.
She said, " No, not then." She then asked
for rice to begin her rice pudding. " How
much ? " was the inquiry. " The same as the
tapioca," was the answer.

" What ! a teacupful ? " inquired the Hermit. She replied in the affirmative, and received the quantity desired, holding out the
same teacup which she had before taken for
the tapioca. She then requested another pint
of milk, and having received it, a second pudding was put in another double saucepan by
the side of its predecessor. After some time
she took out the contents, when they appeared
soft and well mixed, and put them into two
separate basins while she proceeded to break two
eggs, yolk and white. These she mixed both

together on one plate, and then taking a spoon disposed of the egg, dividing it by her eye between the two basins of pudding. While these proceedings were going on, the four Welsh widows were engaged in other affairs, but the Hermit was obviously very uncomfortable, which the Traveller might have perceived, had he not been so well amused in watching the new scholar as not to pay much attention to the countenance of his host. When the novice had divided and mixed the two eggs between her two puddings, she proceeded to the oven, and having endeavoured to judge of the heat by putting in her hand (as she had seen Gwenllian do the day before), she emptied the tapioca into one baking-dish, and the rice into another, and putting both the dishes on the baking-tin, shut them up in the oven.

The Hermit then asked the Traveller, in a low voice, what he thought of the new pupil.

" I think," said he, " that she is most promising, and I have no doubt that the puddings will be excellent. I thought," added he, "that there would not be much difficulty in learning, if she once watched such an expert performer as the widow Gwenllian."

"We shall see," said the Hermit. "I am not so sanguine as you are, but, at all events, I hope that if *you* had perceived any omissions, *you* would have mentioned them?"

The Traveller was discreetly silent. He had *not* observed *any omissions*, or *noted any differences* in the manner in which the pupil had executed on the second day what he had seen the widows do for her instruction the previous morning; but he thought that he had better not make any decided declaration on the subject, lest he should afterwards be proved in the wrong.

At length the dinner-hour arrived. The puddings made their appearance, but *that* appearance was very different to what he had expected. He, however, hoped that the taste would be unexceptionable, and that probably the oven had not been of the right temperature —a point with which *he* was not supposed to be acquainted. But alas! he was doomed to disappointment. The rice pudding was stiff, dry, and tasteless. The tapioca pudding was equally tasteless, and so stiff that it was more like gum and flour baked together than the delicate nourishment produced by tapioca and milk properly cooked—in fact, *both* the puddings *were uneatable*.

" Now," said the Hermit (after the unfortunate failure could no longer be denied), " have you the same confidence you before expressed in your belief as to the facility with which a young female of ordinary capacity may learn, if she is allowed to watch the proper execution of simple cookery performed by expert hands? and do you also think that all those who can cook must also be well able to teach? I am certain that the widows were not only willing but anxious to explain what they thought necessary and to show every process relative to those puddings, and their scholar was equally anxious to learn; but, notwithstanding all this, the first attempt is a total failure, and you yourself, who have now been so long in the habit of observation, and who *might be supposed,* from your education, to have greater powers of memory, fully expected that these puddings would turn out as well as those of yesterday,—and yet, although *you* watched the process of making them both, you did not discover the difference of treatment."

The Traveller confessed his error, bewailed his *shortcomings,* and requested his host to inform him of the cause of the failure.

" In the first place," said the Hermit, " the quantity required of tapioca was two ounces, but it was *not weighed,* but measured in a particular teacup, which Gwenllian is accustomed to use, and which held exactly two ounces; but the teacup which the girl took for herself *held more,* a fact which neither she nor yourself noticed. One pint of milk would have been the right quantity for two ounces of tapioca, but the same teacup was used, and held nearly three ounces; consequently here was another fatal error of proportion in the first start. The third mistake was a total oblivion with respect to sugar—no sugar was added to the milk. With regard to the rice pudding,

T

she *asked* for the ' same quantity' as the tapioca,
whereas she ought to have had *an ounce and a*
half—one fourth less than of tapioca.   To this
she put another pint of milk, instead of which
she ought to have asked for a pint and a half,
being half a pint *more* milk, and one fourth *less*
rice, than was required for the tapioca, as rice
absorbs much more liquid ; but she had forgotten that Gwenllian had half filled the pint
measure again, after having emptied the full
pint upon the rice—here was another mistake
of the same nature.   When the tapioca and
rice were taken off the fire, she put the mixture
into two separate basins, instead of spreading
each on two large flat dishes, by which means
they would have become cool enough to receive
the egg within the time necessary for that purpose ; but, from the thickness of the basin, and
the small surface on which the outward air
could act, both rice and tapioca were too hot
when the egg was added.   To complete the
list of errors, she beat up two eggs together,
instead of separately, and then hastily divided
the whole quantity by her eye between the

two puddings, by which means the unfortunate tapioca got much less than its neighbour, and the rice pudding (which may taste very good *without any egg at all*) had the *largest* quantity of what it *least* required, whilst the tapioca (which I never succeeded in making palatable *without* an egg) had not half its proper share! There was no fault in the temperature of the oven, because Gwenllian had tested it with her own hand, which, by long experience and practice, serves her as well as a thermometer; also the poor novice had unfortunately not observed or remembered that water was to be poured into the baking tin, which caused the puddings to be burnt at the bottom before they were browned at the top; and therefore, between *omissions* and *commissions*, we have had two puddings composed of excellent materials rendered uneatable."

The Traveller admitted that the experiment had not answered as he had expected, and begged to know how the Hermit would have recommended the teaching to be carried on, had he directed the widows?

" I should," replied his host, " have taken care that each act in the progress of the pudding was most carefully explained; the reason being given why such a thing was done, and the consequences which would result if it was omitted, and it is these explanations, at the moment that the process of cooking is proceeding under the eye, which I find are so seldom given, and the ability to give them makes the great difference between one teacher and another, although they may both be equally clever in execution,—but there is a mechanical power, possessed by the majority, of executing a certain routine once learned, which is *much more common* than ability to instruct by the addition of clear explanations, which are most necessary and important for the pupil; and were the observing and reasoning powers more exercised in the *higher classes*, they would be less ignorant of the practical arts of domestic management, and *better teachers*, and those under them would be better able to instruct in their turn; but now, from your account, all is *sotto sopra!* the servants know very little, and the ladies nothing at all ! "

The Traveller vehemently denied that he had ever uttered such a libel on the accomplished females of the nineteenth century ; but the Hermit stoutly maintained that if he had not uttered those words, he had by facts clearly demonstrated that such was the rule, although, of course, there was no rule without some exceptions.

The time had now arrived for the great event to take place of the Hermit's departure to London with his wandering friend ; and as the principal object of this work has been to instil some knowledge of " the Real Principles of Good Cookery," and to awaken a desire in the higher orders to instruct themselves in domestic management (that most important branch of duty), it will not be inappropriate to conclude with a description of the contents of the Hermit's travelling baskets, one of which he insisted upon providing for his friend, the other being intended for himself. The preparation of these wayside provisions were the *last practical lessons in cookery* that the Traveller received in the Cell of St. Gover.

The consternation of the Welsh widows may be imagined when they heard that their master was going from home, the possibility of which they could hardly realize; but when informed that he was going to leave Wales for three months, and, above all, that he was going to London, they uttered lamentations, which proved that they considered his *life* was not only in danger, but his *death* was *certain*; and " O anwyl, anwyl! Beth a wnawn ni!" " Y Meudwy Bonheddig anwyl fe fydd yn sicr o farw! Gwae ninnau!" * was uttered, until the Traveller had heard these sentences so often that the night before his departure, he had a terrible dream.

It required four-and-twenty hours before their agitation had subsided sufficiently to enable them to remember or execute anything that they were told to do, but, at last, a quiet melancholy succeeded to violent and demon-

---

* " Oh, dear, dear, what shall we do ? " " The dear Hermit gentleman will be sure to die. Woe to us ! "

strative grief, and they began the preparations
for the roadside refreshments with much the
same feelings that they would have had if they
had been called upon to cook for the Hermit's
funeral.

Two plump fowls were roasted, having been
basted with fresh mutton suet, to the last twist
of the woollen yarn. They were then enclosed
in the inner tin of a Ffwrn-fach—the Ffwrn-
fach itself was filled with cold water from the
spring—and, after the second lid was put on,
it was sunk altogether in the well.

When the Traveller saw this done, he exclaimed : " This is beyond my comprehension.
I. have seen and heard a great deal of warm water
to surround meat; but why hot chickens are
to be immersed in a vessel surrounded by cold
spring water, and then sunk in a cold well,
I cannot imagine."

" The principle," said the Hermit, " is exactly the same as that upon which some cooks
would plunge a ham, as soon as boiled, into
a pail of iced water. The object is to chill, as
quickly as possible, that which is to be eaten

cold; by which means the juices, which would otherwise run off or evaporate, are staunched up within the flesh; and I am anxious that these chickens, provided for our journey, should be as juicy and retain as much flavour as possible."

Three hours afterwards, the chickens were taken out. A tongue also was boiled, and placed upon a dish. Oranges were then cut across the centre, the core taken out with a sharp penknife, the pulp *cut* round and separated from the rind *without* any adhesion of the white skin; the pulp was put into a basin in lumps, and the juice which remained in the halves of the oranges was squeezed upon it; sugar was sprinkled upon them, and boiling water added, in the proportion of two tablespoonfuls to each orange. They were then put aside till the next day, which was to be the morning of departure.

In the course of the previous day, the widows were very busily engaged in making biscuits * and the rock cakes † (the original recipe for

---

* See Appendix No. XLIV.
† See Appendix No. XLV.

which the Hermit had received direct from
Margaret Cavendish Harley, Duchess of Port-
land), and in carefully washing and re-washing
old-fashioned bottles cased in leather, with glass
stoppers, and two little glass preserving pots also
with glass stoppers. The loaves of rice bread,*
for the sandwiches, were baked the previous
night, as they were better for that purpose
when they were a day old.

The baskets to hold the travelling fare were
those always used by the Hermit for his mountain expeditions, and were made by his Welsh
labourers. They were square, like a box, with
a lid and loop of basket-work, and divisions
in the inside, into which fitted two small tin
boxes, two bottles, one glass preserving-pot,
two wooden spoons, and a fork (made by the
Welsh peasants, who have a remarkable talent
for carving).

All being so far ready, the host and the Traveller retired to rest; when the latter had a
most distressing dream, which he felt he never
could forget, and which, no doubt, was to be

---

* See Appendix No. XLVI.

attributed to his emotions on the eve of departure, combined with the exclamations of the widows, above alluded to. He dreamt that he had been handed over by the Hermit to the four Welsh widows, who were to make him into a "*poten*"—a word which he perfectly understood to mean "pudding." He thought that he struggled in vain to get out of their hands, and that, in reply to his entreaties, they said nothing but "Paid ag ofni!" "Paid ag ofni!"* and that, while he was being cut into mincemeat, the Hermit, with a most sardonic expression, informed him that if, after being boiled three hours in a basin, he could talk Welsh, he would, by his art, restore him to his own proper form; but that he had eaten too long of the best produce of Cambria not to make the small return of speaking the language of those who had provided him with so many good things; and that, if he failed to give this small token of his gratitude, he should remain *a pudding* till he was eaten up by wild dogs. After this frightful dream, he lost all sensation

---

* "Do not fear." "Do not fear."

(even in sleep), until, believing he was awake, but the dream still continuing, he uttered so vehemently, " O anwyl, anwyl, beth a wnaf fi ? " " Beth a wnaf fi ? " *—at the same moment believing that he *was a pudding*, and had jumped out of the pot upon the floor of the Hermit's kitchen—that he was awakened by the violence with which he really had leaped out of his bed, and he lay upon the floor some time before he could understand that he was *not a pudding*, that he had *not* been *boiled*, and that he was *not master of the Welsh language*,— although, in truth, he had been so terrified by the nightmare, that, like Sir Walter Scott's monk,† he could not, for some time, repeat anything but the widows' Welsh lamentations, which were engraven on his memory. At length, however, he recovered, and was able to dress himself, and go down to breakfast.

It was reserved for the last hour before starting to cut or pull the cold chicken meat

---

* " What shall I do ? "   " What shall I do ? "
† The Monk sings the song of the Water Kelpie.   See *The Monastery*, vol. 1. p. 84.

into delicate small pointed pieces taken from the breasts, and which were then laid in a tin box, which had previously been lined with white paper, each morsel being slightly sprinkled with salt. In the other tin box were sandwiches made of the pounded chicken meat and tongue, moistened with the cold jelly of a boiled chicken, which had been flavoured with appropriate herbs. The rice bread was cut into thin pieces of the proper size and shape for eight sandwiches, and pounded meat put between them. Two packets of four each filled each tin box. The oranges were then (pulp and juice) put into the glass preserving pots, the mouths of which were sufficiently wide to admit of a spoon. One bottle was filled with the water of the Ffynon Over, and the other was filled with cold tea, which had been made and sweetened the previous night, and the vessel in which it was contained was put to stand in the well till the morning, when it received the proper proportion of cold scalded (*not clotted*) cream. The centre compartment had also space for narrow strips of rice bread, in-

tended to eat with the chicken; likewise for
the plain biscuits and the rock cakes; also
plums and pears. Both baskets were provided
alike.

At length the Traveller's steed and the
Hermit's pony appeared before the cell with
four or five Welsh mountaineers, all of whom
were called Bechgyn,* although the youngest
had long before seen fifty years, and each of
whom insisted upon seeing their beloved master
to the end of his ride and the beginning of his
perils, and each expecting to have the sole
charge of the much-valued pony named Cymro,
which, next to the Hermit himself, was the
object of their care.

It was thirty-five miles to the nearest
station, and although the Hermit would not
show the slightest fear, having once given his
word not only to accompany his guest, but to
travel by railroad, that he might see it and
judge of it for himself, yet he *shuddered inwardly* when he thought of a mode of conveyance, which, from description, appeared better

---

* Boys.

suited for spirits of the lower regions than for those above ground.

Slowly and solemnly the steed and the pony were mounted. Tears were in the eyes of the widows and the Bechgyn; melancholy resolve on the countenance of the Hermit; and sorrowful regret in the demeanour of the Traveller!

They were to stop, at the end of eighteen miles, by the side of a clear stream, under an ash tree, well known to the Hermit and his attendants, who carried bags of oatmeal for the horses, and said they could procure vessels in which to mix it for them from a cottage, as well as hay, should there not be sufficient pasturage. Here they were to remain three hours, and to refresh themselves with the contents of their baskets, the widows having, by the Hermit's orders, provided each of the mountaineers with a costrel of Glasdwr,* bread and meat, and bread and cheese, with apples in their pockets.

The time has now arrived when the Hermit and the Traveller must take their leave of the

---

* Two parts of milk to three parts of water.

" Gentle Reader," who must imagine them defiling through the wood that leads from the Cell of St. Gover, with the Welsh widows and their handmaidens in mute despair, whilst the Hermit's Welsh harper, who was seated by the ancient Well of Gover, struck the triple strings of his noble instrument, and extemporised an accompaniment to the following Druidic Triad, which he uttered in a plaintive recitative, but with a warning accent, as he watched the departure of his master till he could no longer be seen :—

> " Tri pheth a ddylai dyn ystyried :
> O b'le daeth, b'le mae,
> I b'le yn myned."

Which being translated, signifies—

> " *Three things a man ought to consider :*
> *Whence he comes, where he is,*
> *To what place he is going.*"

For the satisfaction of those who may wish to hear of the *safe* arrival of the Hermit and his friend at the place of *greatest danger*, it may be added, that the five faithful Welsh mountaineers returned the following evening, with the pony Cymro, and informed the widows and all others, that they had beheld the " Meudwy Bonheddig" and his English guest go off in a flame of fire, with a noise which deafened their ears, and a smell that they should never forget, and that no doubt he must come to a fearful end!

THE TRAVELLER'S NOTE BOOK.

TO THE EDITOR OF A COUNTY PAPER.

*Letter shown by the Traveller to the Hermit from a
Gentleman who wanted a Shirt.*

SIR,—I beg to call your attention to the
following distressing facts, for the truth of
which I can vouch, having occurred to myself.
For many years my respected grandmother was
in the habit of presenting me with an annual
stock of shirts, which she cut out and made
with her own hands, my mother having died
when I was an infant. I was thus happily
wel provided till past the age of thirty-one
years, but my excellent grandmother being now
defunct, and my shirts in a very dilapidated
condition, I applied to the wife of a friend for
the direction of any female who followed the

occupation of a sempstress, as my wardrobe required renovation. I did not enter into further particulars, because experience had taught me, that although my grandmother (a gentlewoman of noble descent) no more scrupled to name the word *shirt* than to make a shirt, yet that the great improvements in education had rendered the ladies of the present generation too refined even to know that such a garment was ever worn, far less to name it. The lady to whom I applied gave me the address of a Mrs. Doolittle, residing in the next country town, about three miles distant. I inquired if there was no one nearer in any village, but I was informed there was not, and I accordingly sent for Mrs. Doolittle. When she arrived, I mentioned that I required a set of shirts, and that I would give a pattern which did not require alteration. I was rather surprised by the look I received from the very important-looking personage who had answered my summons, as she neither assented nor dissented, but stood staring, as if she had heard something alarming or insulting. I repeated in other words what I before said, and added, " You *understand*, I require a set of new shirts. You have been recommended to me, and here is the pattern. I wish you to purchase the linen for me, and to make the shirts as quickly as you can." Upon this, she drew up with an air of inexpressible scorn, saying, " I think, sir, there must be some great mistake somewhere ; I never made such a thing in my life, sir, and never professed to do so." " Why, are you not a sempstress ? or what do you call yourself ? " " I go out occasionally to assist in *trimming*, and also take the higher branches at home." " Well," rejoined I, " I thought people who did needlework were called *sempstresses*." " I do not understand that name, sir ; I *never heard it before* ; I was educated in a *very superior* manner, sir." I here recollected having heard my good grandmother say, that " the test of a needlewoman was making a shirt," and that any one who could make a fine shirt properly, was mistress of plain needlework.* I therefore ventured to

---

* If *button-holes* were included.

observe, that I had always understood that "shirt-making was *the* 'highest branch' of needlework;" upon which Mrs. Doolittle replied, with a contemptuous gesture, that "*that* must have been very long ago, before she was born, as her *governess,* who taught all the modern branches of a first-rate education, never allowed such a garment to be mentioned in her presence." By this time I had come to the conclusion that the longer this elegant professor of the "higher branches" remained in my presence, the worse the opinion we should form of each other! I therefore speedily wished her good morning, and applied to another lady to recommend somebody who would not be above undertaking the task of renovating my unfortunate wardrobe, as my requirements were pressing. To prevent trespassing too much on your valuable space, I will shortly narrate that I have had no less than six persons recommended to me as needlewomen, or sempstresses, or whatever their dignity allows them to be called, from three different towns in the same county, and that

there was not one that had ever made a shirt,
though all had been brought up at various
schools; and the only result of my inquiries
has been the disheartening knowledge, that it
is impossible for me to obtain the services of
any one who would undertake to make a fine
shirt, although the population of the above-
mentioned towns averaged respectively 11,000,
6,000, and 2,000, and I was actually informed
that although, five years previously, the smallest
and most unimportant of these towns had possessed an admirable shirt-maker, who was also
a schoolmistress, that she had been removed
from her office, and had left the country, and
a successor had been appointed, who could
neither execute nor teach any manual arts,
employments, or occupations, beyond what the
wooden hook would accomplish, called by the
French name of *crochet*, and which (I was told),
on account of the great expense of fine-coloured
wools, was a much greater tax upon the parents,
than any benefit to the scholars! The person
who gave me the above information with
respect to the departed schoolmistress and

shirt-maker, lamented, as much as I did, the extinction of the art of making shirts, and added, that the *very names* of *trades and callings* were now changed, and that the *elegant nonentities* of the present day were *not* to be called *school-mistresses,* but " *governesses !* " Under these unhappy circumstances, my only resource is to beg for the benefit of your columns, to make known my present requirements, in the hope, that if any female still exists who can make a shirt, that she will be so obliging as to indicate the fact by advertisement in your paper, addressed *to the gentleman in want of a shirt.* I am quite prepared to pay very handsomely, if my pattern is exactly followed.

I am, Sir,

Your obedient, humble Servant,

A GENTLEMAN IN DISTRESS.

POOR LAWS.

THE Hermit recounted an anecdote in reference to the effect of the Poor Laws as follows : —A poor man living on the side of the mountain about four miles distant died, after painful and lingering illness. He left a wife and two or three young children. It was the depth of winter, and the snow covered the ground. His wife inquired of the proper authority how she was to get a coffin, and was informed that she must go to the relieving officer, who lived nearly eight miles off, during which time she must have left the children in the house, or gone out of her way to reach the dwelling of a neighbour, where she might probably have found protection for them during her absence. Fourteen or sixteen miles in the snow, under great distress of mind, would be considered a heavy infliction for a man *under such circumstances ;* but how much more for a woman ? who possibly might not have found the relieving officer at home when she got to the end of her journey. In the present instance, the Hermit

said, that the wretched poor woman thought
that *he* might befriend her, and consequently she
walked three miles in the snow to his cell (instead of eight), and obtained the poor boon she
sought, viz. the Hermit's order for a coffin to
be made for her husband's remains, with the
risk of the parish refusing to pay for it had they
been so disposed, because it was not commanded by the relieving officer! Several other
facts were mentioned by the Hermit, as having
occurred under his own knowledge and that of
his friend, sufficient to cause my exclamation of
" Are we in a Christian country ? " and " Are
these acts in *conformity* with the law ? *or
punishable by the law ?* "

The Hermit believes that all these things are
in conformity with the Poor Law Act, *if so,*
why is such an Act suffered to exist without
alteration and amendment? It also appears that
great cruelty *can* be *legally* perpetrated with
regard to the removal of poor persons who,
notwithstanding a life of industry and an old
age of honesty and virtue, are unable from
bodily infirmity to gain any longer a sufficiency

for their own maintenance. The Hermit mentioned one among many pitiful cases which had been recounted to him by his rich and benevolent neighbour. It was that of a brother and sister who had always lived together, and, though the one was partially crippled and the other was weak, they had managed to earn their bread by their own exertions till they were far advanced in years, when they were necessitated to apply for parish relief. Upon inquiry, it appeared that they belonged to a parish more than one hundred miles distant, although they had resided for so many years in the locality where they had grown old, that they were completely naturalized to the spot. The parish authorities commenced a correspondence, when, after months of wrangling and delay, the distant parties decided that they would not grant any relief unless the two old people were sent to the workhouse more than a hundred miles off, and they *were sent there!*

It appears that the Welsh have such a horror of the workhouse, and are also naturally so very kind-hearted, that numerous instances occur of

peasants and their wives, who earn their daily
bread by hard labour, with children of their
own, have brought up other children who have
been put out to nurse with them after their
parents have died, or have been unable to pay
anything for their maintenance, rather than
surrender them to the parish to be placed in a
workhouse.

The Hermit has a horror of what is *now*
called *centralization.* He says that the order of
the Universe ought to teach mankind that everything is the centre of a small circle, and that it
is contrary to reason to suppose that human
beings requiring various treatment, if collected
together from various quarters in one place in a
huge mass, can ever be properly cared for,
managed, or attended.

On being informed of the enormous buildings now erected in towns for the purpose of
receiving the poor from numerous parishes, he
shuddered with horror at what he was convinced
must necessarily be the dreadful results in various
ways ; and nothing could persuade him that if
each parish, or perhaps two parishes, had a

building appropriated for the reception of such persons as *ought properly* to be called "paupers," and if the remainder of the respectable industrious poor received such out-door relief as was proper under their various circumstances, that it would not only promote virtue and morality, but that it would render the perpetuation of great and long-continued abuses impossible, which must constantly occur in the overgrown communities I described, called "*Union Workhouses*," where all were strangers to each other, and where every tie was severed that was calculated to preserve the best characteristics appertaining to human beings, or Christians.

The Hermit described the Welsh workhouse that he recollected as existing in his own parish about half a century ago, which he then frequently visited. It was an old and spacious farm-house, situated on the edge of a wood by the side of a by-road, with a green before the door on which grew two large walnut trees. It was well supplied with running water, and it was selected as the workhouse for two parishes, the locality being convenient for both. It was kept by an old farmer and his wife, who were enabled to maintain two or three cows on the adjoining land; and he well remembered the inmates of the establishment, of which he gave the following description:—On one of the hobs of the immense old-fashioned fire-place, which occupied a large portion of the side of the spacious kitchen, sat a man called Old Harry (yr hên Harri), who, from some injury, was unable to stand up, and could only move along the floor with his knees raised by means of his hands and feet. Old Harry was a most harmless individual, but he had outlived all his family, and was a proper object for admission into *what was then* a happy home for the innocent and really destitute poor. His pleasure was to be placed on the large stone hob in the recess of the chimney during cold weather, and to sit on the grass under the walnut trees in the warm weather. In the window of this kitchen, a Welsh woman of about fifty spun black wool at a large wheel. She had been for some years in a melancholy and half stupified state of mind; she had no one to

maintain her, and had not sufficient command
of intellect to maintain herself, but as long as
she was provided with wool she was perfectly
happy, and would spin from morning till night
at the large wheel, which gave her exercise as
well as occupation, and which lightened the
expense of her maintenance. A third member
of this comfortable family was a crooked-look-
ing, half-witted boy, called Billo. He might
then have been thirty years of age, but everybody looked upon Billo as a child; he was very
short, but strong and honest, and he was
allowed to go of errands for the neighbours,
and carry small burdens, and assist the good
man and his wife in the various proceedings of
the farm. Billo was a proper object for parish
maintenance, as he also was deficient in bodily
and mental ability to earn his own bread, although he could help those who ministered to
his wants in many ways.

The Hermit added that he also recollected
occasional additions, and a woman with little
children, whose husband had run away from
her, but she was not like a prisoner,—she

might have been supposed to have been a servant of the farm,—cheerful and bustling, she took care of her own children, and was ready to "lend a hand" to anything that was going on ; she was not separated forcibly from any of her family, but she was thankful to find a refuge within reach of her former home in the time of need ; and being near her friends, she was very soon provided for, and enabled to leave the workhouse for service, her relations assisting in the maintenance of her children.

It now strikes me that the friends and relations of persons who are sent to the workhouse would exert themselves, in nine cases out of ten, for the liberation of those within its walls, were all workhouses *within easy reach* of their former homes and connexions. "Out of sight, out of mind," is a true saying. How few relations of those immured in a workhouse *would*, or *could*, go and see their friends, if ten, twenty, or thirty miles off! And how few would fail to do so, from the *weight of public opinion*, (*if not* from affection), when each person in their own locality would know whether they had taken any notice of their distressed friends or relatives, or not!

On this subject I am a convert to the Hermit's theory of the benefit of *small circles,* each centre of which ought to govern its own especial native sphere, all being amenable to general laws; and I certainly read in the newspapers * of the present day enough to know that the workhouses are frequently, if not always, a *frightful conglomeration* of misfortune and misrule, generally accompanied by great cruelty. The management of such establishments can never properly be accomplished by any human beings (however great their talents, and however honest their intentions), without divisions and subdivisions, and the creation and multiplication of expensive departments now

* The appalling disclosures in the *Times* of this year (1866), relative to the sufferings occasioned from the treatment of the sick poor in certain workhouses, had not transpired when the Traveller made this note; these disclosures have since proved that the Hermit did not err in the direful anticipations he entertained of the consequences of the present *monster* system, he *bare outline* of which was described to him by his guest.

unknown! but how much *more* natural, simple, *easier*, and *better* would it be to let *each several locality* have the care of its *own poor*, and thus increase the number of responsible individuals, and render available for the general good the natural interests which must be, more or less, awakened in the mind of each resident for the fate and treatment of his own neighbours, and which can only be secured by having workhouses on a very moderate, not a *monster* scale, calculated for the reception of the paupers of the place who have no moral claim to out-door relief, under the immediate and daily observation of some one or other of the residents of the locality. Doubtless the modern fallacy of supposing that the *bigger* anything is—whether *monster* buildings, or *monster* meetings, or *monster* associations—the better it *must* be, is one of the great mistakes of the present day, which time is constantly developing, and which the Hermit believes will appear more and more palpable as facts are brought to light, to illustrate the study of cause and effect. At present, I could have told him, the aged and honest poor are con-

tinually *forced* into distant Unions, although
they only implore as much relief in money at
home as their maintenance would cost when
taken to the workhouse, but I *did not* tell him
this, because I could not in any way attempt to
defend a practice so totally unjustifiable, and
which ought to be illegal.

OATMEAL.

THE preparation of oatmeal is particularly
well understood in Wales, as well as in Scotland; but, by an extraordinary perversity, the
kilns necessary for its preparation are becoming
very scarce in the Principality, and in many
districts of South Wales the people are beginning to suffer very much from the kilns not
being kept up, or being appropriated to some
other use. Next to *bread* and *good water*, oatmeal may be considered as one of the first
necessaries of life to a rural population; indeed,
in some parts of Wales it still (as in Scotland)
takes the place of bread in many instances; and
when this is not the case, its valuable and

nutritive properties, in sickness and in health, when it is converted into a variety of wholesome and nourishing dishes * by the Welsh, render it to them almost a staff of life; and yet, from the prevalent habit among the higher classes of ignoring or disregarding that which is in their power, many wealthy and philanthropic individuals are perfectly unconscious that the art of preparing oatmeal in Wales may be lost, and in some districts is almost extinct, in consequence of the kiln buildings being otherwise used, while the proprietor is paying a high price for oatmeal from shops which obtain that necessary article from Scotland, the purchaser being totally unconscious that oatmeal could be made to perfection by his own Welsh tenants.

The following amusing recipes for meagre dishes the Hermit allowed me to copy, after a conversation on the unwholesome nature and injurious effects of meagre cookery in general.†

---

* Siccan, Llymru, Uwd, &c.　　　† See p. 179.

DISH OF FROGS.

Take the thighs, and fry them in clarified butter; then have slices of salt eel, watered, flayed, boned, boiled, and cold; slice them in thin slices, and season both with pepper, nutmeg, and ginger: lay butter on your paste, and lay a rank of frog and a rank of eel, some currans, gooseberries or grapes, raisins, pineapple seeds, juyce of orange, sugar, and butter; thus do three times, close up your dish, and, being baked, ice it.

Make your paste of almond, milk, flour, butter, yolks of eggs, and sugar.

In the foresaid dish you may add fryed onions, yolks of hard eggs, cheese-curds, almond-paste, and grated cheese.

TO MAKE A DISH OF MARROW.

Take the marrow of two or three marrow-bones; cut it into pieces like great square dice, and put to it a penny manchet, grated fine, some slic't dates, half a quartern of currans, a little cream, roasted wardens, pippins, or quinces, slic't, and two or three yolks of raw eggs; season them with cinamon, ginger, and sugar, and mingle all together.

DISH OF EGGS.

Take the yolks of twenty-four eggs, and strain them with cinamon, sugar, and salt; then put melted butter to them, some fine minced pippins, and minced citron: put it on your dish of paste, and put slices of citron round about it; bar it with puff paste, and the bottom also, or short paste in the bottom.

TO MAKE A DISH OF CURDS.

Take some very tender curds; wring the whey from them very well; then put to them two raw eggs, currans, sweet butter, rose-water, cinamon, sugar, and mingle all together; then make a fine paste with flour, yolks of eggs, rose-water and other water, sugar, saffron, and

butter, wrought up cold : bake it either in this
paste or in puff-paste ; being baked, ice it with
rose-water, sugar, and butter.*

The above recipes were extracted from a
very curious work in the possession of the
Hermit, by the celebrated Robert May, who
published his " Accomplisht Cook ; or, the Art
and Mystery of Cookery. Dedicated to the
Right Honourable my Lord Mountague, my
Lord Lumley, my Lord Dormer, and the Right
Worshipful Sir Kenelme Digby, so well known
to this nation for their admired hospitalities."
And in the Preface he says, that he values the
" discharge of his own conscience in doing
good " above all the malice of those who
" make it their business to hide their candle
under a bushel ; " and he makes a solemn protest that he " has *not concealed any material
secret* " of which he became possessed in fifty-
five years' experience. He published his work
in the year 1671.

---

* The digestive organs 200 years ago must have been very
much stronger than in 1866, and did much credit to early hours,
air, and exercise.

He was succeeded by William Rabisha, who published his " Cookery Dissected" in 1673, and dedicated his book to " Her Highness the illustrious Duchess of Richmond and Lenox, Her Highness the Duchess of Buckingham, Her Grace the Most Honourable renowned and singular good lady Lady Jane Lane, the Right Honourable good and virtuous Lady Mary Tufton, and the Hon. virtuous and good Lady Agnes Walker; " and, among many wonderful compounds, both meagre, sweet, and savoury, the following, is entitled " *To Potch a Dish of Eggs for a Weak Stomach,*" and gives an idea of *lighter* lenten fare !

TO POTCH A DISH OF EGGS FOR A
WEAK STOMACH.

A handful of good sorrel beaten in a mortar, strained with the juice of a lemon and vinegar; put to it sugar and nutmeg; take sippets, hardened upon a gridiron; lay them on the bottom of your dish, put on them a little strong broth and a spoonful of drawn butter; then pour in your sorrel, and set it on a great heap of coals.

Your eggs, being potched in a little water and salt, take them up, drain from the water, and lay them on your sippets; so cover them, and send them suddenly away. Your sauce must never be hotter on the fire than that you may eat it without cooling again; if you do, it will change the colour of your sorrel, and give your lemon a bad taste.

The following lines from Rabisha's work it ought to be the ambition of every good cook in the present century to *deserve* :—

> " ——— To show the nearest way
> To inform the lowest cook how she may dress
> And make the meanest meat the highest mess ;
> To please the fancy of the daintiest dame,
> And suit her palate, that she praise the same."

LUNCHEON.

I LATELY maintained a fierce argument with the Hermit on the word " Luncheon," which I said was often called " Lunch." The Hermit insisted upon it that no educated person in refined society could possibly talk of " Lunch,"

or " Lunching," but that they must always say
" Luncheon." I assured him that I had heard
persons who, from their birth and rank in life,
might be supposed to belong to refined society,
speak of "*Lunch* " instead of " *Luncheon*," and
of " *Lunching* " instead of " *eating Luncheon*,"
and who said, " *I never Lunch*," instead of " *I
never eat Luncheon.*" My good host, however, maintained that the origin of the word
was from " clutch " or " clunch," the meaning
of which was a *handful*, in contradistinction
to a *full meal*—a small quantity—to appease
hunger when there was no time to sit down to
the table ; and whether he is right or wrong, I
do not pronounce, but it was impossible to help
laughing when he said, " How would it be possible for a refined gentleman when he means to
imply that he has eaten a small quantity of
food in the *forenoon*, to exclaim, '*I clutched*,'
which," (added he,) " he might just as well say
as ' *I lunched.*' Johnson himself quoted Gay as
authority for the word ' *Luncheon.*' "

" I sliced the *luncheon* from the barley loaf ;
With crumbled bread I thicken'd well the mess."

A RAINY DAY.

A LONG conversation upon the waste and mis-management of the present age. The Hermit amused himself with making a calculation, founded upon the account I had given him,* of the number of extra meals and variety of food which it was the fashion to devour in the present day ; and, according to this statement, he said that the *overplus* of food, beyond what was required for health, taken by one individual, would, in one day, be sufficient to maintain one person and a half, giving as much as nature required for health : consequently, in each seven days more than ten human beings might be fed with the extra quantity that is now frequently taken by *one* to the detriment of his own constitution. This calculation was made without reference to the expense of various wines consumed by any one individual in the course of the week; as the Hermit drank nothing but water himself, he could not enter upon the latter point, and I was determined not to assist

* Page 187.

him, indeed, I half repented having given him the details I had already done with regard to eating; but had I supplied him with data upon which to base a calculation of the numbers that might be fed for the value of the quantity of wines which are drunk to the injury of health and the perpetuation of gout, I feared that he would make out so frighful a balance that it would disturb my mind, and I should not be able to sleep at night. I have hitherto taken care not to mention the modern practice of smoking to the Hermit, so very destructive to health; but I hardly suppose my host would believe me, if I gave details on this subject.

CONVERSATION WITH THE HERMIT,

*On the Evils of Artificial Fattening of Cattle, to which he was violently opposed.**

ON referring to the above memorandum, I recollect that the Hermit's objections above recorded were expressed *long before* the outbreak of the Cattle Plague, since which time

* See p. 204.

I have extracted the following passages from the pen of a gentleman * who was qualified, surgically and medically, to pronounce upon the actual consequences, as proved by his professional examination of the wretched animals, which were condemned to suffering and disease, and were in that state pronounced to be first-rate specimens of an art, creditable to science, and to be encouraged for the good of mankind, these poor diseased creatures being afterwards *sold for food!* A calculation of the money and time wasted to produce the diseased meat of each of the prize specimens described in the following paragraphs, would supply a singular balance! And what is the result? *The Cattle Plague!* And who can say that much disease is not produced in human beings (if not the cholera itself) by feeding upon such flesh?

" Certain bodily wants, when ill-suppressed, are soon discovered. The air we breathe may contaminate, but we can often smell, and thereby avoid, an impure atmosphere. Our

---

* On the evil results of over-feeding cattle. By Frederick J. Gant, M.R.C.S. &c. &c.

clothing may be insufficient, but the wintry wind will soon warn us of this deficiency; a bilious head-ache instinctively prompts more active exercise, while fatigue suggests the necessity of repose. Air, temperature, exercise, and sleep are positive hygienic requirements, which severally proclaim their own demand when effective, and thus the tide of life flows smoothly on, each bodily want being wisely suggested by an appropriate, and almost unerring instinctive feeling. But it is otherwise with FOOD. True it is, that we eat when hungry, but this sensation does not prove an infallible guide in our choice of food, still less a criterion of its nutritive quality.

" When visiting the prize animals and others, lately exhibited at the Baker Street Bazaar, I took notes of my observations. One Devon cow looked very ill, and laid her head and neck flat on the ground, like a greyhound. I pointed out these animals to a man who was drawing water, and I asked him if their condition was one of common occurrence. He said, ' I knows nothing of them beasties, in p'ticler, but it's the case with many on 'em—I knows that.'

" I passed on to the pigs. A pen of three pigs happened to be placed in a favourable light for observation, and I particularly noticed their condition. They lay helplessly on their sides, with their noses propped up against each other's backs, as if endeavouring to breathe more easily; but their respiration was loud, suffocating, and at long intervals. Then you heard a short, catching snore, which shook the whole body of the animal, and passed, with the motion of a wave, over its fat surface, which, moreover, felt the cold. I thought how much the *heart*, under such circumstances, must be *labouring* to propel the blood through the lungs, and throughout the body! The *gold medal* pigs were in a similar condition—if anything, worse, for they snored and *gasped* for breath, their mouths being opened, as well as their nostrils dilated, at each inspiration; yet these animals, only twelve months and ten days old, were marked ' *improved* Chilton breed.'

Three pigs, of the black breed, were in a similar state at seven months, three weeks, and five days ; yet such animals the judges ' *highly commend.*'

" When I contrasted the enormous bulk of each animal with the small period in which so much fat, or flesh, had been produced, I naturally indulged in a physiological reflection on the high-pressure work *against time,* which certain vital internal organs, as the stomach, liver, heart, and lungs, must have undergone at a very early age. Now, with the best method of rearing cattle, or that which is most *conducive to their health,* the medical profession are only indirectly concerned; but of the *dietetic value* of animals so reared for food, the profession are, or should be, the immediate overseers and arbitrators.

" These were those to which the judges had awarded the highest prizes, as *specimens* of *healthy* rearing and feeding—viz., *the gold and silver medal prize bullocks, heifers, pigs, and sheep* (which remained in London).

" *This substitution of fat for muscle* is proved by the microscope to have ensued. For when thus examined, the muscular fibres no longer presented their characteristic cross markings, but the fibrillæ within the fibres were entirely broken up, and *replaced* by bright globules of *oily fat*. Each fibre contains an abundance of fat particles instead of fibrillæ within the fibre. The healthy structure of the heart had, therefore, thoroughly *degenerated* by the *substitution* of *fat* for muscle.

" Fortunately, the thin lining membrane (*endocardium*) had not been ruptured, or the animal would have *died instantly*. This might have happened at any moment, on the slightest exertion.

" *This animal, under three years of age, weighed upwards of two hundred stone, and was eating twenty-one pounds of oil-cake a day, besides other food.*

" Within about a foot of the termination of the large bowel was a putty-like mass, one inch and a half thick and about one foot long, and which partially surrounded the intestine. The mass consisted, apparently, of *scrofulous matter.*

" The fat referred to may itself be regarded as the superfluous food with which the animal had been gorged.

" The diseased condition thus produced may be termed *conversion* into fat, as expressive of the *apparent* change which has ensued ; but, on closer examination with the microscope, I would ascribe the change itself to the *substitution* of fat (in the process of nutrition), for the *proper* structural elements—fibrillæ—of muscle, and not to the actual transformation of those elements into fat.

" We should, therefore, expect in vain to replenish our own muscles by the use of such food, nor should animals thus overfed be regarded as prize specimens of rearing and feeding. The heart being *converted into fat*, no longer retains its contractile power, but beats feebly and irregularly. The blood, therefore, now moves onward in a slow and feeble current. Hence the panting breathlessness due to stagnation of blood in the lungs, which the heart labours (in vain) to remove, while the skin and extremities are cold : hence the stupid heavy-headed expression of a congested brain, and the *blood-stained* appearance of meat after death. The slightest exertion of an animal under such circumstances might suddenly prove fatal. Were a man in this condition to present himself at an insurance office, it would *refuse* to insure his life at *any premium. Yet under similar circumstances a sheep is awarded gold and silver medals, and its feeder a prize of 20l. !*

" Under the present system the public have no guarantee, and are not ensured the best if indeed the cheapest food. The bulky withers of a fat bullock are no criterion of health, and its flat tabular back may conceal the revolting ravages of disease.

" The flesh of animals which has been produced by organs themselves diseased, is itself

Y

also necessarily *deteriorated,* and ought not to be regarded as prime samples of human food. These facts will be best understood by pathologists, but they also come home to the understandings, and certainly to the *stomachs* of *the people.* Nor can their feelings fail to respond to the claims of sympathy. The suffocating sighs of those fat pigs are an appeal to humanity.

" If offence come out of truth, it were better that the offence come, than that the truth be concealed."

MEM.*—Conversation with the Hermit about clipping horses, of which he had never heard. He was at a loss for the reasons which could have induced such an extraordinary proceeding. I *would* not tell him what I believed was the original cause, because it would have furnished him with another argument against the great progress of intellect in the present century, but I *do* believe that the real origin of clipping in the first instance was that horses might *appear* to be kept

---

* Page 215.

in what is called " high condition," although belonging to owners who could not afford such expense, but that the practice gained ground from the approval of the majority of those whose duty it was to clean horses, and whose labour was thereby much diminished, and specious arguments were made use of to persuade masters that the animals themselves benefited by such a course of treatment, as the majority of masters possibly do not know how horses ought to be treated any better than the majority of mistresses of families (who have cooks) know how to instruct them to prepare food—but had I said this to the Hermit he would have asked me whether I considered that the stable management in Great Britain generally was more indicative of the improvement of human intelligence than the culinary department in the nineteenth century? In which case I must have answered " No," and subjected myself to additional mortification.

WATER-FOUNTAINS.*

Mem.—Being fearful that I might have exaggerated the destitution of London with respect to water, I have, through a friend (while
still in the cell of St. Gover) referred to docu-
ments belonging to the Metropolitan Free
Drinking Fountain Association, which was
established in 1859, and I find that I might
have said much more, although I should have
only thereby confirmed the Hermit's opinion
that the progress of science has completely out-
run the progress of the cultivation of *sense!*

There were no public drinking fountains in
London till April, 1859. The water used in
the metropolis amounts to one hundred millions
of gallons, and, if formed into one reservoir,
would form a lake seventy acres in extent, and
six feet deep; yet every drop of this enormous
supply must be paid for to water-companies,
who, although by mechanical means they force
water into the houses, make *no provision* for
the wants of the multitudes who traverse the

* See page 224.

streets, and who are as much in want of a draught of water as the travellers of the desert. The resident poor suffer grievously in consequence of an intermittent supply of water, and the absence of free public street supplies ; and, although water-pipes are brought into the houses, it is turned on but once a day, seldom exceeding, and often for less than, half an hour ; and if they have any lack of vessels, or an accident occurs in spilling the water supplied during that short period, they must go *without water* till the next day, as it is *illegal even to buy it from any but the companies*—persons *giving water*, or *selling it* may be *prosecuted !* and every *drop of water* caught by the poor during the precious half hour that it is supplied after being kept in the fœtid atmosphere of a crowded dwelling, soon *becomes poisonous*, and water, which should be a preservative to life and health, is an actual source of fever and death. Under such circumstances, the pumps of London were the only places where many of the poor could obtain water to drink, which were few in number, and at great distances from each other, and in the investigation made of late years as to the cause of the epidemics which spread death and desolation in so many homes, the mischief was found to arise *as frequently* from the *water drunk* as from the air breathed, and the London pump-water was declared to be so impregnated with impure matter from the impurities of foul surrounding soil, that it was almost universally condemned. The Medical Officer of Health for the city of London * stated, that of thirty-six pumps in the City, scarcely one supplied water fit to drink, and the poor were left to choose between the poisonous water in the pumps, and the poisonous water stored up in their own tanks and cisterns.

The *only remedy* was public free drinking fountains, first established in London by Mr. Samuel Gurney, by whom the first drinking fountain was erected on Snow Hill in 1859, at which as many as five thousand people were known to drink in one day. Since 1859, eighty-nine drinking fountains, five cattle troughs, and some dog troughs have been

* Dr. Letheby.

opened by the Society, in addition to which between thirty and forty have been erected in London by private benevolence; and it is estimated in London alone more than *three hundred thousand people* drink daily at these fountains. But yet there are *whole parishes* still *without a single fountain,* and the sufferings that a vast multitude must still experience from thirst, and the horrible results to thousands now ruined in body and soul, occupants of lunatic asylums and prisons, whose state has been caused by being *forced* into public houses and gin palaces to supply their *daily thirst,* is dreadful to contemplate in a Christian country, whilst the sufferings of the poor cattle, sheep, and dogs, are intolerable from the want of supplies of drinking troughs for animals; and the subscriptions of charitable individuals are not sufficient to do a tithe of the work which is still required to place fresh water within the reach of all the poor in London, to whom, as well as to every other class, the sight of running water is in itself a gratification. Running water also serves to clear away any obstruction which might otherwise choke up the overflow pipe, and any supply of water which could only be obtained by turning a cock would *not* answer the purpose required.

A force of police is required specially to protect the fountains, for, in the present corrupt and demoralized state of society, constant supervision is necessary to preserve them from injury. Drunken men are their determined enemies, cups are stolen and taken away, sticks are thrust into the jet, and stones, pipe, rope, buttons, and orange-peel are also frequently used to render them inconvenient or useless, and thus it has been found that fountains erected in London by private benevolence have been so injured that the charitable donors have found they must submit to the expense of keeping their fountains in order, or see their good intentions defeated. The fountains in the care of the Society are alone rendered a permanent blessing by the visits of their own officers of the Society, who regularly inspect them, report their condition, and have damages immediately repaired.

An interesting article by Dr. Wynter contains the whole history of the water supply of London, from the time when the metropolis was interspersed with meadows, and supplied with water from its bournes, its viaducts, and its wells; and when the Thames was a clear river, free from all the impurities that have now converted it *into one great sewer*, until Peter Morris, the Dutchman, obtained a right from the Corporation of London to erect machinery for that purpose in 1580, after which Sir Hugh Middleton proposed to bring a new river into London, from the springs of Chadwell and Amwell, a distance of forty-two miles, when no forcing apparatus was made use of, which system continued till 1782, when water-pipes were carried underground in every direction, and forced up to the top stories, since which time eight water-companies supply the metropolis, and

> " Water, water, everywhere;
> But not a drop to drink."

When the Legislature forced all the water-companies supplying themselves from the

Thames, higher up the stream, it never anticipated the evils which are now apparent. The towns on the banks of the Thames above the highest sources from which any of the water-companies now obtain their supplies, have obtained permission to *drain directly into the river*, and, instead of going up the stream to get nearer the pure element, they are only meeting the refuse and drainage of these towns half-way.

N.B. I *dared not* tell the Hermit that I had heard before I ever saw him, that the favourite and fashionable theory now promulgated, for curing all the evils entailed by want of water in London, is to convey the pure element from the Bala Lake, in North Wales, into the metropolis,—of course *without* the slightest regard to the *robbery* of the *Principality*, or of the injury (to say nothing of the disfigurement) which would result to the inhabitants of that beautiful locality, and were the scheme *not* so very wild, were the expense *not* so very enormous, and were the distance *not* so very great, there would be a probability that it might not be attempted! but as it appears to involve every possible objection, there is cause for the greatest alarm, as the disposition of the present generation is to revel in the excitement of undertakings, which are certain to ruin their projectors, and to materially injure a large portion of the rest of mankind.

Dr. Wynter, however, has committed himself to the opinion, that London may rival Glasgow, which is said to have the purest water in the world, without robbing poor Wales, or going to the enormous expense of bringing water from a Lake in the Principality to London, as water may be had of a pure quality, and in abundant supply, from the gathering grounds which supply the town of Farnham in Surrey. If this is the case, the Hermit might justly say, it is another proof of the proneness of the present age of education and science, to go a hundred miles out of the way, and to spend a thousand times more than is necessary to obtain what is, comparatively speaking, to be found close at hand, but which for that reason is not valued.

The curse of London is certainly want of water, and drunkenness! How has this curse been brought upon London? By the *voluntary acts of mankind!* by the want of reflection, and the consequent misapplication of mechanical talent, under the name of " *Improvements,*" in the nineteenth century.

It seems to me, *since I have begun to think,* that there are several words which have been so long and continually used in the wrong sense, that people are in danger of forgetting their real signification, viz. the destruction of fine old churches, and the construction of modern paltry buildings on their site, is called " *Restoration;* " whilst the words " Ignorance " or " Barbarism," are now applied to those who have retained the knowledge transmitted by their ancestors, of the useful arts of every-day life. Sophistication is called *education,* and a " *superior education* " implies the wilful neglect of instruction in all useful knowledge.

HOLLY—MISTLETOE—IVY.*

In a conversation with the Hermit, in which I gave him some idea of Arboriculture (as at present practised) in many "*highways* and *byways*," especially as connected with Holly in hedges, I omitted to mention the barbarous and ignorant practice (where a standard holly *has* been preserved) of cutting all the branches off close to the stem, up to the top, where a few boughs only are permitted to remain, giving that beautiful tree exactly the appearance of a *besom* set up on end, and which disfigurement is incurable, because the holly-tree never puts out new branches when cut close to the stem.

It is very strange that the propagation of the MISTLETOE is not better understood — its beauty, independent of its medical properties,† as well as its traditional and historical interests, ought to cause its natural history to be more studied, and, consequently, better known; but perhaps it is less extraordinary that this

---

* Page 235. † See Appendix No. XLVII.

should have been neglected than that the Ivy, which, in all its beautiful varieties, is more or less known in every part of Great Britain, should be the object of such *universal persecution*. The Hermit mentioned a fact relating to the ivy, with which I was previously unacquainted, and which I do not believe is generally known, although it is in the power of everybody to see and observe, viz., that when it attains a certain age, and is peculiarly ornamental to the tree on which it hangs, it *ceases* to throw out feelers; consequently, that the outcry that when ivy is old its stem must be cut through, or it will *destroy the tree*, is one of the most remarkable hallucinations of the present age. When ivy is old, it *ceases* to be attached to the stem round which it is twisted, excepting by its folds, which are so completely loose from the stem of the tree that a hand may be frequently passed between the ivy and the tree, while the upper boughs are supported by festoons from branch to branch; consequently, if the ivy is merely thinned sufficiently *above* (when it becomes top-heavy), to prevent too great a weight upon the small boughs of the tree, it cannot in any way injure the tree; and yet ivy, in the state above described, appears to be a favourite mark for the axe to sever. The Hermit pointed out to me several beautiful evergreen trees in the winter, which at a distance I did not identify to be ivy, and I wondered what bright and shining standard evergreens thus enlivened his wood; but he explained that these verdant objects were simply produced by planting ivy (or preserving it when wild) to grow up dead trees, which, being at length entirely covered, resembled standard evergreens of the most brilliant tint. I agree with the Hermit that a series of experiments might be made, with interesting and useful results, to ascertain at what age ivy *ceases* to adhere to the tree against which it grows,—also, the different characteristics of the various sorts of ivy. The Hermit is of opinion that the *very diminutive* wild ivy, which grows especially on walls, the stem of which seldom attains any bulk, and which forms a beautiful network all over the stones, is a great preservative to mason-work, and ought to be specially planted and encouraged against park-walls, in preference to the ivy, generally called Irish, which, however, is not believed to be indigenous in that country.

ROADS, HEDGES, AND BANKS.*

I HAVE had a conversation with the Hermit, on the present frequent *mis*management, and actual *destruction* of live fences, on the sides of high-ways and byways, but he was so anxious that I should return to my lessons in the *culinary* art, that he did not then give me time to tell him the anecdote I was about to narrate, of the discovery of a friend of mine, as to the immediate cause of the miserable system by which the banks, on the sides of roads, are so maltreated, that the hedges and roadside timber are frequently *undermined ;* but he afterwards requested me to write it down, and to illustrate it with my pencil,✝ and expressed his opinion that if I placed the narra-tive in my Note Book, with the sketches, it

---

* See page 238.   ✝ See Plate VIII.

PLATE VIII.

HIGHWAYS AND BYEWAYS, WITH BANKS, HEDGES, AND WATER;
or,
Safety and comfort, shade and shelter, for Bipeds and Quadrupeds.

might some day be of service to those whose property is annually destroyed, while the public safety is endangered, but who either have not opened their eyes to see the evil done, or their understandings to prevent it.

My friend was a landholder, of considerable property, who, having gone abroad for his health, had heard nothing of what had taken place in his own parish for more than twelve months, and on his return he could scarcely recognise the roads around his home. When he went away, there was fine roadside timber, including splendid hollies, and substantial hedges, growing on firm and solid banks—when he returned, it appeared as if an *invading army* had devastated the whole of the environs. The fine and flourishing hedges were cut down to within a short distance of the top of the bank, so as to remove every impediment to bipeds or quadrupeds going over it with ease. The previous winter had been very severe, and the snow had frozen on the small remnant of growing sprays left, so that few and sickly shoots had been brought forth in the summer,

z

which shoots had been quickly disposed of by the cattle and sheep, who, after they had eaten up the few leaves left, amused themselves with looking over into the road, and occasionally making a descent upon it, over the slight obstacles in their way, which an active boy could have cleared with one bound; and which the quadrupeds walked over, or burst through with the greatest ease.[*]

My friend was shocked and distressed by the general disfigurement, and the aspect of barren misery which such a prospect entailed; but being a person of intelligence, he soon discovered that it was *not alone* by wilful and ill-judged cutting down, that such a very rapid decadence of hedges had been produced, but that the *banks* had been *cut away,* and pared down, and *scooped into,* in such a manner, that the natural nourishment of the hedges had been abstracted; and with regard to the hedge-timber, the excavation of the banks had been carried on to such an excess, that the trees had been undermined, and their roots cut through and exposed on the side next the road; whilst

Plate IX.

PLATE IX.

THE DANGERS OF HIGHWAYS AND BYEWAYS WHERE HEDGES AND BANKS ARE NOT FENCES;

or,

A Picture of Peril and Desolation from the destruction of shade and shelter.

the banks in other places being sliced down per-
pendicularly, the roots of the hedge-timber, as
well as the live hedges, were not only visible to
the naked eye, but protruded in some instances,
horizontally, three or four inches beyond the
surface of the soil.

My friend followed up his investigations,
until he made out that in his locality, the
following causes had led to these most lament-
able results, and to injuries, which could not
be remedied for many years, so as to restore or
renew what had been so wantonly destroyed.
The causes were as follows :—

The farmers were annoyed by the unusual stir
which had followed the appointment of new
road surveyors ; and though they might not have
been totally insensible to the disfigurement of
their premises, were certainly more keenly aware
of the time that had been occupied in cutting
down their fences, according to the orders of
the new officers, which officers seemed to have
had but one idea, viz. that the more completely
the hedges were destroyed, and the roads rendered unsightly, and destitute of shade or

shelter, the greater would be the appearance
of their own activity, and the greater credit
they would obtain.   Of the *roads* themselves,
very little notice was taken, excepting to allow
those employed upon them, to excavate gutters
under the banks, and to scrape as much of the
surface away from the *sides* of the road, as to
render them so convex as to occasion frequent
overturns, when vehicles passed each other in
the dark,—in short to imitate the shape of a
saucer turned upside down.

My friend was convinced that some party or
parties must have an especial motive for these
latter proceedings, which were equally subver-
sive of the interests of the public, and positively injurious to private individuals, and he
found that the explanation of the whole was
as follows. The roads had long been neglected,
but the hedges were excellent, though they
might have been in some places a little too
redundant, and required the moderate pruning
of any sprays which protruded over the road
so as to interfere with loaded corn-waggons.
An outcry for mending the roads was raised in

the neighbourhood. The new officials ("*high-ways*" and "*byways*") found the repairs needed (viz. picking up and stoning and making coffer gutters) troublesome, expensive, and tedious, and they thought that if they could produce a rapid transformation by means of cutting down hedges and making *brooms* of the roadside timber, this startling effect would, by the sudden change, impress the public with the reality of " great improvement." Moreover, as they ordered the farmers to be the executioners of their own hedges, their destruction involved no expense, and did not create any extra items in the books,—another advantage so far as the officials were concerned, but the misplaced industry of the race so called " road-menders," was *not* solely attributable to the supervisors, but also to the blindness of the farmers themselves to their own interests, having forgotten the old adage of " robbing Peter to pay Paul," as he discovered that the farmers often gave money or beer to the road-menders (employed by the Highway or By-way surveyors) for slicing down the banks next the road upon which their own hedges grew, by which they believed they were enriching themselves by means of their *enemy's troops*, whereas for every cartload of soil thus obtained by the loss of the banks, they entailed upon themselves the expense of incessant mending and repairing hedges *until quite dead*, and afterwards of keeping up a dead fence without any " tenet " * at hand. It was truly " killing the goose with the golden egg," for between the road-surveyors and road-menders and farmers, the Irish notice might have been practically rivalled, and instead of the sign-post in the Emerald Isle, which announced that " The *improvements* on Market Hill rendered the roads *impassable*," there might have been a notice, " Beware of bulls and other horned animals, as in consequence of the repair of the roads, all live fences have been destroyed and all banks carried away or undermined."

This anecdote, I fear, is not a solitary instance, nor is it exaggerated, but the Hermit laughed aloud when he heard it, and said, gaily,

---

* A word used for the loppings of brushwood used to repair dead hedges.

" What can you expect but *such improvements*
as long as a modern education is confined to
the various arrangements of the letters of the
alphabet, without thought or reflection or
any regard to palpable facts under the eye?
Do you suppose that if any three persons
(or perhaps one) in your friend's neighbourhood, had used either their eyes or understandings, and resolutely and perseveringly opposed this destructive mischief while in its
course, on its *true grounds*—that it could not
have been stopped? Of *course it could*, but it
seems, by your own account, that half the
world are blind, and the other half cripples, in
mind at all events, if not in body."

WALL-FLOWERS.

I have observed that the top of every wall
near the Hermit's abode is surmounted by wall-
flowers, the wild single sort, which are always
the most fragrant, and among which an endless
variety of tints are observable from the young
plants which spring up spontaneously every

year, self-sown afresh, and the Hermit pointed
out some of a violet colour, so that had I not
examined the flowers, I should have believed
they belonged to another species of plant; but
my host confessed that although wall-flowers
grew wild in the locality of his abode, that he
had saved the seeds and sown, not only the tops
of *all* his own walls, but those of *all* his neighbours, which proceeding, he added, had produced the greatest amount of innocent pleasure
to the greatest number of persons at the
smallest expense and trouble, of anything that
he had ever done. He added that this idea
had originated from reflecting upon the bountiful supplies of Providence with regard to wild
flowers, of which, he was surprised to find from
my statements that so little was thought in the
present great world, and that many valuable
species of plants were almost extinct from
being persecuted as weeds, and he thought he
would try the above experiment where at all
events no one would be injured. Its success
was beyond his expectations, and not only did
he himself revel in the increased beauty and

fragrance of his wild *wall-garden*, but he was gratified to find that his poorer neighbours, in fact every one who passed within sight or smell of these delightful flowers, expressed their gratification. A year or two afterwards he added the seeds of the red and yellow antir-hinum (or snapdragon), which had succeeded equally well, and added to the beauty of his wild wall garden without requiring any other nourishment than that bestowed by heaven.

SHEEP'S MILK.

I confess that when the Hermit first told me that his best cheese owed its superiority to the addition of sheep's milk, I thought he was jesting; and although I saw the ewes being milked, and admired the Arcadian scene, I supposed, in my ignorance, that the milk was to *feed the calves!* But I am now fully aware that the milk of that valuable animal (the Welsh sheep), when mingled with that of the cow, produces cheese which is not only excellent to eat new, but, when old, is more like Parmesan than anything else I ever tasted.

The following are memoranda of facts relative to the Hermit's flock of Welsh sheep :—

His lambs were sold when I was with him, about the beginning of July, at 1*l*. each, being then from three to four months old. The ewes were then milked for three months. They were twenty-four in number, and they gave on an average twenty-four quarts a day. The proportions for cheese were one quart o ewe's milk to five quarts of cow's milk, and six quarts of ewe's milk to thirty quarts of cow's milk made a cheese, weighing from twelve to fourteen pounds, of a most superior quality, with the sharpness so much admired in Parmesan. Some of these ewes became so fat after they were dried in October, that when they were killed at Christmas, their weight was from fourteen to fifteen pounds a quarter, and the mutton of the very finest flavour. Of course there was *no stall-feeding*, or *confinement*, or *quackery* with artificial food, but only pastures, often changed, and a good shed to run into at pleasure. The Hermit seldom or ever lost a lamb, but his sheep were supplied with chaff and cut roots in winter, when there was not sufficient grass to support them well.

To give an idea of the profit of Welsh sheep when properly managed, I have made a note of the profits of ten of the Hermit's Welsh wethers, which were *bought* the *latter end of March*, and sold the beginning of the following May; their price was 1*l.* 10*s.*, and they were sold at 2*l.* off turnips. It is also to be remembered that the Welsh wool is a very fine quality, and peculiarly well adapted for cloth as well as flannel, and those native Welsh cottagers who are still wise enough to make use of their wool-wheels, produce a home-spun cloth which, like the brocades of old, is so durable that they may almost be considered as heir-looms. The home-knit Welsh stockings of the black Welsh sheep's wool, are also very superior, and do not need any dye. I also observed that the Hermit's flock was so tame that they followed the shepherd about, and some of them would eat out of his hand, and on remarking that I had always been told the Welsh sheep were so wild that it was impossible to keep them within bounds, I was informed that there was not the slightest inconvenience in keeping Welsh sheep if they were *properly managed*, but that if purchasers chose to go to Welsh fairs or markets, and bought sheep of different flocks, drove them to a strange place, and then took no precautions to reconcile them to their new locality, they would be very likely to find the next morning that their sheep had all disappeared in different directions ; but that if a flock was purchased that had been accustomed to live together, and if they were at first placed in a well-fenced pasturage with plenty to eat, they would soon become reconciled to the change, but when born and brought up on the same spot, they never wished to stray. In short, it appears that Welsh sheep exactly resemble the Scotch Highland cattle—if untamed, untended, uncared for, they are as unmanageable as wild beasts, but when domesticated they are mild, docile, and have no inclination to wander. The Welsh sheep certainly is one of the most *symmetrical* animals I ever beheld, and appears to particular advantage when black, their arched necks, slender legs, small, compact, and well-proportioned, bodies, their long graceful tails, and picturesque curling horns, with their soft dark fleeces and brilliant dark eyes, would render them fit studies for Rosa Bonheur.

GOATS.

THE Hermit's Welsh Goats were differently managed to those I have seen on the Continent, and they are much handsomer animals than the foreign goats, with which I am acquainted. It is surprising that no specimen of the real Welsh goat is preserved in the Zoological Gardens. The Welsh goat being an aboriginal of Britain, ought to be specially protected, whereas it appears that the breed is likely to become extinct. The gallant regiment of the Welsh Fusiliers ought to protest against this neglect of an animal which has always been associated with Welsh regiments and the Principality of Wales.

The Welsh goat has a very picturesque appearance, from its long coat and beautifully formed head. There are two species equally aboriginal; one with magnificent horns, and the other without horns. The Hermit had both kinds, and he made a point of keeping as many as he could without horns, because they were not dangerous to the numerous peasant children who were continually playing with them. The Hermit said that his goats certainly had a predilection for the bark of young trees, and he therefore for many years had adopted the plan of tethering them. Each goat was provided with a leather collar and chain, one end of which was attached by a ring to the leather strap which forms the collar, and at the other end there was a ring which was fastened to the ground by a sharp wooden hook. The goats seemed perfectly happy, their chains were very long, and they were moved twice or thrice a day. They were always brought into a large

yard at night, where they were left at perfect
liberty, with an open shed where they had prun-
ings of shrubs or vegetables or anything that was
convenient, given them to eat. The she-goat
gives when in full milking *more* than *two quarts*
a day. The value of their milk for children
and invalids has been admitted in all ages ; their
milk makes excellent cheese alone, without the
mixture of any other, and the whey is particularly nourishing and wholesome, as well as the
curd which is produced a second time from
boiling the whey. Kids are always marketable,
being excellent food, and their skins very valuable.

FEATHERS.

THE Hermit had a great horror of a feather
bed, which, he said, had been caused by observation of the dreadful consequences to invalids,
or those who were bedridden, of lying in a *hot
hollow*, instead of having a flat cool elastic surface to repose upon, and likewise from knowing that feathers caused, absorbed, and retained

perspiration, and consequently that under any circumstances they were the most objectionable material that could be selected, either for health or convenience, to be lain upon by rich or poor. Feathers, however, seemed to be very much valued in his establishment, and they were carefully preserved and cured in the following manner.

All the feathers were plucked into empty boxes, kept in an outer building, and it was the business of an aged widow, who had nothing to do with the culinary department, as soon as her box was full, to put them into a large high tub which had previously been filled with lime-water, made by putting hot lime into another tub overnight, and filling it up with water, stirring it well, and leaving it to stand for twelve hours, after which, the lime being precipitated to the bottom, the clear lime-water was poured off into the tub in which the feathers were to be immersed, and which being stirred round with a stick, were left to soak for four and twenty hours, at the end of which time the quill of every feather would have burst or cracked at the end in which the animal oil is contained, which has so offensive and unhealthy a smell in feathers imperfectly cured. The feathers were then taken out and put into common washing-tubs, where they were washed in warm water with a little soft soap, and then a sheet being spread over a large empty tub, the water with the feathers was ladled out into the sheet, and the water having drained away, the feathers were placed thinly upon a dry sheet, which was put upon a square frame (or *cratch*) composed of thin strips of wood nailed together, and fixed on the top of four upright sticks in the sun (if in summer), or else suspended to four hooks fastened in the ceiling of the Hermit's kitchen in winter. As soon as the feathers were dry, they were taken away by the featherwife, who stripped them, cutting off the hard part of the quill with a pair of scissors, and by practice she was so expert, she almost mechanically placed in their respective heaps the finer and the coarser down, which at the end of the day she put in paper bags and hung along the beam of the ceiling.

A A

This occupation is particularly well adapted for old women, who can sit near a fire, and pursue this employment in the winter, as a means of subsistence. The Hermit had a little building on purpose, where there was a good fireplace, and a long beam for the feather-bags; the contents of which were perfectly sweet, and as downy and *fluffy*, as if they had never been wetted. They were appropriated to making quilts for the winter and pillows.

The Hermit said that it was not from the custom of his country he had learnt this, as he must admit that the Welsh were *too fond* of feather-beds; but that although he did not wish to introduce the *rolling balloons* of the Germans, called Eider-down quilts, he thought that much gratitude was due to that nation, for the sensible idea of putting feathers over instead of under human beings in the winter.

The Hermit's bedsteads had strips of wood at the bottom (*no sacking*), on these were placed a very deep, but very soft mattress, filled with oat-straw, or beech-leaves, but not those dreadful inventions, called by the French name of

" *Palliasse,*" although never seen in that country. These mattresses had two openings in the seams, by which means the straw or leaves could be levelled by the hand every day, and the contents could be changed every year, or oftener if necessary, in the course of half an hour. Over a mattress of this description, a wool mattress was placed, with a small quantity of horse-hair, mixed with the wool in the centre, to increase the firmness and elasticity. Feather pillows completed the equipment of the bedding ; and the upper, as well as the lower mattresses, were all made at home, and consequently easily re-made when necessary.

MOLES.

These little animals were special favourites of the Hermit, who said that they ought to be preserved for their utility, as well as protected for their harmlessness. He considered that their hillocks, of the finest earth, were an excellent top-dressing for grass, and that half the

money spent in paying mole-catchers would be
much more profitably bestowed in paying for
spreading the mole-hills at dawn of day. I
suggested that if moles were never destroyed,
they might become so numerous as to get into
his garden, and throw up their mounds over
the young plants. He said, in that case they
must be kept under and it would be only necessary to kill them in certain restricted localities,
and these would be exceptional, but that the
usual way of trapping them by letting them
fall into deep empty boxes, out of which they
could not crawl, and leaving them to die of
famine, was a disgrace to humanity. The
Hermit did not like my remark that their fur
was as fine, if not finer, than sealskin, as he
was afraid it might lead to a still further destruction of his favourite little underground
ploughmen, and insect - destroyers ; and, he
added, if the undeniable talent for mechanics
which characterised the present age had not
yet invented a merciful method of putting
these innocent little animals to death when *no*
benefit was derived by their flesh or skins, that

nothing was to be expected but an increase of cruelty, if any profit was to be obtained from the latter. I informed him of the existence of the excellent Society for the " Prevention of Cruelty to Animals," and he asked me, " how it was that all these years it had *forgotten the moles ?* " which question I could not answer.

BEES.

THE Hermit has a large establishment of bees, to which industrious insects he is not only particularly partial, but he has a sort of respect, I might almost say *reverence*, for them, which is very general among his country-men, and which surprised *me*, although he appeared to be *as much* surprised at my know-ing so little about their habits or their treatment; but still I was able to inform him that there were in England many scientific Apiarians, who had made the treatment of bees their especial study. He asked me whether the study had led to a great increase of bee-keepers in England

generally, but I told him that the houses or
boxes recommended for their abode were so
very expensive, and required such very neat
joiners' or cabinet-makers' work, that it was
impossible to expect that any but those in
affluent circumstances could keep bees; this
unfortunate remark has brought a storm down
upon my devoted head, as I unfortunately
furnished my host with a new argument in
support of his opinion, that everything he hears
from me proves that the present age is anything
but an age of common sense.

There is, however, no doubt that the
Hermit's bees thrive remarkably well, and that
so far from their houses or their management
being complicated or expensive, they are neither
one nor the other; and for the benefit of my
friends, I have made sketches of the hives,*
which are all double, a small one at the top,
and a large one at the bottom. It appears that
the bees fill the top hive for the Hermit, and
make further provision for themselves in the
lower hive.

---

* See Plate No. X.

PLATE X.

No. 1. Top Hive (on its Mat), 6 inches high, and 10 inches diameter.
2. Mat, 11 inches diameter ; Hole, 2 inches in circumference.
3. Lower Hive (without Top Hive), 11 inches high, 16 inches in diameter, with Hoop 3 inches wide.
4. Lower and Upper Hive together, Mortared round the Hoop.
5. Wooden Scoop.
6. Jug for Keeping Bees' Winter Food, with Flat Top to be tied over. TOTAL VALUE OF THE WHOLE . . 4s.

In the month of July, the Hermit takes off the top hive, which is generally full of the finest honeycomb. He replaces it with another the same size, leaving the contents of the lower hive undisturbed. The lower hive has a flat top, with an extra round of straw on the outer rim, within which the upper hive fits, and the hole in the centre of the top of the lower hive admits the bees from one to the other. There is a simple hoop of wood at the bottom of each of the lower hives, which the Hermit had neatly mortared round outside, so that there could be no egress into the hive, for any insects besides the bees themselves, who entered by one small aperture cut purposely in the hoop. Everything else was made of straw, worked in the usual beehive fashion, roll upon roll of straw, fastened together with strips of thin willow.

The Hermit had fifty double hives. I requested one of the widows to weigh a small top hive *empty*, and another of the same size *full*. The empty hive weighed one pound and a half; the full hives six pounds and a half; consequently at the rate of five pounds for the owner's share, my host's bees produced an average of two hundred and fifty pounds of honeycomb, all filled with the purest honey, for there never is either bee-bread or young bees in the upper hives.   I was informed that there is no absolute necessity for the round mat of straw which I observed under each of the top hives, though it was convenient and useful, as the hive was more easily lifted off without disturbing the bees below, in a manner which would *not* be the case if the upper hive rested only on the top of the lower hive, without having any independent platform; and as bees carefully fill up every crevice which admits light, or might give admission to insects, the upper hive is generally cemented round the edge to whatever it is placed upon, and therefore to take it off suddenly produces a great wrench and disturbance throughout the establishment, entirely avoided by the little mat, which, having a hole in the middle answering to the hole in the top of the lower hive, admits the bees from one to the other.   When the bees swarmed, they were hived in the lower hive, and the hole at the top had a cork in it; but the evening after (if they had settled quietly) the cork was withdrawn, and the top hive with its mat put in its proper place, and as soon as the bees were thoroughly at home, the hoop of the lower hive was mortared round with a trowel, after dark, a piece of white paper, pricked full of holes, being placed over the entrance attached by four pins to the hoop (while the above operation was performed), to prevent the bees from coming out.

The Hermit's bees were always fed from the month of November, till the spring blossoms rendered it no longer necessary. Their food was so inexpensive that the Hermit never permitted the question of their being sufficiently provided with their own honey to prevent their having the offer of *supper* every night, during the period above mentioned, as he said that, if they did not require it, they would not eat it, but it very seldom happened that they did not take the whole quantity, except in very hard frosts, when they are in a state of torpor.

Their food consisted of treacle, in the proportion of one teacupful to two of water, boiled together, in a jug plunged in a saucepan of boiling water, with as much salt sprinkled in as gave it the very slightest saline flavour.* This mixture was kept in jugs with narrow spouts and flat tops, over which thick brown paper was tied, to keep out the dust; and every night two of the widows went to each hive, with a candle, the jug of boiled treacle and water, and scoops made of elder or other wood, which they placed in the mouth of each hive, leaving the portion outside which was not hollowed. They filled each scoop with as much of the prepared food as the cavity would hold without overflowing. The first thing in the morning the scoops were withdrawn, and, being well washed, were put to dry in the house, on a shelf, till the following night. If the bees left any of their food in the scoop, it was not washed out, but withdrawn during the day, and replaced the next night in the hive from which it had been taken.

---

* Appendix No. XLVIII.

When the spring is sufficiently advanced for the bees no longer to require food in the hive, they will not take it; but as the weather is very uncertain, and the sun and a few flowers may tempt them out for two or three days, after which a change may take place, to prevent their obtaining any food abroad, the Hermit's widows were frequently obliged to recommence feeding between the end of February and April. The Hermit explained that feeding the bees not only kept them strong and vigorous, but that it saved a great deal of time with regard to their labours in the spring; as, if they had a good stock of honey for their own use, they begun the sooner to work for their master, and in good years the top hive may be changed twice between June and September.

The Hermit was very indignant at the idea of joiner's work or cabinet-maker's work being necessary to make houses for bees; and he said there was no greater mistake than to suppose that bees could only thrive under one aspect; — that a little observation might convince any one interested in the subject that bees will thrive in various aspects, provided they are sheltered from wind, and they have easy access to pure but shallow water, where they can drink without danger of being drowned; also that where the locality will not admit of a safe watering-place for the bees, fresh water should be placed twice or thrice a day in shallow pans, in the shade, near the bee-house, which, if possible, should have a projecting roof of stone-tile to screen them well from the rays of the sun.

A little penthouse of this description, built against the wall, with the ends boarded or bricked up with a shelf from end to end (which shelf ought to be about an inch from the back wall), is quite sufficient for all useful purposes connected with bees. If stone-tile cannot be had, the roof should have double boards as a protection against the sun, and it should be plastered inside, and whitewashed inside and out every year, and frequently swept between the hives and examined, to see that no ants or snails, or other insects or reptiles, have taken up their abode in the bees' dominions, which is often the cause of their deserting their hives.

While I was with the Hermit, the widows were terrified one morning, at seeing a long black tail, and part of a black body, at the entrance hole of one of the hives, and I then had ocular demonstration of what before I never believed, viz. that mice *would* venture to interfere with bees, as a mouse attracted by the smell of the honey, of which they are particularly fond, and being, no doubt, very hungry, had entered the hole of one of the beehives in the night, or early in the morning. It appeared that the mouse had only been able to squeeze little more than its head and its forefeet into the hive, when it was so violently attacked and stung by the bees, that it died without being able to extricate itself, and, no doubt, had it not been discovered soon, it would have caused the death of all the inhabitants of the hive from suffocation, the body having swelled and filled up the entrance.* The Hermit's bees knew the widows that fed them as well as possible, and were not alarmed by the introduction of the scoop in the evening,

* A fact.

and the evil consequences were explained to me of ever feeding bees in the daytime, or putting their food on the outside of the hives at *any time*, as such a practice not only distracted their attention, and prevented the bees from following their regular routine of daily duties, but attracted their enemies, and subjected them to the continual annoyance of wasps, hornets, and other as troublesome, though less powerful insects.

On the approach of winter, a quantity of dried fern was placed between the back of the hives and the back of the bee-house, and over the top of the hives. Fern is considered better than straw, less likely to harbour insects and birds, and more tough and lasting. The fern is removed when the bees begin their spring work, and the bee-house is well swept from cobwebs or any other impurities. Care was also taken to prevent weeds or flowers from growing underneath the shelf on which the hives are placed, and the Hermit preferred paving-stones, or pitching, as not affording any harbour for insects or reptiles. He said that it was remark-

able, that although few people were ignorant
that the bees, in a state of nature, made the
hollow of a tree or a rock their chosen resi-
dence, and always selected a place impervious
to the rays of the sun, yet that he had repeatedly
noticed the bees were often exposed to the
fierce heat of the sun, without any reflection as
to the torture those valuable little labourers
must endure, if the top of the hive became so
warm as to affect their honeycombs by partially
melting their wax, also that bees required as
much protection from the sun *over* their hives,
as from the rain, but in front of their hives
wind was their greatest enemy, and they should
be so placed as to be able to issue forth and
return home, without being blown over, which
frequently occurs when the bee-house faces the
windy quarter. When they swarm, their new
hive should be rubbed with balm-leaves (but
not daubed with beer and sugar), and every
empty hive should be boiled in a copper of
clean water, and well dried, in the month of
April, to be ready when wanted, as without
boiling it would be impossible to ensure them

from insects (or their eggs) having a domicile between the straw bands.

I find I have myself imperceptibly acquired something like habits of industry, and of interest in objects which before would no more have occupied my mind than a blank wall would have gratified my sight, and time has fled so fast, from the multiplicity of occupations with which I have been diverted, that I look back with surprise to the length of time that has elapsed since I made the last entry in this Note Book, and with still greater astonishment do I recollect, that very soon after I returned to the Hermit's cell, on my culinary apprenticeship, I resolved to commence these memoranda, not so much with a view of recording useful information, as with the intention of turning my host into ridicule, by writing parallel columns of my own counter experiences, which were to be shown in triumph at the conclusion of my visit; but *where* are the refutations which I *intended* to produce, by my own observations and practical knowledge? and Echo answers, *where !*

I have at last persuaded this venerable Welsh Hermit to go to London. I expect great amusement, if not improvement, from his remarks upon what he may see and hear there in the nineteenth century, although I do not believe that, in scenes so totally different from those in which he had lived for more than half a century, he will be able to impart much instruction to myself or my friends.

As I perceive the last pages of this note-book have been devoted to the INDUSTRIOUS BEES, I cannot do better, on leaving Wales, than to dedicate the remaining space to the subject of a Welsh poem, written by a learned Welsh antiquarian,* upon those exemplary and mysterious insects. The contents of this poem in many respects expressed the sentiments of my venerable host, who was enthusiastically devoted to the bees, and in various conversations on this favourite subject he gave me an idea of the meaning of the above-mentioned

---

* Gwalltr Mechain.

B B

composition, but he was very unwilling to allow me to take any notes, as he had a dread that some attempt might be made to turn the poem into English rhyme, and he said that it was utterly impossible in English to do anything like justice to Welsh composition; that English *prose* might give an *inoffensive* outline or *idea* of the sentiments expressed, which (from the different construction of the languages) English rhyme could never do, yet that any man who really comprehended the Welsh language as well as the English tongue (or *vice versâ*) would never be guilty of the absurd attempt of translating Welsh poetry into English verse, excepting for the purpose of giving an incorrect and erroneous idea of the original.

Having promised faithfully that I would never assist or encourage such an objectionable proceeding, I was permitted to make the following notes from memory, which give a general notion of the subject:—

The Welsh bard recounts that the Druids knew through a dream or vision that the bees were originally inhabitants of heaven,* where they received the blessing of the Almighty; but for the sins of man were sent to the earth to *teach* the human race that *diligence was happiness.* The model of good government is described as displayed by the bees, who (Queen and subjects) each perform their various duties in unison, each executing with regularity, method, and precision, their allotted work, according to the various powers and qualifications bestowed on every member, their system of government being such that the wisest of men might gain instruction from them, and learn many things which would be most conducive to the general welfare of nations.

There is also a description of the fine balmy mornings in May, when the ascending sun summons the bees from their homes, and when (light-winged) they start off with the opening day, and disperse themselves over the country, collecting materials of various kinds, from leaves and flowers, with which to form mansions for

---

* There is a tradition that the bees were white before the fall of Adam in Paradise, but afterwards became brown.

the young generation and food for their support, collecting that honey which is so much prized in every quarter of the world. In seven days, when the young bees are able to fly, they are not subjected, like mortals, to long and painful tutelage and confinement, but they are taught early to exercise all their powers fully and freely, to observe and recognise every leaf and flower, and to know the difference of forms and colours, yet the greatest wonder relating to this marvellous race is, that however much they may take from the flowers, " *Nid ydyw y ddeilen meillionen ddim llai*" (*there is not one single petal of trefoil the less*). The bees have various modes of expression, and they thoroughly *understand their own language*, in which there are many idioms, and which is always harmonious. When the weather changes, and high winds arise, and oblige the bees to return home, they do not return to idleness because they return to safety, and are surrounded by comforts. Unlike weak-minded man, the bees have always work ready, and adapted for all circumstances, and they are equally occupied, whether under the canopy of heaven or in the shelter of their own homes, where they replace, arrange, and repair everything with the utmost discretion, and such true wisdom, that everything they do promotes stability as well as health and cleanliness. Maidens may well be instructed by the bees. Fools might learn of them (were fools capable of receiving instruction).—Matrons of every rank ought to study the bees, who demonstrate in their daily life *the beauty of diligence,* as well as *the use of industry,* and who, in the midst of all their labours, are so neat and comely, that they appear like gems when poised upon the flowers of the garden.

Yet can it be believed that, by the perversion of human intellect, man wilfully murders these lovely and innocent winged beings, for the sake of eating their stores? Yes! senseless man actually destroys the labourers provided by the Almighty, who cheerfully work from morn till eve, and, by their unremitting industry, collect honey enough to satisfy the utmost greediness of the human race, as well as to maintain themselves and all their generations, also reared to labour, and which are by the hand of man now suffocated in their cradles! Man has no right thus to use the arrows of death, and to oppose the ordinance of God.*

The poem concludes with an emphatic aspiration, in which I (the Traveller) most heartily concur.—The Poet invokes prosperity for all the Bees in the world, wishing them the continuance of wisdom and intelligence to maintain their beneficial hosts, with hopes that the Ancient Britons may ever have means to live, be contented with their lot, and thankful to their God. The words of the original are these :—

> " Mawr gynnydd fo'n dilyn holl Wenyn y wlad,
> Mawr synwyr i feithrin—mawr fyddin mor fad,
> Fel y caffo yr hên Frython fwyn foddion i fyw
> I'w byd yn foddlonus—yn ddiolchus i Dduw."

---

* " *Thou shalt not muzzle the ox when he treadeth out the corn.*" How much more unjustifiable to kill thousands and tens of thousands of Bees, whose lives are not merely harmless but abundantly useful and profitable, and whose dead bodies do not benefit either man or beast!

LONDON.

WE have arrived in London.   I am disappointed! I had expected that the Welsh Hermit would have been more impressed by the grandeur and progress of the human intellect from his first journey on a railway ; but alas ! he is much more struck by the *inconveniences* than by the *wonders* of that mode of conveyance, and says that if he makes the acquaintance of any anatomists in the metropolis, he will entreat them to give lectures to enlighten the railway companies and the builders of their carriages as to the fact that the relief and repose of the human frame cannot be promoted by having a large protuberance, or hump, in the wrong place, in the back of each of their carriages, so that, instead of the neck of a tired traveller being *supported*, it is *thrust forward* exactly in the place where it ought to fall back, and, *vice versâ*, a hollow is provided opposite the back, where a projection is most required.   The blinds of the railway carriages caused him much astonishment and indignation. The sun was hot and glaring. We had to change to other lines three times. The carriages of each line had different sorts of blinds. The first had springs which were all out of order ; the next had no springs, but rings on a rod, the consequence of which was, that there might as well have been no blinds at all, as the draught produced by the velocity of the motion blew the unfortunate blinds in every direction, and there was no alternative but to be *blinded* or to draw up the window and *shut out the air.* The third change was not an improvement, although it is impossible to say whether it once might have been so, as one window was *minus* any blind at all, and the other blind was in shreds. On complaining to the guard, he said " *they were under repair.*"

I almost repent having induced the Hermit to take this journey; he is *very intractable ;* his satirical humour seems to increase, and alas ! his sharpness of perception also.

Our journey was unlucky; there was an accident to a luggage train before us, and the wreck was so great that the broken carriages

could not be got out of the way in time for us
to pass, and we were obliged to walk through
the wreck in the dark, to take our places in
another train, which had been telegraphed for,
and was waiting on the other side of the heap
of ruins, by which transit we lost all our
luggage, and obtained the trunks of other
passengers.

I only hope the Hermit will not publish
all the particulars of his first railway journey,
as it might bring down the shares of one of
the lines, in which I have a large stake, which
would be a cruel addition to the loss I have
previously sustained of one finger and part of
my thumb, and all my good looks !

There is certainly no progress made as yet
towards inclining the Hermit to the belief that
the nineteenth century is an age of remarkable
intelligence or special improvement, and he
continues to declare obstinately that if the ends
produced by the present bad system of education, (so conducive to ignorance, through neglect
of observation and reflection,) were printed in
parallel columns with the benefits which have

been derived by the undoubted progress of
mechanical talent, that the balance of benefits
would be on the *wrong side* of *happiness,*
morality, general utility, and *general intelli-*
gence. However, I will try to keep up my
spirits, and commence a new note-book, as a
record to look back upon of the visit of the
Hermit of St. Gover to London in the nineteenth century.

END OF TRAVELLER'S NOTE BOOK OF 1866.

APPENDIX.

CONTAINING

RECIPES GIVEN BY THE HERMIT TO THE TRAVELLER,
AS COOKED IN THE CELL OF ST. GOVER.

APPENDIX.

BOILED FOWL.

WEIGHT of fowl, three and a half lbs. ; a quarter of a pint of cold water to each pound. Fill the outer vessel with water, and let it simmer very slowly for two hours and a quarter, unless the meat of the fowl is tender and fit for eating sooner, which can be proved by trying it with a fork. Pour off the broth, which ought to be about a pint of strong chicken broth, and when cold will be a jelly. The bones of the chicken, after the meat is eaten (or all taken off), are to be broken up, and stewed in a digester for two or three hours, with a pint of water to every pound of bones ; then pour the liquor off, which ought to produce about half a pint of jelly, and the bones are to be re-broken, and put into the digester again, with a pint of water to every pound of bones, which will, of course, weigh *less* than before the first stewing. They are to remain between one and two hours stewing, then pour off the liquor, which ought to produce more than a quarter of a pint of jelly. The bones to be broken the third time, and subjected to the same process, with a pint of water to the pound, their weight being again diminished : the liquor ought to produce a quarter of a pint of jelly. Thus, a fowl or three pounds and a half weight will, under proper management, on an average, produce, *besides the meat,* more than a quart of jelly stock, first and last, including the pint produced by the first boiling.

N.B.—It must be remembered that slight differences as to produce will be found, according to the sort, the quality, or condition of poultry, as well as butcher's meat : but the receipts given in this work have been written down from actual practical experiments, often repeated, and the variations in the produce are, on an average, trifling, excepting where the meat has been *very fat,* and when that is the case in butcher's meat, the same quantity of jelly stock must *never* be expected as when the meat is lean, inasmuch as the fat will *not* produce gravy; consequently, when there is a great overplus of fat, less water should be allowed to the weight of meat.

In the proceeds from the Hermit's fowl, the oil on the top of the jelly from the first boiling measured a quarter of a pint, and the fat collected from the surface of all the jellies amounted to a quarter of a pint.

Total produce of Hermit's fowl (*besides the meat*) :—

> Jelly stock, 1 quart.
> Oil   ,,   ¼ of a pint.
> Fat   ,,   ¼ of a pint.

PARSLEY SAUCE FOR BOILED FOWL.

Two ounces of fresh butter, cut in little bits, put into a double saucepan, with as much flour as will make it into a stiff paste ; then add two tablespoonfuls of milk ; stir well, add six tablespoonfuls of water, continue to stir till it is quite hot and the thickness of good cream. The above is *now* plain melted butter, and ready for parsley sauce, which must be made by previously having had the parsley washed very clean, and picking every leaf off the stems ; put a small teaspoonful of salt into half a pint of boiling water, boil the parsley in this for ten minutes, drain it on a sieve, mince it fine, or bruise it to a pulp, and stir it into the melted butter prepared as above described.

FRICASEED COLD CHICKEN.—(Page 33.)

Chop very fine leek-roots, celery, a small quantity of turnip, and some persons like a *little* carrot. Put the whole into a saucepan with sufficient top fat (if from chicken stock *all the better*) to form a thick pulp when thoroughly incorporated with the chopped vegetables (the whole of the vegetables together being about two ounces), stir briskly over the fire for ten minutes; then shake in as much flour as will make it a stiff paste, stirring well for five minutes longer, then put the whole into a double saucepan in which is three-quarters of a pint of chicken stock, which has been previously warmed, and after well stirring, again leave it to stew slowly for three-quarters of an hour, then pass the whole through a wire sieve into a basin, and pour what is strained back into the double, adding two tablespoonfuls of cream, after which the flavour must be improved as required, by stirring round a sprig of orange thyme, or any other herb wanted, and, if the flavour of celery and onions is not sufficient, it is now to be increased by stirring round pieces of either of those vegetables, and taking them out as soon as sufficient taste is obtained. The meat of the cold chicken is to be cut or pulled into long pointed pieces, and put into the sauce, where, being well stirred, it is to remain until thoroughly warmed through, and the chicken flavour imparted to the sauce. This will take a few minutes more or less according to the heat to which the hot water on the outside is exposed,—the slower the better, as, if the water is kept fiercely boiling instead of barely simmering, the chicken will be beat to pieces; whereas having already been once dressed, it ought only to be done the second time sufficiently to have the chicken flavour imparted to the sauce, and the flavour of the sauce absorbed by the chicken.

In the Hermit's mode of cookery in separate double vessels, any dishes can be kept warm without injury for a long while, should the dinner by any accident be retarded.*

---

* The reader of this recipe, who may possibly be acquainted with the copper tray called a Bain-Marie, to hold hot water, which is used by professed cooks to keep their sauces from burning, and may probably suppose that that contrivance was *unknown* to the Hermit, and that *his* system of double vessels for cookery was only a clumsy substitution for a scientific invention, beyond his knowledge or his reach ; it is, therefore, necessary to add, that it was in consequence of the *total inefficiency* of the copper tray, called a Bain-Marie, to effect the objects which it was the ambition of the Hermit to attain, that he discarded the Bain-Marie altogether, as an expensive and cumbersome addition to his kitchen, which took up a great deal of room, and did very little work, and was totally inadmissible where there was not a very large stove.

C C

No. II.

ROAST LEG OF MUTTON.

Leg of mutton weighing five lbs. ; put on the hook attached to the yarn, which hangs from a crank (see page 40), 24 inches from the fire, basted with clarified dripping, or suet. Keep an earthen pan on the bottom of the screen next the dripping-pan ; after basting, ladle all the gravy, or liquid fat, out of the dripping-pan into the earthen pan, from which it can be taken as often as needed to baste, and again returned. A leg of mutton of this size will take about three hours ; half an hour before it is finished, put it four inches nearer the fire ; put half a pint of boiling water in a watering-pot with the rose on, salt to taste, and pour over the joint slowly, which will produce a great increase of gravy, and when browned again after the watering, and well basted, sprinkle flour all over it with a flour dredger, and again baste to froth it. The gravy to be served with the meat should, if possible, have been saved from a previous joint, and warmed in a double saucepan ; but, if not practicable, the gravy should be taken out of the dripping-pan after the watering, and placed in a basin or dish to cool, and when the fat is sufficiently congealed to be removed, the clear gravy can be rewarmed in a double saucepan, and would be ready to be served with the meat by the time it is frothed and dished.

JELLY FROM THE BONES OF ROAST LEGS OF WELSH MUTTON.

The bones of roast Welsh legs of mutton, broken small, and put in a digester with three pints of water, produced a pint and a half of jelly after stewing slowly for three hours; the bones being re-broken and put down again with a pint and a half of water, after stewing for two hours produced three-quarters of a pint more jelly. The bones being broken the third time, and put down with one pint of water, produced one-quarter pint more jelly. Total quantity of jelly from a pound and a half of leg of mutton bones, two pints and a half.

No. III.

STEWED BEEF.

Trimmings of half-rounds of beef cut in pieces for pies, 6 lbs.

Brisket, stewed same time, 15 lbs.

C C 2

Beef altogether, 21 lbs.

Onions, celery, leeks, turnips, and carrots about four soup-plates full, a soup-plate holding about 1 lb. of chopped vegetables.   Suet, or top fat, 1 lb.

N.B.—The suet or top fat which is added to stewed beef to make it more mellow, should always be added the last thing over the vegetables, because otherwise it would prevent the juice and flavour of the vegetables from penetrating into the meat.

Water two quarts and one pint, being a quarter of a pint of water to every pound of beef.   Stewed in double vessel for twelve hours, produced six quarts of stock, which when cold was a strong jelly; and the fat when cold taken off the top weighed two pounds and a half.

It must always be remembered that the fatter the meat the less stock will be produced; nothing is so wasteful or unwholesome for household purposes as over-fat meat, or fat produced by oil-cake and forcing feeding, and such animals are, moreover, scarcely ever free from disease.

The sauce for this stewed beef (if eaten hot) is prepared from its own jelly stock in the same manner as hashed mutton, with addition of turnip and carrot balls (or shreds) stewed till tender in broth.   (See page 64.)

No. IV.

HASHED MUTTON.

Cut as much mutton as is required from the remainder of a roast leg in pointed pieces.* Fry one ounce and a half of onion, and the same of celery chopped fine, and one ounce of turnip, with a sufficient quantity of fresh top fat, cut in small pieces, from soup or broth, stirred round and round over a stove or fire in a clean tin saucepan for ten minutes; then add as much flour as will stiffen it into a paste of the consistency of wet mortar, and stir round and round over the stove for five minutes more; then add a sufficient quantity of the jelly from the bone of the leg of roast mutton, to be of the consistence of thick pea-soup; then pour the whole into a double saucepan, in the outside of which there must be a sufficient quantity of boiling water to fill within an inch of the top of the inner saucepan. Let the whole simmer gently for a quarter of an hour or twenty minutes; then pour through a wire sieve and return into a clean double saucepan, which replace on the stove; taste, and if it requires any further flavouring of herbs or vegetables, add them; then put in the pre-

---

* See description, page 60.

pared pieces of meat, stir well, and let it remain in a very slow heat for half an hour, when it will be ready for the table.

No. V.

SIMPLE WHITE SOUP.

One pint of veal stock and one pint of brown stock in a large basin; place the basin over a saucepan of boiling water on a stove or fire, add an onion cut in half, three or four pieces of celery slit in variousplaces to let out the juice, a sprig or two of basil and marjory (if in winter these herbs may be used in powder, having been bottled* in the summer); place a plate over the top of the basin, and the lid of the saucepan on the plate to keep in the heat; let all simmer together, the water in the saucepan being kept boiling under the basin for forty minutes; then add four tablespoonfuls of cream and macaroni cut small, after having been previously stewed till tender in mutton broth or veal stock.

---

* See page 75, on preserving and bottling herbs.

THE WHITE SOUP OF GOVER.

Put one quart of veal stock in a double saucepan to warm, then chop fine six ounces of onion, six of celery, four of leeks, six of pumpkin, four of carrots; stir the whole in a single saucepan over the stove for ten minutes, with as much top fat as will make them into a pulp, without burning or being oily; then shake in with the dredger as much flour as will form the whole into a pulpy *paste*, stirring briskly for five minutes more; then add the whole mass to the hot veal stock in the double saucepan, and let all stew slowly together surrounded with boiling water for an hour and a half, frequently stirring; then pass through a wire sieve, return into a clean double saucepan, add whatever flavouring is deficient, either in salt or herbs, with six spoonfuls of cream; let the whole be well stirred and thoroughly hot, and it is ready for the table.

N.B.—More or less cream can be added according to taste, and it is better flavoured if the cream is added before it is put through the wire sieve,.to which some persons may object for reasons given by the Hermit; * but whether before or after, an additional

---

* See page 113.

flavour of herbs is generally required, and sometimes more onion after the cream, which can be done by adding pieces of vegetables or sprigs of herbs until the additional flavour has been obtained, when they can be taken out before it is served.

N.B.—The stocks used for the above soups are the jelly produced by boiling or stewing in a double vessel either veal or beef, till in perfection for eating (as described by the Hermit), in the proportions of a quarter pint of water to one lb. of meat (bone and flesh together); if very fat, less stock will be produced.—*Nothing is worse economy than overplus of fat.* When *broth* only is wanted *half* a pint of water to the pound may be used.

THE HERMIT'S GRAVY SOUP.*

Five pounds of lean beef cut in small pieces, (trimmed from the inside of two half-rounds before they were salted,) fifteen pounds of brisket of beef, four pounds of onions, leeks, turnips, and carrots, all finely chopped, in the proportions of one pound of onions, one pound of celery, half a pound of leeks, quarter of a pound of turnips, quarter of a pound of

* Page 65.

carrots. Suet one pound, water two quarts and one pint, being a quarter of a pint to every pound of meat, stewed in double twelve hours, by which time the meat was not overdone, but very tender and juicy. The produce was five quarts and a pint and a half of stock, which when cold was a clear jelly; fat taken off the jelly when cold weighed two pounds and a half.

N.B.—Had the meat been fatter the produce of soup would have been much less, and there would have been waste in eating the meat from disproportion of fat to the lean. The arrangement of the meat, &c. in the inside vessel, was as follows:— First, brisket; then the trimmings on the top of the brisket; second, vegetables; third, a sprinkling of salt on the vegetables; fourth, suet also on the vegetables. By attention to this order of things, the juices of the vegetables drawn out by slightly salting are distilled through the meat, while the suet is also slowly melted, and enriches the meat as it passes through; the superabundance, after the meat is saturated, is all again collected from the top of the jelly stock when cold. By this process of slow cooking in a double vessel two very important objects are gained; the first being the *impossibility* of *burning* or *entirely spoiling* the meat *or the soup;* the second, that more soup is obtained than the quantity of water which is put to the meat; whereas upon the old system *much less* soup is produced than the quantity of water put in, because the liquor is *boiled away* and *wasted.* The trimmings thus cooked make the best beef family pies, the bottom part of the jelly stock being used for the gravy, which not being so transparent as the upper part is not so well adapted in appearance for gravy soup, but is especially savoury and well-flavoured. The brisket itself is ready to be served next day, with the sauce recommended by the Hermit.* *No skimming* while hot is *ever* required for *any of the recipes in this book.*

The gravy soup, as well as other soups, will generally require some extra flavouring of herbs and vegetables when warmed for the table, which warming must always be in a double saucepan, or a basin over a saucepan of boiling water: the *latter* is the most delicate.

No. VI.

HASHED MUTTON (SIMPLE).

Prepare the cold mutton as directed in No. 4; salt it slightly, flour it lightly, turning it well over

---

* See page 64.

with two forks; put it into a double saucepan, with a sufficient quantity of jelly from the bones of mutton previously flavoured with onion and herbs; let the meat remain in this sauce in a gentle heat, frequently stirred for three quarters of an hour before it is served. If there is no jelly from mutton bones, clear gravy from roast mutton, similarly flavoured, would be very good.

No. VII.

MUTTON PIE.

Neck or loin of mutton, five pounds, cut in chops, put in a double saucepan with *half a quarter* of a pint of water to the pound; add one pound of vegetables chopped fine (onions and celery equal quantities, turnips and carrots half the quantity); a sprinkling of salt. Stew for two hours; when the meat is sufficiently tender, take it off, pour the liquor into a basin to cool, and cut the meat off the bones, removing also the superfluous fat. When the liquor is cold take the solid fat off the top, and the stock will then be in a jelly; add this jelly to the meat which has been cut off the bones, and place the whole in a thick crockery basin over a saucepan of boiling water until the jelly has melted amongst the meat, and the whole is warmed through; then remove till the next day, when the meat will be imbedded in the jelly which will have cooled round it, and of which it will have absorbed a great deal. The meat and jelly can then be placed in layers in the pie-dish, and there ought to be (if done properly) considerably more jelly than is required for gravy for the pie, which overplus is to be kept back; a little fresh parsley chopped small is to be sprinkled between the meat.

The paste for the pie is to be made with six ounces of flour, three ounces of the top fat, taken off the mutton jelly, and put on the fire in a saucepan with a quarter of a pint of water; when the water boils make a hole in the middle of the flour and pour in the boiling water and mutton fat by degrees, mixing the fat in with a spoon; when well mixed, knead it till of the proper stiffness, and dredge the board with flour to make it smooth; cover your pie, make a hole in the top, and form a little ornament with a small stem to fit into it. Fill your baking tin with water under the pie-dish to prevent too great a heat to the bottom: when the paste is baked the pie is done. Screw out the top ornament and pour in as much liquid mutton jelly as the pie can receive, which must be previously warmed in a double saucepan; replace the ornament, and serve the pie.

N.B.—A pie after baking will always take a good deal of extra gravy, but it will not take nearly all that the meat has produced when properly done, and of which there ought to be more to spare, which can be used for soups or sauces, or added to mutton broth.

No. VIII.
PEA-SOUP (WINTER).

One pint of peas soaked in the well for twenty-four hours; stew three hours in a double saucepan with one pint of bone stock, and a quarter of a pound of finely-chopped onions, and a quarter of a pound of celery; rub through a wire sieve, put back again into the double, add one pint and a half of good broth or stock, and stew one hour more, with one onion split in half, and three pieces of split celery, and a little fresh or powdered basil; add salt and powdered or fresh mint, with marjory, and orange thyme to taste. The above soup may be varied by adding a quarter of a pint of cream before the last onion and herbs are put in; and the Hermit occasionally had rice stewed in new milk in a double saucepan, and added instead of the cream, on which occasion fried bread was not served, which was done when the pea-soup was made without rice.

No. IX.

GREEN PEA-SOUP (SUMMER).

Chop all together *very* small, three lettuces, two cucumbers, half a pound of spinach, half a pound of onions, half a pound of leeks. Let them be stirred in a single saucepan for ten minutes with a quarter of a pound of fresh top fat from beef stock until in a pulp; meantime, have prepared in another double a pint and a half of veal or beef jelly stock from stewed beef or boiled veal, also one pint of old green peas, which have also been stewed and pulped through a wire sieve; add to the stock the pulp of the peas and other vegetables; flavour according to taste, by stirring round at last pieces of split celery, a little basil and mint to taste, and serve, having a quarter of a pint of young and tender peas ready boiled to throw in before it is served up. The Hermit sometimes added pieces of cucumber about an inch long, which had been previously stewed in beef or veal jelly stock.

N.B.—Two pounds of green pea-shells chopped or pounded, will produce excellent pea-soup, treated in the same manner as the old green peas in the above recipe, and will be found very convenient when peas are scarce.

No. X.

BEEF-STEAK.

Place beef-steaks in a large single saucepan, or stew-pan, over the stove ; turn them about until browned on both sides *without being burnt,* with an ounce of top fat from beef stock ; take about two dozen of button onions, and boil till tender, in as much water as will cover them, in a double saucepan; then take the beef-steaks, (about five pounds,) and, when browned, put them with the gravy that has been extracted, into a double, and add to them the water which has boiled the button onions, two ounces of celery chopped small, one ounce of carrots ditto, two ounces of onions ditto ; let the steaks stew with the above from one to two hours, or till tender, then put into a basin, pour all their gravy over them, straining the vegetables out, and leave them till the next day, when the fat, which will have congealed on the top, is to be removed, and the basin with the steaks and gravy placed on a saucepan of boiling water to warm, and if the button onions are liked, they can be added ; also a quarter of a pound of potatoes, cut in little balls or dice, are to be fried in a quarter of a pound of top fat, of a golden yellow, a quarter of an hour before they are wanted. They are to be put on a doubled clean cloth upon a flat dish, and placed in the screen before the kitchen fire, being turned to remove all superfluous fat, and being perfectly hot and dry, are to be put into the gravy with the steaks when served.

No. XI.

TO PRESERVE GAME OR POULTRY, OR ANY SORT OF MEAT, WHEN REQUIRED TO BE KEPT LONG BEFORE IT IS EATEN.

Roast the poultry or game exactly the same as if it was to be eaten immediately ; by the time it is ready have a sufficient quantity of fresh suet (beef is preferred) melted in a double saucepan, put the game or poultry into a pan or vessel sufficiently deep, and pour in *hot suet* till over the top ; keep in a cold place, and when wanted, cut it out of the suet, which will easily be broken off the game, and place the birds in a basin with a very *little* pure broth under them, put the basin over a saucepan of boiling water, cover with a plate, and as soon as the birds have slowly been warmed through, during which process they must be turned, they are ready for the table, with the addition of some pure gravy from something similar, or else from roast mutton. The suet which has melted into the broth will congeal on the top when cold, and can be taken off.

N.B.—It is seldom remembered that dressing meat, *after* it is tainted, will not remove the taint, though it may render it less offensive and unwholesome; consequently, those who wish to preserve meat, game, or poultry in hot weather, must dress it *before* it is tainted.

No. XII.

BAKED FILLET OF VEAL.

Stuff the fillet with stuffing made of finely chopped suet, lemon-peel, and bread crumbs, leek root finely chopped, a little orange thyme, nutmeg, pepper, and salt, pounded with one egg; after it is filleted and stuffed, put two ounces suet or fresh top fat from stock of soups (veal the best) on the top of the fillet after placing it in the iron (outer) part of Ffwrn fach without the inner tin. Place over it (if to be had) a piece of the rind from cold boiled pork, with about a quarter of an inch of the fat adhering to

D D

it ; add one quart of water, put in an oven of steady heat, not sharp, and *take out* all the fire from under the oven as soon as it is in. A fillet of veal of seven pounds will take about three hours. When done, the gravy must be poured off, and when cold will be in a firm jelly.

N.B.—If the veal was baked in the tin double of the Ffwrn fach, in addition to the outer vessel itself, it would produce more *gravy,* but the objection to this mode of cooking is that the veal will not then *brown outside ;* but if the fillet is only wanted for eating cold, for mince veal, &c., or making the Hermit's pies, it had better be done in a double vessel to produce more gravy, and the meat will taste equally good or better. If required to be eaten hot, it can be served next day warmed in a double, with some of its own gravy.

No. XIII.

TONGUE BOILED.

One of the Hermit's salt* tongues, which weighed two pounds, stewed six hours in a double saucepan, with one quart and one pint of spring water, and six ounces of fresh suet. When done the tongue was

---

* For Salting Tongues see No. XXXIX.

tender but firm, and the water in which it was boiled being kept till cold, all the suet that had not been absorbed by the tongue was taken off from the surface when solid.

TONGUE ROASTED.

A favourite Welsh dish, and a very excellent one. Wash a fresh tongue well, and when quite clean cut off no more of the roots than will make it stand well on the dish; chop fine equal parts of onions and celery, and half as much of carrots and turnips, and pile them all along the tongue; sprinkle freely with salt, and add half a pound of fresh top fat from soups, or (if not to be had) use chopped suet, but the former is best; then bind up the tongue, with the vegetables and the fat upon it, in two or three folds of thin "*whity brown*" paper, which must be tied on. The tongue is then ready for roasting, and must be well basted, the paper being previously thoroughly greased. A short time before it is done, cut the string, take off the paper, and brown it before it is taken down. The best gravy is that from roast beef, but roast mutton is also suitable. It is customary to stick in a few cloves round the top before it is sent to table, but this is more ornamental than useful.

No. XIV.

HERMIT'S RABBIT FRICASEE.

Two rabbits cut up, weighing four pounds and a half; one pint and half a quarter pint of water, stewed for three hours, produced a pint and a half of jelly. Put away for the next day, then take the pint and a half of rabbit jelly and put on in a double, with two ounces of onions and the same of celery, chopped *very fine*, and a pint and a half of milk; let it stew altogether for half an hour; then put in the rabbit, which has been previously cut in moderate sized pieces, and floured, and let all stew together in the double, frequently stirring, for an hour, slow heat.

If a richer and more delicate dish is required, the vegetables should be stirred over a stove, in a single saucepan, for ten minutes, and then made into a paste with flour, and stirred for five minutes more, and the whole put into a "double" with the rabbit jelly and a little new milk or cream, and after being stirred half an hour put through a wire sieve, returned to the double, then put in the pieces of rabbit for half an hour before serving, which in this case should not be floured.

No. XV.

HERMIT'S BOILED SHOULDER OF MUTTON.

Weighed three pounds; onions, half a pound; celery, half a pound, chopped fine; marjory and a small sprig of orange thyme.

Put in a double with one pint and a half of water, and water boiling round for two hours and a half. Produced one quart of good broth, the meat being tender and juicy.

ONION SAUCE FOR BOILED SHOULDER OF MUTTON.

Cut up four onions and stew in a double with a little water till tender; then pour off the water and mix half an ounce of flour with it; then add half a pint of milk, and stir well till of a proper consistency, then pass through the wire sieve and return into the double saucepan; stir well, and when quite hot it is ready to pour over the boiled shoulder of mutton or over boiled rabbits.

No. XVI.

HERMIT'S SAUSAGES.

Quarter of a pound of roast or baked pork, quarter of a pound of baked veal, two ounces of cold boiled tongue, an ounce and a half of onions chopped very fine, an ounce and a quarter of sage, flour well, add pepper and salt to taste; pound well in a mortar, and make into very thin, short, round sausages; beat up one egg well, and glaze the sausages with it, then roll them in two ounces of fine bread crumbs, and fry in boiling-hot top fat (from soup stock) until the sausages are a fine golden brown: if they are at all greasy, put them on a soft hot cloth on a flat dish in a screen before the fire, and turn them on the cloth till they are perfectly dry, before serving.

N.B.—Where pork is used it can be baked in the same manner as directed for the fillet of veal; but if no more is wanting than the quantity to make sausages, it is better to cut up a quarter of a pound of raw pork and a quarter of a pound of raw veal, and half a quarter of a pint of water and a little salt, which can be baked slowly in a double Ffwrn fach, or it can be stewed in a double saucepan till the meat is fit for eating. When it is not convenient to provide pork or veal, cold stewed beef, or indeed any cold meat, will make very good sausages, if pounded, with the addition of a little finely-chopped suet, and well flavoured with sage.

No. XVII.

THE HERMIT'S COLD VEAL PIE.

Bake (or stew in a double) a pound and a half of veal, with not quite a pint of water, and a little orange thyme, some small bits of fresh lemon-peel, and a very small bit of mace. Bake or stew till the veal is in good eating order; it will take more or less time, according to the tenderness of the meat, but, whether baked or stewed, it must be done *very slowly*. When done pour off the gravy, which will become a jelly, and put the meat away till the next day ; then pound the veal very fine in a mortar, with a sufficient quantity of boiled salt tongue to give it sufficient saltness and flavour; moisten while pounding with as much of the jelly stock from the veal as will make it into a stiff paste, the consistency of mortar; rub the inside of the dish well with olive oil or top fat; then stick small pieces of dry vermicelli all over the bottom of the dish; line the dish (over the vermicelli) with paste—(the same paste as that in the recipe given for mutton pie)—then put in the pounded meat, press down close and *flat* to the top of the dish, and cover over with the same paste. Bake for an hour in a slow oven with water in the baking-tin under the dish, and when cold it will turn out of the dish *topsy-turvy*, the vermicelli adhering to the paste: when eaten the end should be cut off straight, and slices taken off from one end to the other. The above pie is also excellent for sandwiches.

No. XVIII.

SALT DUCK.

For a common-sized duck, a quarter of a pound of salt, to be well rubbed in and re-rubbed, and turned on a dish every day for three days; then wash all the salt off clean, put it into a double with half a pint of water to the pound, and let it simmer steadily for two hours. Salt boiled duck, with white onion sauce, is much better than roast duck.

No. XIX.

GREEN PEA-SOUP.

See Appendix No. IX.

No. XX.

ROOT OF TONGUE SOUP.

Cut off the roots of a fresh tongue, wash well in separate waters, and then leave them to soak in a pan sunk in a stone trough or well over which fresh water is constantly running, for half an hour, then take them out and place them in the inner tin of a Ffwrn fach, with half a pound of vegetables, viz. celery, onions, leeks, turnips, and carrots chopped fine, equal parts of each excepting carrots, of which there must not be more than *one small root* chopped small ; sprinkle a little salt over the vegetables, and let all stew slowly with water boiling round until the roots are thoroughly done ; then strain the soup off into a pan, place the roots on a dish till the next day, and the vegetables will be excellent mixed in broth for family use. The following day the soup will be a jelly, from the face of which the fat must be removed. When the soup is wanted, put the jelly into a large basin or pan over a saucepan of boiling water ; when hot, taste, and add any herbs required for flavouring, or any additional vegetables, if wanted, can be put in and stirred round till sufficient flavour is obtained.

The best parts of the roots of tongue are to be cut in neat squares or mouthfuls, and put into the soup to warm before it is served. No water need be added to the roots beyond what they will imbibe in the well.

No. XXI.

TO CLARIFY FAT.

All fat which is not used fresh should be clarified in the following manner. Cut up the fat in very small pieces, and put it into a large double saucepan, which should be kept on purpose; when perfectly liquefied from the heat of the water which has been boiling round it, pour it into a very large pan holding four or five gallons of boiling water, and stir the liquid fat briskly with a stick round and round; let the whole cool, and next morning the fat will be on the surface in a white cake, which can be cut round and across with a knife and taken off in pieces; the under part of each piece should be scraped, if any impurity adheres to it; the cakes of fat can then be broken up and put into little pans, holding from one to three pounds each, which being placed in the screen before the kitchen fire, will melt again, and on being removed to a cold place will congeal, and, if wanted for keeping long (if the pans are not filled too full), a piece of linen or calico, or even paper, can be placed over the top, and a piece of wood (like a bung) can be pressed down on the fat with the cloth, or calico, under it, by which means the air is excluded, and the fat will keep for some time.

N.B.—The pan to hold the boiling water into which the fat is to be poured should also have boiling water put into it to stand for half an hour *before* the fat is ready; this *first* water being poured off, the pan will have *become hot*, and the second supply of boiling water will be scalding hot when the liquid fat is poured into it; but otherwise the cold pan would have abstracted so much heat from the boiling water that the water would no longer be hot enough for the purpose of clarifying and purifying the fat properly. The fine fat which is obtained from the boiling and stewing of beef, veal, and mutton, only requires one clarification for keeping, but *dripping* from roast meat should have *two*, and, as a general rule, fat should be kept separate according to its sort. *Dripping* should never be mixed with any other fat, and fried fat (which should have two or three clarifications) is always inferior for any other cooking purpose, and should also be kept by itself, whilst the flavoured fats from beef and veal are best for savoury cooking purposes when *un*-clarified, if used fresh, as they possess all the *aroma* of the vegetables with which the meat has been stewed.

No. XXII.

BREAD SAUCE.

Two ounces of fine bread crumbs, half a pint of milk, one small white onion whole, four black pepper-corns whole. Stew for forty minutes in double sauce-pan, stirring well; then add two tablespoonfuls of cream; stir again, and take out the onion and the peppercorns before the sauce is served.

No. XXIII.

THE HERMIT'S MARROW-BONES.

The marrow taken out of the bones weighed five ounces. The bones weighed three pounds. The bones were broken small with an iron hammer, and put into the digester with three pints of water, stewed slowly on the stove for four hours. The marrow taken off the top when cold weighed five and a half ounces, under which was one pint of fine jelly; the bones were re-broken and stewed again with two pints of water : the marrow when cold weighed one ounce and a half, and there was three-quarters of a pint of jelly. The bones were broken the third time and stewed with one pint and a half of water for three hours ; one ounce and a quarter of marrow was produced and a quarter of a pint of jelly. The marrow altogether weighed thirteen ounces and a quarter. The total of jelly was two pints. The marrow taken out of the bones before they were stewed was put into a double saucepan with a quart of cold water, and simmered till the marrow had melted. But when wanted for mince pie *meat*, it is *not* to be clarified. When *clarified*, it is for *mince pie paste*, or other pastry. (See Mince Pies, page 444.)

No. XXIV.

THE HERMIT'S SOUP FOR POOR PEOPLE.

Three pints of peas, soaked in the well all night; then put in the double with three quarts of water, and stew five hours. Chop very small, onions, celery, leeks, turnips, and carrots, three pounds altogether; stir in single saucepan over stove with a half pound of top fat for *ten minutes*, add one pound of oatmeal, and stir again well for five minutes more ; then put them into the double, together with twenty quarts of broth from boiled beef (not oversalted) or bone stock, to stew for an hour. Any pieces of dressed meat to spare can be cut up and added at last.

No. XXV.

THE HERMIT'S SHEEP'S-HEAD BROTH.

Two sheeps' heads, weighing five pounds and a quarter. Put in double with a quart and three quarters of a pint of water, two ounces of onions, three ounces of celery, four ounces of leeks, four ounces of turnips, three ounces of carrots, and a bunch of sweet herbs, all chopped small, stewed slowly for five hours. Broth produced three pints and a quarter. The meat taken off the bones after boiling weighed one pound and a half, and the bones two pounds. The bones were then broken small and put into the digester with two pints of water, stewed for five hours. Jelly produced, one pint. The bones were then re-broken, and stewed with one pint of water for two hours and a half: jelly produced, three-quarters of a pint. Total of good broth produced from two sheeps' heads, two quarts and one pint, to which the meat was added cut up in mouthfuls, and put in at last.

No. XXVI.

HERMIT'S CHICKEN BOILED IN A JUG.

Weight of chicken, three pounds; water, three quarters of a pint. Put together in a jug, the jug being placed in a saucepan of boiling water, and covered over with a saucer; boiled two hours and a half; produced one pint and a half of jelly. The meat was then excellent for eating. The bones weighed, after the meat was taken off, three quarters of a pound; broken up and stewed two hours in a digester with three pints of water, produced one pint and a half of jelly; re-broken and stewed the second time in two pints and a half of water, produced a pint and a quarter of jelly.

Total produce of Chicken.—One pint and a half of best chicken broth or jelly; two pints and three-quarters of jelly from the bones: nourishing jelly in all, two quarts and a quarter of a pint.

No. XXVII.

MINCED VEAL.

Cut (not chop) three-quarters of a pound of veal in small squares thus ▧; chop fine, onions and celery one ounce each, add a *little* thyme* and parsley; put the whole into a single saucepan, with half an ounce of fine top fat from soups (veal to be preferred); stir incessantly on a slow heat for ten minutes; add half an ounce of flour; stir five minutes more; then put the whole into a double saucepan, in which has been previously warmed half a pint of veal stock; let all stew together for a quarter of an hour; then strain through a wire sieve and return it into the double saucepan; add two tablespoonfuls of cream, stir well, and then put in the cold minced veal; stir well again, and let it remain in the double in a slow heat for half an hour before it is served.

No. XXVIII.

HARICOT OF MUTTON.

Boil twelve button onions till tender, and having cut up a neck of mutton into cutlets, put them into a single saucepan or stewpan, stir them round and round on the stove over a steady heat until browned, but not burnt, then put them into a double; take half a pint of the water in which the onions have been boiled (while quite hot) and add to the mutton cutlets,

* Orange Thyme.

adding also two ounces of raw onions or leeks, ditto celery cut in pieces, one ounce of turnips, and half an ounce of carrots cut small, a nosegay of orange thyme, basil, and savory, and a sprinkling of salt. Let all stew together slowly till the cutlets are tender, then pour off the gravy, and put it away where it will cool *as speedily as possible ;* leave the cutlets and vegetables in the double, taking care that the vegetables are both over them and under them, and leave them on the stove to keep warm, but not in any fierce heat, adding the boiled button onions which had been put aside, that they may *warm* while the *gravy is cooling ;* as soon as the fat can be removed from the top of the gravy, take it off, and pour the gravy back upon the cutlets and vegetables, and as soon as it is hot it is ready to serve with the gravy and button onions, which must be separated from the chopped onions or leeks. Some turnips and carrots must have been stewed till tender in another double saucepan (*previously*) in beef jelly stock to add to the above : the carrots require to be boiled for half an hour longer than the turnips.

E E

No. XXIX.

LOBSTER SAUCE.

Take a fresh hen lobster full of spawn, put the spawn and the red coral into a mortar, add to it half an ounce of cold clarified marrow, pound it quite smooth, and rub it through a hair sieve with a wooden spoon, pull the meat of the lobster to pieces with forks, put it in a basin and pour a small quantity of vinegar over it, just enough to give it sharpness; cut one ounce of fresh butter into little bits, put it into a double with a dessert-spoonful of fine flour, mix the butter and flour together into a paste before you put it on the fire, then stir in two tablespoonfuls of milk over the stove (with the water boiling round the double); when well mixed add six tablespoonfuls of lobster jelly, stir all the same way, and when thoroughly blended, and the consistence of cream, put in the meat of the lobster to which the vinegar was added, but previously drain it well from the vinegar by laying it on a cloth for a minute or two; stir the lobster and the sauce together till the lobster is hot, and then having at hand a small empty double saucepan with boiling water, pour a small quantity of the lobster sauce into the empty double, and mix in the lobster paste made with marrow till thoroughly blended, then pour the whole back to the lobster, and after well stirring it is ready. The lobster jelly is made from the shell of the lobster, which having been previously broken small and stewed well in a very clean digester, and treated in the same way as bones, will (when cold) produce a jelly highly flavoured with lobster, which adds very much to the flavour of the sauce.

N.B.—The lobster paste made with the coral and spawn is chiefly valued on account of the scarlet colour it imparts to the sauce, and also for its taste, but its scarlet colour will be destroyed by too long exposure to great heat; it is, therefore, very desirable that it should be put in at the very last, and mixed as quickly as possible. Where fish is continually eaten, a digester should be kept solely for stewing fish-shells or bones.

No. XXX.

SHRIMP SAUCE.

Take the shells of the shrimps, pound them slightly, and stew them with a very little water in a double saucepan for two hours; the shrimp water thus made is then to be strained off, and used instead of plain water, exactly in the same manner as ordered in No. 29 for Lobster Sauce, being added to the butter, flour, and milk. When the sauce is thus made, nothing more is wanted than to put in the shrimps, and, stirring well, let them stew for about a quarter of an hour.

N.B.—The reason the Hermit did not recommend the shells of shrimps to be put into a digester, was because they are in too small a quantity to require it, and sufficient flavouring can be very well extracted in a small double saucepan.

No. XXXI.

SOUTH WALES SALMON.

As soon as a salmon is killed it ought to be crimped, by making incisions between the head and the tail, two inches wide, and one inch deep. It should then be put in cold water (well water is best) for one hour, then put it on in a fish-kettle (if too large cut it in three) with as much cold water as will cover it; one quarter of a pound of salt, and as much vinegar as will make the water slightly acid. As soon as the water is scalding hot, (but *not to boil,*) take it off and pour the water into a pan and put it away in a cold place, leaving the fish in the strainer, and placing the strainer with the fish upon it over the pan of hot fish-water to cool together, where it should remain till the next day, when the fish should be placed again *in* the fish-kettle with the same water in which it was scalded, and when it is again warmed it is done. *It must not boil.*

When there is more dressed salmon than can be eaten, it is particularly good fried in batter. It should be slightly sprinkled with salt before the batter is added, and if there is any Granville fish sauce ready, or to spare, a little of it put on the pieces of salmon under the batter is a great improvement.

No. XXXII.

PRESERVATION OF JELLY STOCKS FOR SOUPS IN SUMMER AND WINTER.

One of the numerous mistakes which are made with respect to the preservation of stocks in *summer*, is that if a basin or other vessel holding a hot liquor is put in a pan of cold water, it will not only speedily cool the stock, but that if left there it would preserve it longer; whereas the fact is, that unless the vessel containing hot liquid can be left in running water, or have the cold water surrounding it continually changed, a hot pan or basin, with hot soup, will speedily warm the cold water into which it is plunged, and in warm weather it is thus *kept* in a tepid bath, and will turn sour sooner, instead of the heat being carried off by the outward air. Another mistake is very common with reference to the removal of fat which congeals on the top of stocks. In cold weather the surrounding atmosphere cools the vessel containing the broth or stock as quickly as the fat rises and congeals upon the surface; but in warm weather the stock remains warm underneath the congealed fat, and therefore if the fat is not speedily removed after it is cold, there is great danger of the stock speedily turning sour underneath from being kept for a length of time in a pan which remains warm without any air on the surface; but in cold weather, when the pan is cold, and surrounded by a cold atmosphere, and the stock has from that cause become a cold jelly, there is no danger of the above result; but, on the contrary, the fat being allowed to remain on the top keeps the air from the jelly and tends to its preservation; notwithstanding this a good manager will always have the stocks scalded frequently, by placing the pan over a saucepan of boiling water, taking care to break up the jelly by stirring it up with a wooden spoon from

the bottom, by which means the heat sooner pene-
trates, and there is less danger of a careless cookmaid
removing the pan before the liquor is thoroughly
heated through, in which case it is certain to turn
sour.

No. XXXIII.

WELSH MUTTON CHOPS.

Cut the chops off the neck of Welsh mutton; do
not remove the fat, and trim as little as possible; broil
on a gridiron over a sharp fire; sprinkle with a little
pepper and salt; take care not to scorch or to let the
gravy fall upon the hot stove; serve in a very hot
dish with their own unadulterated gravy; do not add
butter or any made sauces: about ten minutes will
finish them. The Hermit considered that mutton
chops never were so good as when served between
two hot plates separately to each person. Mutton
chops cut from a neck or loin, and fried in batter the
moment they are taken off the gridiron, make an
excellent dish. They should be fried in top fat from
veal or beef soups. The batter is one tablespoonful
of flour mixed with as much milk as will make it a
smooth paste; add one egg beaten up; dip the chops
hot into the batter, and fry for about five minutes in

a stewpan : a little salt may be added to the batter if liked, and chopped vegetables, but they are not necessary.

No. XXXIV.

BOILED EGGS.

Eggs only require to be put into cold water, whatever their size may be, and when the water boils the eggs are done.

No. XXXV.

BAKED APPLE DUMPLINGS.

Peel and core the apples ; then make a thin paste with two ounces of flour and one ounce of fresh butter ; rub the butter through the flour, then wet the paste with a quarter of a pint of milk, in which the yolk and white of an egg has been beaten up ; when well blended, roll the paste out and cut it into squares ; put one apple in the centre of every square of paste, and fill the hollow out of which the core was taken with sugar ; wrap the paste neatly round the apple, so as to be quite round. Glaze with white of egg and a little white powdered sugar, and bake in a slow oven for half an hour.

No. XXXVI.

GRANVILLE FISH SAUCE.

One small anchovy well pounded in a mortar, one shallot chopped fine, two tablespoonfuls of sherry, half a tablespoonful of best vinegar, six whole black peppercorns, a little nutmeg, and a very little mace. Simmer the above ingredients altogether in a double saucepan, stirring well all the time, until the shallot is soft; then take an ounce of butter in another double saucepan, with as much flour as will make it into a stiff paste; add the other ingredients which have been stewing, and stir it well till scalding hot for about two minutes, then add six tablespoonfuls of cream: stir well, and strain. This sauce was considered by the Hermit to be a difficult and complicated recipe to execute.* The only written recipe he possessed was old, very vague, and unsatisfactory; but, nevertheless, the sauce was made in perfection under his directions, and the traveller wrote down as well as he could what he saw executed, and was informed that when properly made it was even better the second day than the first, and only required to be warmed over a saucepan of hot water. It is suitable

---

* See page 176.

for salmon and every other sort of fish; but the Hermit drew his attention to the impossibility of any one making it either good or twice alike who was deficient in the organ of taste; as if the anchovy or shallot was larger or smaller, or the butter not the very freshest and best, or if there was too much or too little nutmeg and mace, or if the cream was of a different consistency, the flavour would be altered, and the greatest discretion is necessary in using mace, which, if overdone, the whole is spoiled. The written recipe belonged to the Hermit's family papers, but his mother understood how it ought to be made, and had personally taught the grandmother of Gwenllian.

No. XXXVII.

MEAGRE SOUP.

Chop fine three turnips, four potatoes, four onions, one carrot and lettuce, four ounces of bread crumbs : put into a single stewpan with four ounces of top fat; stir briskly ten minutes over a hot stove; then add a spoonful or two of flour, sufficient to make it into a stiff pulp; then add two quarts of bone stock,*

---

* Roman Catholics cannot have the slightest objection to the Hermit's bone stock, which is made from bare bones of

and after stirring well all together, pour into a double saucepan, and let it stew slowly for three quarters of an hour; then add a pint of boiling milk, stir well, and pass through a wire sieve; return it into the double; add any seasoning required of salt or herbs, &c., and it is ready to serve: it can be eaten with fried bread like pea-soup, or larger pieces fried and put into the soup at the last.

No. XXXVIII.

TO SALT BEEF.

Round of beef weighing fifty pounds; divide it as evenly as possible through the whole length. Lay it with the skin undermost and the fleshy part uppermost; cut gashes across the thickest part from one end to the other, taking care not to cut it through. Cut off all the ragged pieces, and *reduce* the thickness of the inside flesh *where necessary*, so that it may be

---

cooked meat, after every shred of meat has been taken from them, and is perfectly tasteless, but is a much lighter and more wholesome medium than the quantities of butter with which it is customary to make meagre soups. The one is *as much* an animal product as the other. Fat is always allowed instead of butter, and is much more wholesome in all savoury cookery, when treated in the manner practised in the cell of the Hermit.

filleted in a good shape, to secure which object a person salting must roll it round to try what the shape will be, and trim it until it will make a firm and compact round; take out all sinews and slimy particles, and wipe the meat thoroughly dry with a clean cloth, carefully cutting out the kernels; also trim the end of the flap, and cut it into a tapering shape. Have a pound of finely-pounded salt ready in the oven or hot closet, and sprinkle the warm salt into all the gashes and interstices of the meat; then rub in the whole of the remainder of the salt with the hand until the meat has acquired a greyish-blue tint, and there is no place left of a bloody red colour; bestow half a pound upon each half-round in this manner, and then putting them full length, with the skinny side next the stone, leave them to drain into a pan, which is to be placed conveniently to receive the brine below the salting table; rub another quarter of a pound of hot salt into each round the same night, ditto the following morning, ditto the following evening, do the same on the third morning, by which time each half-round will have had a pound and a half of hot salt rubbed into it. On the third afternoon place both the half-rounds in a large pan with a sufficient quantity of brine to cover them, composed of a gallon of cold water to a pound of

PLATE XI.

I

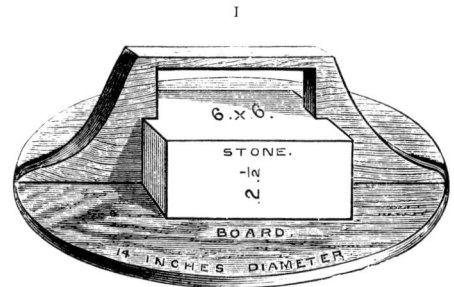

2

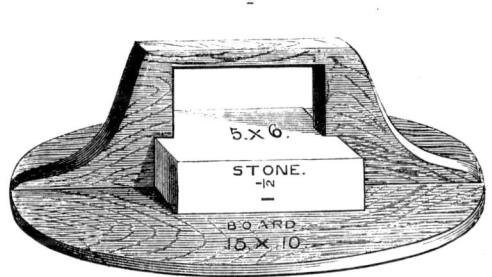

No. 1. Wooden Board and Handle, with a square Stone fixed in the
centre for Weight, to keep Salt Beef and Pork under the
Pickle.

No. 2. Ditto ditto for Tongues, adapted for a long Pan.

salt; turn them about well in the brine the same evening; the next morning the pickle will be quite bloody, and must be thrown away; then cover the rounds with a cold boiled pickle of the same strength, the salt and water of which must be boiled the previous evening that it may be *quite cold* and ready for use; turn the rounds every night and morning, and whenever the pickle is muddy or bloody it must be exchanged for fresh boiled cold pickle of the same strength. Boil the beef at the end of five or six days. If you wish to have the liquor of use for the poor, and the beef not oversalted for eating, it is always better to have a pan for each half-round if it can be managed, as they are easier to turn and better attended to.

No. XXXIX.

TONGUES TO SALT.

Cut off all the roots,* wash well and scrape clean, and rub well with hot salt night and morning for two days, until they are no longer slimy; especially rub the salt well into the parts where the roots have been cut off; then put the tongues into a pan and cover with pickle made as follows :—Three quarts of water,

---

* See No. XX., Root of Tongue Soup.

one pound and three-quarters of common salt, quarter of a pound of saltpetre, quarter of a pound of bay salt, quarter of a pound of brown sugar, an ounce of black peppercorns, a little thyme ;* boil well all together, and put to cool, and when cold cover the tongues. They are ready for use in a fortnight to three weeks; the time differs according to the size and age of the tongues, but a little experience will soon teach a cookmaid by the touch when they are sufficiently hardened. If from any circumstances they are left in pickle until they are too salt, the evil can be remedied by soaking in spring water before they are boiled, and if very much oversalted, the water in which they are boiled should be poured off when they are scalding hot, and fresh boiling water put in to finish cooking them.

No. XL.

FRESH PORK TO DRESS.

Pork for pies should be deprived of all superfluous lard, and then stewed in a double in a quarter of a pint of water to the pound of meat, a little onion and

---

* The above recipe was given to the Author by Mr. Howell (man-cook), 68, Park Street, Grosvenor Square, and has been often tested.

celery cut small, and a little salt, till the meat is tender. The gravy should then be strained off and the meat put aside; the pieces of onion and celery can be picked out. The next day, the cold fat being removed from the surface of the gravy, it will be found a finely-flavoured and delicate savoury jelly. The pork meat can then be cut into proper-sized mouthfuls if for large pies; superfluous fat, bone, or sinews being taken off, and a sufficient quantity of the jelly put into the baking dish for gravy. If properly done there will always be more than sufficient, and the overplus can be used to fill up the pie after it is baked, as directed for mutton pie (see page 395), and is very good for soups.

For roast pork always take off the rind, leaving only as much lard adhering to the meat as can be eaten with it; *scotch* it across and across, and sprinkle with sage and onion very finely chopped; baste well; it will soon brown outside, and when brown take it down, put it into a double, and put the greater part of the gravy with it, reserving only enough to dish it with, which put aside; put half a quarter of a pint of boiling water in the double to every pound of pork, and, keeping water boiling round it, finish it off in the double. The gravy that has been put aside after the cold fat has been removed

from the top is to be re-warmed and dished with it.
Pork can of course be roasted entirely before the
fire, but the advantage of cooking it in the above
manner is, that it yields a great deal of extra gravy,
which, when deprived of the fat, is excellent for
family pea-soup.

Pork sausages are preferred by the Hermit when
made of the meat of pork previously dressed in a
double, or the remains of pork pies, the meat to be
pounded in a mortar, as directed in No. XVI. If
pepper is desired for pork pies or sausages, it should
be added at the last, as pepper would spoil all the
overplus pork jelly stock for soups.

No XLI.

HAMS TO CURE.

Beat or roll the ham well with a rolling-pin on the
fleshy side, rub in one ounce of saltpetre and three
ounces of salt, well mixed, finely powdered, and warm ;
take one pound of pounded common salt, and one
pound of treacle, mix together and make thoroughly
hot in a double saucepan, then rub into the ham well
by degrees (one spoonful at a time) till the whole is
absorbed—it will take an hour to do it properly ; let it
lie one night, the next day rub in half a pound more

of common salt pounded fine, rub it in evenly all over the ham, let it lie till brine runs from it; then turn the ham in its own pickle, and rub it well every day till it begins to shrink, and it may then be hung up in an airy place and dried very gradually. Three weeks or a month is the ordinary time to cure a ham.

N.B.—After the first rubbing with saltpetre the ham must be placed in a long pan, out of which it can be taken, and put upon the stone to rub in the treacle and salt, but it must be kept in the pan or the pickle will be lost. Hams cured in this way, as in all others, should be used before they are old and rusty, but when used in the above manner they are particularly good dressed very fresh, and small hams from porkers should be cured in this way when required for eating cold.

No. XLII.

BRAWN.

Soak a fresh pig's head in cold salt and water—one pound of salt to a gallon of water—for twelve hours, changing when bloody; then boil in a double till tender with as much water as will cover it; chop small, sprinkle pepper and salt between each layer of the chopped pig's head until the brawn tin, or mould, is filled, then put on the wooden lid which fits within the mould, but rises above it, and place a weight upon it; the next day it can be turned out. It must be kept in a bran pickle if not eaten immediately.

Pigs' ears and pettitoes can be done in the same way, and added to the pig's head, unless wanted otherwise. The jelly from boiling the brawn (if it has not been too much salted) is a good addition to soup for the poor.

PICKLE FOR BRAWN.

Take as much water as will more than cover the brawn in a pan, mix in as much bran as will thicken it, add salt *in the proportion* of one pound to a gallon; simmer altogether in a double for two hours; strain it, and pour it off to cool. When cold, pour it off gently into another pan, keeping back the sediment; then add in the proportion of one quart of vinegar to the gallon, and then pour over the brawn.

No. XLIII.

TAPIOCA PUDDING FOR CHILDREN OR INVALIDS.

Tapioca two ounces; put in a double with one pint of milk, sugar to taste, and a bit of lemon-peel;

when the tapioca is thoroughly soft and blended with the milk, put it to cool on a flat dish; when cold put it into a basin, and mix in one egg beaten up, white and yolk together; it must be well stirred in through the tapioca to be thoroughly blended; bake with water in the baking-tin, so that the bottom of the pudding may not be burnt before the top is done.

RICE PUDDING.

Rice, one ounce and a half, put in a double with a pint and a half of milk; sweeten to taste. Let it stew till thoroughly soft; flavour with lemon-peel if liked; put upon a flat dish to cool; when cold beat up one egg, yolk and white, and mix thoroughly through it; bake with water in the baking-tin, for reasons above given.

RICE PUDDING WITHOUT EGGS.

Two tablespoonfuls of rice, two teaspoonfuls of white sugar, one pint and a half of skim or new milk; put altogether in a baking-dish, fill the baking-tin with cold water, and put in a steady slow oven for two hours; if the oven is very slow, it will take three hours.

No. XLIV.

CIL GOVER BISCUITS.

Two pounds of flour, half a pint of milk, and half a pint of water; knead well, and roll and beat hard for half an hour with the rolling-pin till the paste is so stiff it will crack; cut out the biscuits of the size marked below, and about a quarter of an inch thick, prick them, and bake in a quick oven.

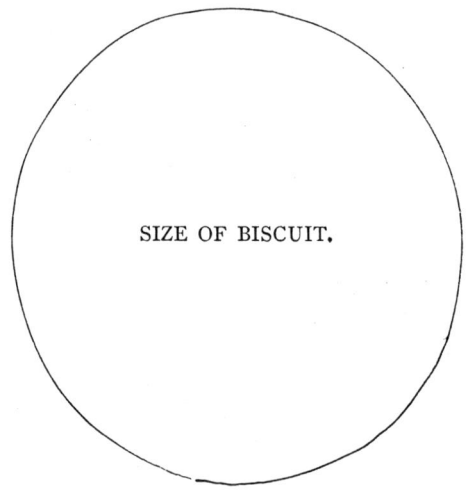

SIZE OF BISCUIT.

N.B.—A great deal depends on the heat of the oven; it must be *as sharp as possible without burning*. The biscuits when properly done are slightly browned, or mottled, in patches over the surface. These biscuits are particularlv wholesome for invalids and children. The Hermit's patients often recovered upon them when they could not eat any bread; and in fevers these biscuits broken in small bits, and soaked in cold water from the spring, frequently agree when no other nourishment can be taken.

No. XLV.
THE HERMIT'S ROCK CAKES.

Four ounces fresh butter, six ounces fine sugar, six yolks of eggs, and one pound of flour; beat the butter to a cream, then add the eggs, the sugar, and the flour; mix into a stiff paste, and add four whites of eggs and beat all together well for a whole hour; add previously caraway seeds, or currants well plumped to the flour. Drop the mixture on the baking-tin in rough pieces about the size of a large walnut and the shape of little rocks. Bake in a quick oven for twenty minutes.

N.B.—Two persons are required to beat these cakes by turns for an hour. They keep well in tin boxes.

No. XLVI.

THE HERMIT'S RICE BREAD.

Six pounds of flour and one pound boiled cold rice well mixed through the flour; then add a quarter of a pint of barm, leave it to rise for half an hour, then knead it with the water in which the rice was boiled, and in half an hour it is ready for baking, if the barm is good. Bake for an hour in a moderate oven.

RICE BREAD (ANOTHER SORT).

Boil a quarter of a pound of rice till quite soft, put it on a sieve to drain, when cold mix it well with three-quarters of a pound of flour and a spoonful of barm; let it stand for three hours to rise, then knead it up, and roll it in about a handful of flour so as to make it dry enough to put in the oven; about an hour and a quarter will bake it. It should not be cut till a day or two old, and then looks like a honey-comb.

No. XLVII.
FOR ST. VITUS'S DANCE.

Take as much mistletoe (that which grows on the whitethorn) and moss from the bark of the ash-tree as three quarts of water will cover, boil them till they are reduced to three pints; strain it, and, when cold, take a teacupful three times a day.

N.B.—This prescription actually cured a Welsh boy when all other means had failed.

No. XLVIII.
BEES' FOOD.

One teacupful of treacle and two of water. Simmer it for half an hour with a little salt in a jug plunged in a saucepan of boiling water; keep in a cool place, and tie the jug over with paper; feed the bees by pouring a little every night into a wooden scoop, which put into the hole of the hive, and take out the first thing in the morning.

PASTE FOR APPLE OR OTHER TARTS. *

Take four ounces of fine flour on the board, rub one ounce of fresh butter through the flour, mix the yolk of one egg smooth in a quarter of a pint of skim milk, wet the flour with the mixture to a proper temper, roll it out, then line the edge of two tart dishes, put in the fruit and cover with the paste, which will be sufficient for two tarts; the white of the egg is to be beat with a fork upon a plate till it is in small bubbles, then put it evenly all over the top paste of the tarts with a feather, put the tarts in the baking-tin into which cold water has previously been poured, place them in the oven for a few minutes until the egg froth is sufficiently set to be sugared,

---

* The *un*numbered recipes are those which are not referred to in Hermit's lessons.

take them out, strew sugar over them quickly, and replace them in the oven till baked sufficiently.

N.B.—Practical experience alone can teach the proper heat of the oven; it is not absolutely necessary to put them in the oven before they are sugared, but some persons succeed better in making the rough glaze by doing so; others produce exactly the same effect by sugaring the white of egg as soon as it is put on, before the tart is placed in the oven.

QUINCES FOR ADDITION TO APPLE TARTS.

Cut the quinces in quarters. To five pounds of fruit put three pounds of sugar and half a quarter of a pint of water; put them in pint jars; put plates or saucers over the jars, and let them simmer very gently for three hours placed in boiling water; put the peels in with them, and take them out when done; the overplus of syrup may be bottled, and also used to flavour tarts. It will prevent waste of sugar if the peels are stewed the first hour without sugar, then take out the peels and add the sugar, and simmer for two hours longer.

TO DRY HERBS.

Cut the herbs on a dry day just before they flower; cut off the hard parts of the stems, and dry

the tender tops and leaves in an oven (or hot closet
or screen) between two dishes, as quickly as possible,
provided they are not burnt; pick off the leaves
while hot, pound them well in a mortar, and put
them into well-stoppered bottles; they ought to be
green but crisp. The best time for drying herbs is
when they are in bud.*

BASIL is in the best state for drying from the
middle of August and three weeks after.

KNOTTED MARJORAM, from the beginning of July
and during the same.

WINTER SAVORY, the latter end of July and
throughout August.

SUMMER SAVORY, the latter end of July and
throughout August.

THYME, LEMON-THYME, ORANGE-THYME, during
June and July.

MINT, latter end of June and during July.

SAGE, August and September.

TARRAGON, June, July, and August.

CHERVIL, May, June, and July.

---

* All good managers should keep this calendar by them,
and take care to gather their herbs when in bud (not blossom);
and those who have a gardener should give him a duplicate
list, that the herbs may not be sent in for winter preservation
when past their prime.

Burnet and Basil, June, July, and August.

Parsley, May, June, and July.

Fennel, May, June, and July.

Elder Flowers, May, June, and July.

RASPBERRY VINEGAR.

Bruise eight pounds of raspberries and pour on them three pints of good gooseberry or sugar vinegar, let them stand *twenty-four* hours, frequently stirring them with a wooden spoon; put six pounds of loaf-sugar, broken in large lumps, into an earthen vessel, and the fruit and vinegar into a jelly-bag, wrung out in boiling water; let it drop upon the sugar till the juice is drained out, pressing it gently now and then; pour the liquor into a preserving-pan, and let it simmer until it boils up slowly over a moderate fire, and when cold bottle it. When wanted for use, put one or two spoonfuls in a tumbler of spring water, and, if too sweet, add a few drops of vinegar when drunk. A stone jar is the best to boil it in, set in a vessel of boiling water.

DUCHESS OF BEDFORD'S TEA-CAKES.

Take two pounds of fine flour, three ounces of pounded sugar, four ounces fresh butter, four eggs well beaten, one large tablespoonful, or half an ounce, of barm (or German yeast), one pint of new milk; melt the butter in the milk, which must be warmed, mix all together and beat it well; let it stand one hour, then put it in well-buttered small round tins; let them be *well proved.* Bake in a quick oven twenty minutes.

RHUBARB JAM.*

Boil an equal quantity of rhubarb cut up, and gooseberries before they are *quite ripe*, with three-quarters of a pound of crystallized moist sugar to one pound of fruit. When boiled, it will make an excellent jam, similar to apricot.

It will keep some time in a cool dry place, tied down as usual.

APPLE BREAD.

Boil twelve apples till soft; core and peel them, break them up, and pulp through a sieve; put sugar to taste, and mix them with twice its weight of dough, and bake them in a very slow oven.

---

* This receipt was given to the Hermit by the venerable Mrs. Faulkener, of Tenby, South Wales, aged ninety-three, for many years landlady of the principal hotel there (*then* the White Lion).

THE HERMIT'S MINCE-PIES.

Squeeze the juice out of three large lemons, boil the rind (till a straw will go through) in several waters to extract the bitterness; chop them fine, add half a pound of sweet almonds pounded fine, one pound of currants, one pound lump sugar, one pound raw marrow, cinnamon, nutmeg, and a *very little* mace; mix it up to a proper consistency. The currants must be very well cleaned and plumped by pouring boiling water on them, and drying in dry cloths before the fire, and picking them well. To be baked in very small tin pattipans, the paste being made with clarified marrow, *not butter.*

A COMPLICATED VEAL PIE, BUT VERY GOOD, TO BE EATEN COLD.

Quarter of a pound of suet, quarter pound bread crumbs, a tablespoonful of parsley leaves chopped fine, a small quantity of tarragon and basil chopped fine, half a tablespoonful of lemon thyme, ditto sweet marjoram chopped fine and eschalot, all to be chopped fine, and pounded, also one tablespoonful and a half of rind of lemon, cut as thin as possible, and pounded with a lump of sugar that has been well rubbed on the lemon before the peel has been cut off, chop and pound a small quantity of lean dressed ham or tongue. Bake raw lean veal in a Ffwrn fach with one-quarter of a pint of water to the pound, and put pure fat over it (its own is the best) in a very slow oven, or stew it in a double saucepan. After it is done pour off the gravy, which will become jelly, cut in very small pieces, and pound it in a mortar with all the above ingredients moistened with the veal-jelly; and after all are thoroughly mixed and pounded together, beat up the yolk and white of an egg, mix it with all the pounded ingredients, then beat it all well together again. Put a layer of very thin boiled cold ham at the bottom of the dish, then add the forcemeat till the dish is full.

It must be moistened with the jelly stock which came from the veal. The dish is to be first lined with puff paste, and carefully baked with water in the baking-tin, well soaked through in the oven, and yet not dried or burned. When cold, to be turned upside down.

THE WELSH HERMIT'S FAVOURITE CHICKEN AND LEEK PIE.

Boil a chicken as directed in No. I., cut it up into tidy pieces, not too large, flavour the chicken jelly which it will have produced with a little salt and celery, onion, and various herbs to taste; scald some small leeks by pouring boiling water upon them, then split them, and cut them in pieces about an inch long; lay the pieces of chicken in the pie-dish with slices of cold boiled tongue, the pieces of scalded leeks, fine-chopped parsley, and the chicken jelly flavoured as above described. The paste to be the same as ordered for mutton-pie, No. VII. Fill the baking-tin with water; when the paste is done take off the top ornament, and with a jug pour in through the hole in which it was placed three tablespoonfuls of fresh cream previously heated, by placing the jug containing it in a saucepan of boiling water ; replace the ornament, and serve.

N.B.—Mutton, beef, and veal make excellent pies prepared in the above manner; but the veal also requires tongue or ham intermingled with it, and a very little pepper as well as salt may by some persons be considered an improvement to mutton and beef, though the former is not necessary, and it is more wholesome without spice.

THE HERMIT'S MUTTON STEW.

Necks and scrags of mutton, eight pounds, cut up , celery, half a pound, chopped small ; onions, half a pound, chopped small ; water, two quarts. Stew in the double three hours. It will produce two quarts and one pint of good broth. Next day, cut off all superfluous fat and bare bones ; put the meat on again in a double, with as much of the clear broth as is sufficient to moisten the stew, with half a pound more raw chopped onions and four pounds potatoes which have been boiled and cut up ; all the fat must be previously removed from the broth when cold. The whole to stew together for one hour.

N.B.—There is always more broth produced than is required for the stew, and the overplus can be kept for use as clear, pure mutton broth, as the stronger flavour required for the stew is obtained by the chopped onions added with the potatoes, and any overplus of the sauce which is to spare when the stew is dished will resemble, potato soup, and is an excellent addition to other thickened soups.

ROAST HARE.

Hares in general when roasted have black heads, ears burnt to tinder, and the top of the shoulders, and very often the whole body, scorched and dried up. The proper way to roast a hare is first of all to soak it in several waters for an hour and a half (and having got rid of all the blood from the neck by cutting the neck-string, and pouring warm water over the incision to effect the above purpose) ; the hare must then be well dried, and a piece of paper saturated with liquid fat put all over the head and neck, under which there must be as much pure fat as can be tied on under the paper. Lay slices of cold boiled pork or bacon all over the back, which should also be covered with oiled paper for the first three quarters of an hour. The paper can afterwards be taken off, and the bacon also, when nearly done, to finish the roasting ; brown it and froth it. The hare must also be continually well basted. The art in roasting a hare is to prevent its being dry, and yet to have it brown and well frothed at the last ; it will take from one to two hours according to the size ; it should be tied upon a spit with skewers and roasted horizontally. Spits should never be put *through* anything that can possibly be avoided.

The meat remaining from roast hare should be hashed in the jelly made from its bones, treated exactly in the same manner as directed for other bones. They will make more jelly than required for hashing the meat. If the hash is not all eaten, it will make excellent hare soup with the overplus of the jelly. If more stock is required, the jelly from the bones of other game or poultry can be used also, and the whole flavoured

with herbs and vegetables as required, the remainder
of the hash to be added half an hour before it is
wanted.*

HARE STUFFING.

Two ounces of beef suet chopped fine, three ounces
of fine bread crumbs, half an ounce of parsley, marjoram, winter savory and grated lemon-peel, half an
ounce of shallot, nutmeg, pepper, and salt. Mix
with the white and yolk of an egg. If not stiff, it
is good for nothing; put it in the hare, and sew
it up.

GOOSE OR DUCK STUFFING.

Two ounces of scalded onion, one ounce of green
sage leaves, four ounces of bread crumbs, yolk and
white of an egg, pepper and salt, and some minced
apple. The flavour is much milder if the onions are
scalded previously.

VEAL CUTLETS.

Veal cutlets should be half an inch thick, cut round
and flattened; the trimmings which come off the
veal (by cutting them round) should be put into a
double saucepan with two or three spoonfuls of water,

---

* Three pounds of hare bones will make three pints of hare
jelly.

G G

and finely-chopped leek roots, orange thyme, and marjory, and a small piece of lemon-peel. Stew them slowly two hours, and then strain off; while the gravy is being made the raw cutlets should have a few drops of lemon-juice squeezed upon them on a dish, and some chopped sweet herbs sprinkled over them; take all the fat off the veal gravy as soon as cold; chop very fine two ounces of leek roots, one ounce of celery, and a quarter of half an ounce of carrot, and stir in a single saucepan over the fire, with the fat obtained from the veal gravy ; if any additional fat is wanted, let it be taken from veal stock or chicken stock. Stir the vegetables and fat together briskly for ten minutes, then add as much flour as will make it into a soft paste, and stir five minutes more; then add the whole mass to the veal gravy, which should be ready heated in another double saucepan, and, when it has simmered for three quarters of an hour, add two tablespoonfuls of cream ten minutes before it is strained; return the sauce, without the vegetables, into the double saucepan, and it is ready to dish with the cutlets; but if any additional flavour is wanted it can be previously added. The cutlets are to be rolled in egg and bread crumbs, and fried, in the same way as fish, in clarified top fat. The veal trimmings, after the gravy has been made, will be useful to make sausages, after being pounded in the mortar with a little veal jelly, and a little boiled ham or tongue, and flavoured with sage.

WELSH LEEK BROTH OR SOUP.

Blanch five or six fine winter leeks by putting them for five minutes in boiling water, after cutting off part of the head, leaving some of the green leaves attached to the roots; having split each leek in half lengthways, and cutting one half in three or four pieces, then add them to a fowl trussed· for boiling, with half a pint of water to the pound weight, in a double stewpan, adding a little celery chopped small, and herbs and salt to taste. Let the water boil slowly round in the outer vessel until the chicken is tender and nearly fit to eat, then put in two dozen French plums whole; draw the saucepan aside to keep hot, but not to overboil the fowl. In about half an hour the plums will be plump and fit to eat, before which time take out the fowl, cut it into neat pieces, removing the bones, and put the pieces into the tureen, pouring the leek broth or soup over them, the leeks being then partly in pulp. If too thick, some additional veal or chicken jelly can be added to it. The plums are eaten with the meat and vegetables.

SHOULDER OF VEAL BOILED.

The jelly stock from veal boiled in the following manner was the usual foundation for the Hermit's white soups.

Shoulder weighing ten pounds, celery half a pound chopped fine, onions half a pound chopped fine, water one quart and half a pint; stewed in double till the meat is fit for eating.

It produced one quart and a pint and a half of stock, which when cold was a firm jelly.

The next day the shoulder being *re*-warmed in a double in its own stock (which is improved thereby), can be served with the following sauce:—Milk, one pint; water, one quarter of a pint; one pint and a quarter of bone stock; half a pound of rice; suet or veal's top fat, two ounces. Stir well, and stew in double three hours and a half, with four ounces of pounded ham or cold boiled pork, or else salt to taste, with finely-chopped onion: five minutes before it is served put in two or three ounces of fresh chopped parsley, and again stir well. The above sauce is not only a palatable accompaniment with veal, but an excellent foundation for a family white soup afterwards. Fried bacon or sausages can be served as accompaniments.

N.B.—The *cruel* practice of bleeding calves before they are killed, to make the meat unnaturally white, destroys the flavour of veal, and renders a meat which is not light of digestion really unwholesome.*

GLAZE OF COW'S-HEEL.

Scald a fresh cow's-heel to get the hair off; then, after well scraping, crack it across in several places, and chop up and put it in a digester with four quarts of water, and stew till it is reduced to two quarts; then pour into a pan till the next day. Then take all the oil off the top, and bottle it for the use of the stables. (This is pure neat's-foot oil.) The jelly under it will be hard, and is the material to make glaze, which is coloured by stirring quickly over the fire till it becomes a fine yellow bronze, and is thick enough to adhere to the spoon. There is less waste if coloured with a little burned sugar, as it requires less boiling down for colouring.

N.B.—The cow-heel bones ought to be done a second and third time; *re*-broken with fresh water in digester; and will make stock each time. Second time, put two quarts of water and reduce to one

---

* This cruel practice is not followed abroad, which is the reason that veal often agrees there with those who cannot eat it in England.

quart; third time, one full quart, and reduce to one pint.

It it much less wasteful to procure a cow's-heel for glaze than to allow glaze to be made of trimmings of meat, &c. &c. Glaze is *only* for *ornament* to *varnish* meat. It is not supposed to be eaten, but, *if* it is put on food, it *ought to be wholesome.* The usual custom of making glaze of what is called "*anything*," but means "everything," otherwise eatable, destroys a large quantity of food for no good purpose.

MUSHROOM CATCHUP.

Full-grown mushrooms are the best for catchup; cut them across and across stems and skins, put a layer at the bottom of an earthen pan and sprinkle with salt, and continue till you have used all the mushrooms you have ready; sprinkle moderately with salt over every layer, let them stand three hours, then pound them up in a mortar, and let them stand two days, stirring them up with wooden spoons twice every day; then pour the whole mass into jars, and to every quart add half an ounce of whole black pepper, ditto allspice; put the jars into an outside double surrounded by boiling water; let the water boil slowly and steadily round them two hours and a half, then take out the jars and pour the juice through a sieve into a clean double saucepan, and let the water boil around it for one hour more, then pour it into a jug or basin, and let it stand in a cold place till the next day, when very gently pour it off into half or quarter-pint bottles which have been rinsed out with spirits of wine; cork close, and cement. If it is ill-corked and not kept dry, it will spoil. The pepper-corns and allspice should be bottled with it, and the strainings can be made use of for hashes, &c. &c., if not kept longer than two or three days. The sub-stance of the mushrooms which is left behind after straining, should be pressed down flat on a plate covered over with another plate, and dried in a hot closet, or in a screen before the fire. When dry, pound and put in bottles, and use in the same way as catchup, where mushroom flavour is desired.

N.B.—Mushroom catchup is generally made with *putrefied* mushrooms, and, even when mushrooms are fresh, it is customary to keep them so long in a pan mashed, or unmashed, that they are unfit for use, the best flavour being gone and the mushrooms in a very unwholesome state. The mushrooms should be as freshly gathered as possible for catchup, and should never be kept longer than is recommended in the above recipe.

THE HERMIT'S BREAD AND BUTTER PUDDING.

Cut rice bread (see page 437) of two days old in thin slices, without crust, butter thinly with cold butter, fit them into the tart-dish you intend to use, then take them out and pour three-quarters of an inch of rather thick batter (flavoured with sugar and lemon-peel) into the bottom of the dish. Put the dish into the oven for three or four minutes to consolidate the batter, then take it out and lay a layer of slices on the batter, then pour out of a jug a sufficiency of *thinner* batter (similarly flavoured) to moisten the bread, then sprinkle a layer of currants well plumped, then another layer of slices of bread, pouring in batter in the same manner over each layer until the dish is filled to within half a quarter of an inch of the top; then make your batter thicker, so as to be of the same consistence as the first layer in the bottom of the dish, and with this (*thicker*) batter fill the dish evenly to the edge, and bake with water in the tin. If properly made it will be firm and yet light, the batter at the bottom will keep the bread from drying up with too fierce a heat, the thicker batter on the top ought to *cover* the upper layer of currants, and prevent that common but very unpleasant effect of having the slices of bread at the top of the dish scorched and curled up, and covered with currants burned to a cinder. The object of having thinner batter poured between the layers of bread is to soften the bread, as otherwise the bread would not absorb the batter and be flavoured by it.

WELSH CARROT PLUM PUDDING.

Half a pound of raisins, half-pound of currants, half-pound of suet chopped fine, one ounce lemon-peel, one nutmeg, two large carrots, and two tablespoonfuls of flour; mix all well together, but the carrots must be boiled and pulped previous to mixing with the other ingredients, and the whole must be boiled two hours.

ANOTHER.

Half-pound of flour, quarter of a pound of suet chopped very fine, quarter-pound bread crumbs, three-quarters of a pound grated carrot, quarter of a pound of raisins stoned, quarter of a pound well-washed and plumped currants, quarter-pound brown sugar, beat up *two whole* eggs and the yolks of four in a gill of milk; grate a little nutmeg into it, and add it to the former. Boil at least one hour.

FAMILY PLUM PUDDING.

Flour twenty-six pounds, suet seven pounds, raisins nine pounds, currants four pounds, sugar four and

a half pounds.   If not eaten the day boiled, boil half
the time the first day and the other half the second,
or only warm through the second time, as over-
boiling makes the plum puddings too soft.

Cow-heel is an excellent substitute for suet in
making plum puddings.   It must be well boiled previously, and not chopped too fine.

The subjoined pudding casket,* made of tin, was

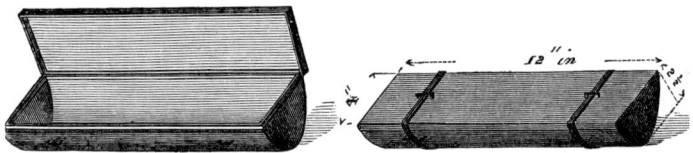

invented by the Hermit for boiling plum puddings
when made in rolls to be cut in slices, the Hermit
having observed that when plum puddings were boiled
in cloths *only* the water became a sort of *raisin and
currant soup*, and that the waste of ingredients altogether was considerable.

Each pudding turned out of these tin caskets can
be divided into *ten* thick slices.   The Hermit had a
wooden gauge for the widows with *points* at equal
distances, and each pudding was thus marked in a

* These Plum Pudding Caskets are to be had of Richard
Jones, Tinman, Abergavenny, South Wales.   Price 1*s.* 6*d.*
each, or 1*s.* 3*d.* by the dozen.

moment (as soon as turned out) and cut up in the most exact manner. A thin piece of cloth laid under the lid after the tin is filled is all that is required, and the lid, being shut, is tied round with strong pack-thread passed through the loops in the lid; and when twenty or thirty puddings are boiled at the same time in a boiler, five or six can be tied together, and taken out of the boiler when done with a hook by a loop in the string.

ROWLEY POWLEY PUDDING.

Skin and chop one pound of beef suet very fine, put it into a mortar and pound it well, moistening with a little sweet-oil until it is the consistency of butter.

Put one pound of flour upon your pastry slab, make a hole in the centre, in which put a teaspoonful of salt, and mix it with cold water into a softish flexible paste with the right hand; dry it off a little with flour until you have well cleared the paste from the slab, but do not work it more than you can possibly help; let it remain two minutes on the slab, and then lay the prepared suet on the paste; press it out flat with the hand, then fold over the edges of the paste so as to hide the suet, and roll it to the thickness of half an inch; fold over one third, over which pass the rolling-pin; fold over the other third, thus forming a square; place it with the ends before you; shake a little flour over and under, repeat the rolls and turns twice more; flour a baking sheet, lay it in a cool place for half an hour; then roll twice more, and put in a cool place for a quarter of an hour; give two more rolls (making seven in all), and it is ready for use.

Roll it out and cover with jam; tie in a loose cloth, and serve up cut in slices. This pudding may also be boiled in a bason and turned out.

BREAD PUDDING.

A pint of bread crumbs in a double saucepan with as much milk as will cover them; the peel of a lemon, a little nutmeg, and a bit of cinnamon; boil about a quarter of an hour, sweeten, take out the cinnamon and add two eggs, beat all well together. If baked, it will require half an hour; if boiled, more than an hour.

QUEEN CHARLOTTE'S ORANGE PUDDING.

Take two oranges and one lemon, grate the peel off them and mix with the juice, into which put a quarter of a pound of sugar and the yolks of five eggs; then make a little paste for the bottom of the dish. It must be baked slowly in a moderate oven, but yet be browned at the top.

APPLE SNOW.

Roast four or five apples that look white, work the pulp through a sieve; take the weight of one egg of pulp, the same of powdered sugar; beat up the apple sugar and the white of an egg together until they become as white as snow. When nearly beaten up, put in as much ground alum as will cover a sixpence, and, when quite beaten, put it very lightly piled in a dish. If liked, cream or custard can be eaten with it.

Preserved raspberries or strawberries can be used as well as apples.

LEMON CREAMS.

Rub three lemons with sugar until the aroma is absorbed, squeeze the juice of one upon the sugar, put it in a large china bowl, add a quart of cream, and whisk it continually till the froth arises; take it from the top with a spoon, and place it on a sieve; put it in the glasses a short time before it is sent to table. It will take nearly half a pound of sugar to sweeten a quart of cream with the lemon-juice.

LEMON JELLY.

Eight sheep shanks broken up and put to soak over night in cold water; then put on the fire or stove in a digester with two quarts of water, and stew until it is reduced to one; but if done in a double saucepan, one quart of water will be sufficient, and double time required, but there will not be any danger of waste. Pour off to cool, and the next day take off all the oil from the top, and what will not come off with a spoon can be wiped off with a clean soft cloth, or absorbed with soft paper. The jelly ought to be very firm, so that it would cut up in pieces: to one quart of jelly put half a pound of lump sugar broken up, the peel of one lemon and the juice of three lemons, three eggs, whites and shells; beat up together, whisk the whole over the stove till ready to boil, then draw it off sufficiently to keep it simmering slowly for a quarter of an hour, putting hot cinders or hot charcoal on the lid of the stewpan; then, having the jelly bag ready and warm, having squeezed it out in scalding water and suspended before the fire with a basin under it, pour the jelly through the jelly bag, return the first strainings back a second time into the bag till all has run through. The jelly is then finished, and may either run into a mould or be allowed to cool in a basin and cut out as wanted. Shank jelly is lighter of digestion than calves'-foot jelly, and quite as good for every other purpose.

TURIN STICKS.

Two pounds of white flour, two ounces of fresh butter. Rub the butter well into the flour ; add two teaspoonfuls of baking powder, and sufficient pure cold spring water to mix it into a *stiff* paste ; cut into little lumps of equal size, roll out into long thin sticks as quickly *as possible;* bake in rather a *quick* oven.

PUMPKINS.

Few vegetables are so little understood, and, consequently, so much undervalued in Great Britain, as pumpkins. Perhaps Gower, in South Wales, is the only part of the United Kingdom where pumpkins are grown as an article of diet by the rural population from their appreciation of their nutritive qualities; and there they are to be seen as on the Continent, hanging from the ceilings for winter store, in cottages and farmhouses, and any little spare corner in the field or garden is made use of to place the small mound in which to sow a few pumpkin seeds. The varieties of this plant are so numerous that it would

be beyond the limit of any cookery book to attempt
an enumeration of comparative merits, from the
Vegetable Marrow to the Turk's Turban and the
Yellow Pumpkin, which grows to such a size as to fill
a wheelbarrow, but, as the Hermit was fully aware of
the merits of this vegetable, it will not be out of place
to note shortly from among his recipes a few of the
modes in which pumpkins are available, wholesome,
and nourishing in cookery. For white soup they can
be used alone, with merely the addition of onion, celery,
and sweet herbs for flavouring, in the same manner
as the numerous vegetables mentioned in the White
Soup of Gover. (See page 391.) They are excellent when boiled, sprinkled with salt and sweet herbs,
and fried in egg and crumbs, like soles. Also plain,
boiled in slices, and served with brown gravy. In
Gower they are added to hashed meat, made into pies
with apples, and put into soup. There is also a dish
made by the natives which seems to evince an Eastern
origin, which is made of pumpkin, mutton, and currants. Pumpkins have one peculiar quality in addition
to a good deal of natural sweetness, which is, that
they will absorb and retain the flavour of whatever
they are cooked with; this where fruit is scarce* is a

---

* The Hermit was of opinion that the great scarcity and
dearness of fruit in Great Britain, which is severely felt by the

very important characteristic, as the pumpkin is both wholesome and nourishing in itself, but, not having any flavour, its imbibing the flavour of any fruit if mixed with it is an especial advantage. If stewed with plums, it tastes exactly like them in puddings and tarts; the same with apples, rhubarb, or gooseberries and for savoury cookery it would be difficult to say in what dish it may not be used with advantage as an addition.

In America there are an endless variety of puddings of which pumpkins are the principal ingredient; and they are very easily grown. On one occasion they appeared in a field of mangel-wurzel in South Wales,

poor, arises from the *want of attention to hardy sorts of fruit* with which the climate of Great Britain will agree. In many parts of Germany, where the climate is much more severe, and where also there is a great deal of rain, there is abundance of fruit; pears, plums, and peaches, and in many places *standard apricots*. It is very true that the fruit is frequently very inferior in flavour to the fruit from English walled gardens, but it is equally good and wholesome when stewed or preserved. It is very singular that the Horticulturists of Great Britain do not pay more attention to the introduction of those kinds of fruit-trees which are hardy and bear abundantly, instead of sacrificing everything to the magnitude of specimens. *Fruit for the million* is much wanted. The purple peach (of Bonn), which is hardy and a standard, seems to be unknown in Great Britain. The pulp as well as the juice is the colour of a mulberry. (*Traveller's Note.*)

H H

to the great surprise of the owner, as it was not in that part of the Principality where pumpkins were grown. The seeds had been accidentally mixed with those of the mangel-wurzel; they were treated in the same manner, and they came to as great perfection as if they had been grown in a garden. This sort was the large orange species, called in some places " Turk's Turban," around which there is a beautiful strip of narrow network exactly resembling nun's lace: this species is particularly sweet and hardy. There are very few kinds of gourds or pumpkins that are not edible; but some of the ornamental kinds are uneatable, or have medical properties, such as the colocynth, which so closely resembles an orange in appearance.

LOSS IN ROASTING A WELSH LEG OF MUTTON.	LOSS IN ROASTING AN ENG-LISH LEG OF MUTTON.

	s.	*d.*
Weight before roasting,		
5¼ lbs. at 10*d.* per lb. . .	4	4½
Loss by weight of bone, 10		
oz. at 10*d.* per lb. after		
roasting	0	6¼
Balance	3	10¼
Fat, 4 oz. at 4*d.* per lb., loss		
at the rate of 6*d.* per lb. .	0	1½
	3	8¾

	s.	*d.*
Weight before roasting,		
12 lbs. at 10*d.* per lb. . .	10	0
Loss by weight of bone,		
1¾ lb. at 10*d.*	1	5½
Balance	8	6½
Fat melted away, taken from		
dripping-pan, 3 lbs. 2 oz.		
at 4*d.* per lb., loss at the		
rate of 6*d.* per lb. . . .	1	6¾
	6	11¾

Loss in Welsh mutton, 7¾*d.* in 4*s.* 4½*d.*, or 31 in 210, nearly one-seventh; consequently, more than half the saving in food as compared with English mutton.

Loss in English mutton, 3*s.* 0¼*d.* in 10*s.*, or 36¼ in 120, nearly one in three; consequently, more than double the loss in English mutton as an article of food.

The foregoing Table will show that the loss on an English leg of mutton is nearly *one* in *three*, while the loss in the Welsh leg of mutton is only *one* in *seven !* the loss being more than one-half *less* in Welsh mutton than English. It must also be remembered that in the *ordinary* manner of roasting the fat above-mentioned would either be utterly lost, or not worth above 2*d.* a pound, so that the loss in English mutton would in reality be much greater. In roasting the English leg of mutton no basting fat was needed; in the Welsh leg one-quarter of a pound was used, and one-quarter of a pound was taken from the dripping-pan afterwards. In the *ordinary* method of cooking, the bone would be a clear loss in *both* cases; but *even* the Hermit's jelly from the bone would not go very far towards repairing the loss of 3*s*. o$\frac{1}{4}$*d*. in every ten shillings! And if the Hermit's process of basting and clarification of fat was not adopted, the 1*s*. 6*d*. in the above Table set down to the *credit* side must be added to the loss, or at least one-half of it. There are few greater errors than to suppose fat, large animals are either wholesome or economical.

THE HERMIT'S BAKED BEEF FOR CHRISTMAS.

Take half or whole rounds of beef, cut and prepared as described (see page 427), roll them up, and skewer them into rounds, and put each of them into the outer part of a (round) " double " (see Plate 4), which is made of iron, or galvanized iron; place on the top of the round of beef, a *star* of wood the proper size to go

within the top of the vessel, then put a stiff paste of

coarse brown flour (or flour mixed with bran) over the star to prevent any evaporation, and pour in as much water with a sprinkling of salt as will rise to about two inches, then put on the lid and bake in a brick oven; the time must, of course, depend upon the size and weight of the rounds. When done the paste at the top will look like gingerbread,* the gravy will be very strong and abundant, and the meat will be juicy and nicely browned. The gravy being poured off, and the fat taken from it when cold, it is *re*-warmed to dish up. The Hermit, when he required a number of these rounds dressed at once for a Christmas feast, used to bake them the day before, and the next day *re*-warmed them in the inner doubles in their own gravy, with hot water in the outer vessel, on a large stove. In this way they were all done punctually to the same time, equally well cooked, and an abundance of extra gravy without grease. Where a brick oven is not to be had for baking meat, the iron oven should always have *all* the fire *taken out* before the meat is put in. Meat should be baked very slowly, and be well covered in a vessel with a close-fitting lid. The ignorant practice of putting meat into open baking-tins not only entirely ruins the flavour of the meat, from the bad taste imbibed from the vapour of the fat

---

* Very useful pounded to thicken soup for the poor.

(frizzling in the iron oven), but it is very wasteful, dries up the meat, destroys the gravy, and *taints the oven* to such an extent that, if bread or cakes are baked in it afterwards before it has undergone a long and laborious purification, they would be flavoured by the same taste as pervades a house from the odour of fat frying upon hot iron.

MUSHROOMS.

Wild mushrooms are generally brought in, in larger quantities than are required for immediate consumption unless made into catchup, and, as the mushroom season is always very short, the overplus of mushrooms can be preserved for two or three days to be as good as if freshly gathered, if cooked in the following manner :—Peel the mushrooms, cut off the stems, sprinkle a little salt in the inside of the flap, and put on each flap a bit of clarified marrow about the size of a very small bean, and place them one over the other in half-pint or pint jars (the outer side down and the flap up), put the jars to stand in vessels of boiling water, and let them simmer slowly, with a bladder over the top of the jar, for an hour or two, according to the number and thickness of the mushrooms ; then put them away in a cold place. These mushrooms will be good for several days, and taste as if fresh gathered. When used, take off the marrow, if it has congealed on the surface, and put the mushrooms on a soup-plate upon squares of toast saturated with their own gravy, which will have exuded from them in the jars, put another soup-plate on the top, and warm the whole over a saucepan of boiling water. The stems and peelings of mushrooms ought to be chopped up as soon as they are taken off, and put into small jars, with a little salt, and simmered with boiling water round them in the same manner as the mushrooms: the liquor distilled from them can be used *while fresh* for flavouring sauces and hashes.

The Hermit was very partial to mushrooms, and considered them not only wholesome for persons in ordinary health, but so nutritious that he believed them equal to meat, and questioned me closely as to the improvement of their cultivation in the present age, but I did not distinguish myself by my answers, for I really could give no account of them, excepting that rich persons had mushroom houses, where they were produced by artificial heat in the winter, and that mushroom spawn was generally purchased and was expensive, but I did *not know* whether naturalists or horticulturists had discovered any means of cultivating them in the open ground, or securing the preservation of mushrooms from one year to another in places where they spring up spontaneously, though I had often heard surprise expressed at the abundance of mushrooms in some years and the absence of them in others, in the same ground; and this being the sum and substance of my knowledge, I was taunted repeatedly, at the expense of my " *scientific friends,*" who had not turned their attention to a natural production so beneficial to rich and poor, and about the natural history and cultivation of which so little (according to my report) appeared to be known; and I was advised to offer a prize for new discoveries on the subject!

GOOD FAMILY BREAD (WHITE).

Five pounds of fine bran to 28 pounds of flour.

GOOD BROWN BREAD.

Two pounds of bran to four pounds of flour.

N.B.—The brown bread, or household bread of old times, is now hardly to be met with, and is rare even in Wales, the reason being that the millers do not grind and prepare the flour in the same way as formerly, when the pure corn, having been sent to be ground, was returned by the miller with the bran and flour altogether; and in every house there was a good-wife or *widow*, who sifted the flour required for each baking, removing only the large flake bran. Bread thus made is very superior in flavour to the bread now generally used, but where the above plan cannot be followed, it is best to mix fresh sifted bran with the flour. The *flavour* of bread is in the bran, and in the absence of bran it is *flavourless*, much less wholesome, and not at all more nourishing.

WELSH PAN OR POT BREAD.

Take three pounds and a half of brown flour (flour which has only had the coarser bran taken out of it), put it to rise with about two tablespoonfuls of barm, and, when risen, mix it and knead it in the usual manner; then put it into an iron pot or a thick earthen pan, and turn it topsy-turvy on a flat stone, which should be placed on the ground in the middle of a heap of hot embers, made by burning wood, peat, or turf; cover the pot or pan entirely over with hot embers, leave it to bake, and when the ashes are cold take it out. This mode of baking produces most excellent bread, but of course it cannot be practised economically except where such rural operations are carried on as provide the necessary quantity of hot embers for other purposes within a convenient distance of the house.

OATMEAL CAKES.

Make a stiff paste with oatmeal and water or skim milk; then form it into balls with the hand about the size of small eggs; then shape with the hand round and round to the size of a small cheese-plate or large saucer; when one oat-cake is formed the right shape and thickness, turn it and shake dry oatmeal all over it; then take another, put it in the middle of the oat-cake you have made, and form that in the same manner upon the first made; when well tempered, turn it, and shake dry oatmeal all over it, and proceed in the same way until you have got eighteen oat-cakes one on the other, remembering that each must be turned, and that dry oatmeal must be put between every one, and they must be turned and *re*-turned, and shaped with the hand, until they are all of the same texture, as thin as is possible without breaking. When dry enough to put on the bake-stone (heated to the required point which practice alone can teach), bake them one at a time; have a clean cloth folded to the proper shape, and press the cake down flat on the bake-stone, where it should remain until it is of a nice light brown colour. The upper side of the cake is to be glazed before it is taken off the bake-stone; the glaze is made with egg and milk, and a little sugar is generally added, but that is only a matter of taste; some persons like a

little sugar mixed with the oatmeal of which the cakes
are made. As each cake is taken off the bake-stone
it is laid across the rolling-pin that it may dry in a
hollow shape; and as each cake becomes hard and
crisp, they are again put one on the other, and are
always served and kept in a pile. The rolling-pin
must not be used in making these cakes, all must be
done with the hand, and they must be flattened and
worked round and round with the hand until they
are almost as thin as a wafer. Great skill and dexterity, as well as practice, are necessary to make these
cakes well, which when once attained, the process is
very quickly executed. The *thin Welsh-oat cake* is
particularly wholesome, and often agrees with invalids
of weak digestion better than bread; they are sometimes eaten with cold butter or cheese, or eaten dry
with milk or tea.

THICK WELSH BARLEY CAKES.

Take fine barley meal and make into a stiff dough
with skim milk; roll out to the size of a small bake-
stone, about three-quarters of an inch thick, and bake.
It is eaten with cold butter.

THIN WELSH BARLEY CAKE.

Mix fine barley meal and milk together to the consistency of batter, and pour slowly on the bake-stone

out of a jug until it has formed a circle the size of a small plate, then let it bake slowly. It ought to be very thin but soft, like a pancake or a pikelate; it is likewise eaten with cold butter.

CIL GOVER BUNS.

One pound of flour, two ounces of currants well plumped, quarter of an ounce of sugar, and a tablespoonful of barm. Melt an ounce of butter in a quarter of a pint of milk; glaze with the yolk or white of an egg. The above quantity will make twelve buns.

Mix the barm * into the flour with a little warm milk, and leave it to rise for half an hour; then knead, and let the dough rise for one hour before baking. Bake twenty minutes in a moderate oven.

TEISEN FRAU GWENT A MORGANWG.†

One pound of flour, three ounces of currants well picked and washed, a little sugar (and spice if liked); mix into a thick batter with one pint of sheep's milk-cream, butter the tin of a Dutch oven and drop it in and bake before the fire. Care must be taken in turn-

---

* *Barm* (called *Yeast* in England) is a Welsh word, although found in English dictionaries.

† Short cakes of Gwent and Morganwg.

ing; it can be cut in any shape. Cream of cows'-milk may be used, but sheep's-milk cream is best for these cakes. A variety of the Teisen Frau are made by rubbing six ounces of butter in one pound of flour and two teaspoonfuls of sugar made into a stiff dough with new milk, or sheep's-milk cream; roll it out half an inch thick, and cut to size required; bake on a bake-stone, or before the fire in a Dutch oven.

FOR HARVEST. WELSH APPLE OR RHUBARB CAKES.

Stew apples or rhubarb till soft, in a basin placed on a saucepan of boiling water. If the former, take off the peel and take out the core when done, and mash with a little brown sugar to taste. If the latter, pour off the overplus of juice for other purposes. To every five pounds of flour rub in two pounds of clarified fat, roll out the paste the size of a large baking-sheet, spread the apple or rhubarb pulp all over the square sheet of paste, then lay another thin layer of paste on the top and fasten the edges together. Bake, and when cold turn it out of the tin and cut it up in squares. Another plan of making these cakes is to form the paste the size and shape of a small cheese plate, or large breakfast saucer; put the fruit over one-half of the round and turn the other half over it, making a half-moon ; then glaze and bake in a quick oven. Jam of any kind can also be used in this way for Welsh harvest cakes.

WELSH HARVEST BUNS.

One pound of flour and two ounces of clarified fat rubbed through the flour, one ounce and a half of currants, one ounce of sugar, a tablespoonful of barm (or one teaspoonful of baking powder), wet the above quantity with skim milk. It will make four very large buns or cakes.

N.B.—The two foregoing recipes were used by the Hermit for the supply of his work-people during harvest, and no people ever worked better. The cold *glâsdwfr* (one quart of milk to three quarts of cold spring water) was supplied throughout the day to men, women, and children. If the weather was hot, the milk was always scalded previously to preserve it from acidity. At four o'clock, warm tea ready mixed in jugs with sugar and milk, was taken out to every one at work, with the above harvest buns, also a piece of cheese and part of a loaf of home-made bread for those whose appetites required more than two of the above buns. At eight o'clock or earlier (if they desired it) tea was sent out again in the same manner, with bread and cheese for each person.

The apple, rhubarb, or jam cakes were used as a variety, instead of buns occasionally. It was very rarely that there was any illness during harvest among those engaged in it. Mowing commenced at three or four in the morning, and the work (when the weather was favourable) continued as long as they could see in the evening, often till past nine o'clock.

The Traveller heard it remarked, that the children employed in the Hermit's harvest always "grew fat" during that period, having good appetites and as much wholesome food as they could eat : *no fermented liquors* of *any sort or kind* were *ever given ;* the usual hour was allowed for dinner at twelve o'clock, and they supplied themselves also with breakfast as on ordinary occasions. The *glâsdwfr* when mixed in the above proportions never disagrees with the digestion ; it is cooling, refreshing, and nourishing without being heavy ; but if a larger proportion of milk was used it would disagree. In some places in Wales " *dwfr blawd ceirch* " is used instead of milk and water; this is made by putting boiling water on oatmeal, stirring it well, and letting it stand all night, and the clear water is taken off the next day for drinking.

In noting down the above particulars, I (the

Traveller) asked the Hermit how he avoided the introduction of intoxicating liquors in harvest time?   He
replied :—" My aim has been to preserve or restore all
the *good* old habits of my country, and utterly to repudiate all immoral introductions which ruin the health
as well as imperil the soul.   Harvest *especially* is the
time when we should *do what is good,* and not *teach* and
encourage wickedness.   Many and many a man, woman,
and child are taught to drink in harvest time, from the
want of other sustenance than intoxicating liquors."

WELSH TOASTED CHEESE.

This celebrated national dish of Wales will appro-
priately conclude the present collection of recipes,
which were especial favourites in the cell of the Welsh
Hermit, and which, in honour of his Principality,
is here given in the original language as well as in
English.   Welsh *toasted* cheese, and the *melted* cheese
of England, called " toasted cheese," are as different
in the mode of preparation as is the cheese itself ; the
one being only adapted to strong digestions, and the
other being so easily digested that the Hermit frequently gave it to his invalid patients when they were
recovering from illness, and found that they could often
take it in moderation without inconvenience when the
appetite and digestion were not sufficiently restored

to take much, (if any) meat, without suffering.*—
Cut a slice of the real Welsh cheese made of sheep
and cow's milk,† toast it at the fire on both sides, but
not so much as to drop; toast a piece of bread, less
than a quarter of an inch thick, to be quite crisp, and
spread it very thinly with fresh cold butter on *one*
side (it must *not* be saturated with butter), then lay
the toasted cheese upon the bread and serve immediately on a very hot plate; the butter on the toast
can, of course, be omitted if not liked, and it is more
frequently eaten without butter.

CAWS WEDI EI BOBI.

" Torrer darn o gaws Cymreig gwneuthuredig o
laeth defaid a gwartheg, pober y ddwy ochr o flaen y
tân ond nid cymmaint ag i ddiferu; craser tafell o
fara (llai na chwarter modfedd o drwch) yn grych, a
thaener ymenyn newydd oer yn deneu iawn ar un ochr
iddo (rhaid iddo beidio cael ei lenwi o ymenyn), yna
rhodder y darn caws pobedig ar y bara, ac anfoner ef
i'r bwrdd ar ddysgl boeth yn ddiattreg. Gellir peidio

---

* The same observation will apply to the Welsh sheep's-
milk cheese *without toasting*, which can often be taken with
bread or biscuit and a glass of cold water, with benefit by
invalids with weak digestions.

† See page 346.

rhoddi ymenyn ar y bara crasedig, os dewiser, ac yn amlaf bwytteir ef hebddo."

Here ends the Traveller's Book of Recipes, obtained from the Hermit of the Cell of St. Gover, though only a portion of those known and practised under the directions of the venerable recluse. The Traveller departed, as has already been mentioned, to London with his ancient but active Welsh host, regretting that he had not been able to fill another book with a list of the various wild plants yet undestroyed in that part of Wales where he had so long resided; the virtues of which were well known to the Hermit and his native countrymen, and whose Welsh names in many instances indicated either their appearance or their medical and curative properties.

December, 1866.

FINIS.

INDEX.